The Nicolson House at 821 Piedmont Avenue, now an inn on the National Registry of Historic Places, where Sallie Clayton wrote her memoirs. (Photograph courtesy of the author)

Requiem for a Lost City

A Memoir of Civil War Atlanta and the Old South

Sarah "Sallie" Conley Clayton

Edited by
Robert Scott Davis Jr.

Mercer University Press
1979 - 1999
Twenty Years of Publishing Excellence

ISBN 0-86554-622-3 MUP/H466

The paper used in this publication meets the minimum requirements of American National Standard for Information Sciences— Permanence of Paper for Printed Library Materials, ANSI Z39.48-1984.

Library of Congress Cataloging-in-Publication Data

Clayton, Sarah Conley, 1845-1922.

Requiem for a Lost City: A memoir of civil war Atlanta and the Old South / by Sarah "Sallie" Conley Clayton; edited by Robert Scott Davis Jr.

pp. 6 x 9" (15 x 22 cm.)

Includes bibliographical references and index.

ISBN 0-86554-622-3 (alk. Paper).

1. Clayton, Sarah Conley, 1845-1922 Diaries. 2. United States—History—Civil War, 1861-1865 Personal narratives, Confederate. 3. Georgia—History—Civil War 1861-1865 Personal narratives. 4. Atlanta (Ga.) Biography. 5. Women—Georgia—Atlanta Diaries. 6. Atlanta (Ga.)—History—19th century. 7. United States—History—Civil War, 1861-1865 Social Aspects. I. Davis, Robert Scott, 1954- . II. Title.

E605.C595 1999

973.7'82'092—dc21 99-25581

CIP

For Dr. Harriet Amos Doss

She taught me a great deal about a profession
and about being a professional.

Were these the same people—these haggard, wrinkled women, bowed with care and trouble, sorrow and unusual toil? These tame, pale, tearless girls, from whose soft flesh the witching dimples had long since departed, or were drawn down into furrows–were they the same school girls of 1861?... To think with what gay insouciance we laughed, danced, flung gay jests, while we stood upon the brink of a grave that, ere long, swallowed all that was brave and beautiful.

—Miss A. C. Cooper of Atlanta
quoted in "*Our Women in the War*"

Contents

PHOTOGRAPHS

ACKNOWLEDGMENTS

The editor would like to acknowledge the kindness of E. Lee Shepard, senior archivist of the Historical Society of Virginia, without whose help Sallie's memoirs would certainly have remained buried in the unprocessed holdings of the Society. Kathy Best, Gordon B. Smith, Keith Bohannon, Frank May, Lucy Singleton, Helen Mathews, Bill Simpson, Madeline Anthony, Eric Montgomery, and Carl A. Anderson helped in many ways, as they have so many times before (so much that I forgive Carl for what happened to my car while I poured over a previously misplaced chapter of Sallie's manuscript at the HSV). Franklin Garrett again easily proved to be the single greatest source of Atlanta history. Dr. Harriet Amos Doss of the University of Alabama at Birmingham reviewed the manuscript and provided invaluable advice, including the suggestion to contact Mary D. Robertson of Savannah for sources on Civil War women's studies. Shirley Knight helped with the introduction and Virginia Steele Wood of the Library of Congress kindly checked the biographical card catalog of that institution's Local History and Genealogy Room for this project. Kenneth H. Thomas, Jr. used his extensive genealogical knowledge of Georgia to provide information on important family connections. Bill Smedlund kindly loaned his microfilm of Civil War Atlanta newspapers. Elizabeth Ford gave valuable help in wading through the unindexed maze that is A. A. Hoehling's book, *Last Train From Atlanta*, for all of the references to the Claytons. Gus Welborn, Betty Lott, and Iman Humaideh gave support when it was needed.

The help of the staff of the Southern Historical Collection of the Wilson Library of the University of North Carolina must be especially acknowledged. Their manuscript holdings and those of the Atlanta Historical Society make Atlanta's Civil War history among the best documented of any Confederate city. Charles S. Longley of the Boston Public Library brought to my attention the Civil War newspapers of the Boston Athenaeum and Stephen Z. Nonack of the latter institution made them available to me for research. The microfilm collection of state and federal Civil War records assembled at Wallace State College, Hanceville, Alabama through the support of Dr. James C. Bailey, the college president, helped make the annotations here far more complete than they might have been.

The Southern History Collection of the Birmingham Public Library lives up to a reputation of being the one of the best such local history resource centers anywhere. The completeness of the annotations to this memoir is due in part to the service provided by Yvonne Crumpler, Elisabeth Willauer, Grace Reid, Francine Cooper, Jim Baggett, Roger Torbert, and the other members of their helpful staff.

Robert Scott Davis Jr.
Blountsville, Alabama

INTRODUCTION

> Mr. Scheer led me to the Virginia Historical Society and the Rev. Clayton Torrence, its executive secretary. Here, appropriately, I was seated at a desk Robert E. Lee once had used and given the Sallie Clayton papers to read. Long years had passed since Sallie set down her memories of Atlanta during the war; Sallie had died, the papers were crisp, the ink faded; but the sentences were still alive, brimming with the ardor and the sadness of vanished dreams.
>
> —Earl Schenck Miers[1]

> The most important thing in a book is often what is not written.
>
> —Jean-Jacques Annaud

THE MEMOIRS OF THE PARTICIPANTS IN THE AMERICAN CIVIL WAR APPEAR enormous in number and broad in scope. However, too few civilian memoirs remain, excluding the sensational and the fragmentary. For example, for every socialite and female spy who wrote a self-serving memoir, hundreds of thousands of other southern women sent their men to war, suffered the deprivations of the home front, provided for families, worked in hospitals, kept households together, rebuilt their lives, and memorialized their Confederate dead. The war and the aftermath remains no less their fight and struggle. Too little of the South's Civil War literature came from these civilians and now, in trying to see the total reality of the American Civil War, we suffer in our knowledge of the era for not having more of their reminiscences.[2]

---

[1]Earl Schenck Miers, *The General Who Marched to Hell: William Tecumseh Sherman and His March to Fame and Infamy* (New York: Alfred A. Knopf, 1951), 342.

[2]For some of the related reminiscences of women during the war see Camille Kunkle, "'It is What It Does to the Souls': Women's Views on the Civil War," *Atlanta History* 33 (1989): 58-70; George C. Rable, *Civil Wars: Women and the Crisis of Southern Nationalism* (Urbana: University of Illinois Press, 1989); Joan E. Cashin, ed., *Our Common Affairs: Texts from Antebellum Southern Women* (Baltimore: John Hopkins University Press, 1996); Katherine M. Jones, *When Sherman Came: Southern Women and the "Great March"* (New

Since the growth of social history in the 1960s and the current efforts to study the Civil War era as more than political and military history, interest in the civilian history of this period has rapidly expanded. Nothing similar has occurred since the flurry of publications about and by women at the turn of the century, during that era's national interest in the Civil War South. The scholarship of Carol Bleser, Mary D. Robertson, Elizabeth Fox-Genovese, Catherine Clinton, and others represents important new interpretations of that era, based in the surviving writings of the participants.[3]

A very few documents, however, provide enough detail of interest to use in a modern *Annaliste* style of social history built around a biographical record. One such document, the memoirs of Sarah "Sallie" Conley Clayton (Mrs. Benjamin Elliot Crane), illustrates something of what we have missed for Atlanta, "the Crossroads of the Confederacy." Decades after the Civil War, elderly and in ill health, Sallie put pencil to scrap paper to privately record her memories. Her memoirs appear here, in print, for the first time.

The quantity and quality of Sallie Clayton's memoirs provide exceptional information on the Civil War South. Other reminiscences of Civil War Atlantans, especially by women, survive in the extensive holdings of the Atlanta Historical Society and the Southern Historical Collection of the University of North Carolina at Chapel Hill. However, these writings seldom exceed a few pages in length, even when padded with genealogical and other extra information. Sallie's memoirs consists of more than one hundred hand written pages, without extraneous information, and even hint at more stories not written.

While other memoirs concentrated largely on only one or a few places within a very limited time, Sallie's adventures spanned from floods in Augusta to gun boats in Montgomery to an army tent in Chattanooga. Readers will regret that in her writings, unlike the way people appear in the well known works of Mary Chesnut and Sarah Morgan, we do not learn even more of the family members, acquaintances, and strangers, famous and obscure, who pass through Sallie's memoirs.

Although other Civil War memoirs writers did not minimize their roles

---

York: Bobbs-Merrill, 1964); and idem., *Heroines of Dixie: Confederate Women Tell Their Story of the War* (New York: Bobbs-Merrill, 1955).

[3]See Catherine Clinton, "In Search of Southern Women's History: The Current State of Academic Publishing," *Georgia Historical Quarterly* 76 (1992): 420-427.

in their writings as Sallie did, frequently they shared, as a common feature with her, a supernumerary role in their own lives. Such other memoirists as Sarah Morgan and Mary Chesnut also did not head or operate households or have any real say in their own lives during the war years of which they wrote. They also, like Sallie, recorded very little about their respective lives after the war, when they no longer merely observed but also had some personal independence in and control of their lives.

Sallie's decision to tell her story from the view point of a background observer also reflects her family environment. The Claytons, although a prominent and wealthy family before and after the war, remain largely unnoted in Georgia history. While participants in the Atlanta society, they never took a leadership role, just as she seldom assigned herself a central role in the events that she described in her memoirs. Allusion to this background position appears in an unsigned article on early Atlanta, written many years after the Civil War, wherein the writer remembered Sallie and her sisters as "among the girls in the exclusive sets."[4]

The planter Claytons, however, in wealth and prominence exceeded almost any other family in Georgia, at a time when the state had more plantations of over a thousand acres than anywhere else in the South and where sixty-four hundred people each owned the twenty or more slaves required of persons considered as planters.[5] Both sides of Sallie's family had owned slave plantations for generations. The fourth child of the ten children of William Wirt (1812-1885) and Caroline Maria Semmes (1819-1893) Clayton, Sallie was born in Athens on 9 April 1845. Her father changed careers with the times. Before Sallie's birth, he and his brother Edward Patrick Clayton were dry goods merchants in Athens. William later

---

[4]Unsigned article in MS 391, Box 1, Folder 36, Atlanta Pioneer Women's Society Papers Collection, Atlanta Historical Society.

[5]Samuel Carter III, *The Siege of Atlanta, 1864* (New York: Bonanza Books, 1973), 25. The 1860 Federal census of Cass County, Georgia credited William Wirt Clayton with real estate worth $17,000 and personal property worth $46,000. The latter included the fifty slaves on his Cass County plantation. Seventh Census of the United States (1860), Cass County, Population Schedule and Slave Schedule, microcopy M653, reel 114, 795, and reel 143, 367, National Archives, Washington, DC. An Atlantan wrote, in June 1864, of Cass County as the wealthiest county in Georgia. *Louisville* (KY) *Daily Press & Times*, 28 June 1864, 1, c. 4. Also see Lucy Josephine, *The History of Bartow County Formerly Cass*, 1933 reprint. ed. (Cartersville GA: Tribune, 1933; reprint, Easley SC: Southern Historical Press, 1976), 209. Cass County consequently had various academies for boys and girls of the planter class, from throughout Georgia.

served for many years in the Georgia legislature. He prepared the Clayton-Gartrell Resolutions that presented a states' rights argument for Georgia's slave-owning planters during the national crisis of 1850. W. W. Clayton came by this support for secession honestly. His father, Augustin Smith Clayton (1783-1839), despite being a leader in the largely unpopular Federalist Party, still earned fame as a Georgia state court judge and congressman. A Georgia county was named in his honor. Historian Gordon B. Smith identified Augustin Clayton as the premier Georgian to call for nullification/secession in 1831.

However, W. W. Clayton also led the way to a new South, even before the Civil War. Retiring from politics shortly after 1850, he next became a planter in Cass, now Bartow, County, Georgia, when the railroads opened that area to the profitable plantation economy. Agents for R. G. Dun & Company described him as having fine business qualities and as being very intelligent, with a personal wealth of $40,000-$50,000. At that time, Cass County became a model of plantation society and one of the wealthiest counties in Georgia. In 1859, Clayton again changed his profession and lifestyle when he moved his family from his Talla Tanarrah plantation near Kingston (a town that he owned) to Atlanta, where he served as cashier of the Georgia Railroad Bank. With the end of the war in 1865, he started over in the rebuilt and reconstructed city of Atlanta. He sought and received a pardon from Congress for his support of the Confederacy. As an Atlantan of the New South, he served as cashier of the Merchants Bank of Atlanta (which he also founded), second president of the Atlanta Chamber of Commerce, treasurer of the Western & Atlantic Railroad, and tax collector for Fulton County.[6]

The family of Sarah's mother, Caroline Maria (daughter of Washington,

---

[6]William Clayton-Torrence, *Rootes of Rosewall* (n.p., 1906), 74-80; *Southern Banner* (Athens GA), 17 June 1842, 3, c. 6; William B. McCash, *Thomas R. R. Cobb: The Making of a Southern Nationalist* (Macon GA: Mercer University Press, 1983), 23, 33, 137-138; Georgia vol. 5, 202, 204, R. G. Dun Collection of Credit Reports, Baker Library, Harvard Graduate School of Business Administration; William W. Clayton Pardon File, HR 40A-H21.8, RG 323, Records of the US House of Representatives, National Archives, Washington, DC; James H. Broussard, *The Southern Federalists 1800-1816* (Baton Rouge: Louisiana State University Press, 1978), 193, 252; P. Clayton, *A Vindication of the Hon. Augustin S. Clayton* (Washington, DC: G. S. Gideon, 1855); and Robert H. Welborn, "Augustin Smith Clayton," in *Dictionary of Georgia Biography*, eds. Kenneth Coleman and Stephen Gurr (Athens: University of Georgia Press, 1983), 196-198.

Georgia planter Andrew Green Semmes and his second wife Mary Robertson) also knew prominence. Her relations included her Confederate martyr brother General Paul Jones Semmes, and second cousins Confederate Admiral Raphael Semmes and Louisiana Confederate Senator Thomas J. Semmes.[7]

With the writings of such Confederate women as Frances Thomas Howard (Sallie's former teacher), Eliza Andrews, Mary A. H. Gay, Phoebe Yates Pember, and Mary Chesnut, as well as Francis W. Dawson's compilation, "*Our Women in the War*," available as inspirations, Sallie began her memoirs of these families and their lives in the Civil War. A reference in the memoirs implying that her relation by marriage, Anna Barnard Hunt, still lived, suggests that she wrote that passage before Mrs. Hunt's death on 3 January 1910. Her reference to the late B. J. Semmes shows that at least part of the manuscript was written after his death on 29 January 1902. She wrote the entire book length manuscript in pencil on the back of the pages of an examination to become a doctor taken by W. T. Kimsey on 17 March 1897 (likely scrap paper from Sallie's doctor son-in-law). She did not include any chapter headings or plan for the book and attached changes and additions to the original draft with straight pins. For some passages she wrote alternative drafts. Parts of these manuscripts end with incomplete sentences, proving that some of her writings perished.

What does survive tells the story of a city, a nation, and a society under a wartime siege that ended with not only defeat but the destruction of all three. As a teenager in Atlanta, Sallie Clayton witnessed the events before the city fell to General Sherman and its final destruction in November 1864. When her memoirs opened, Atlanta, the fastest growing city in Georgia, had moved from the fifth to the third largest city in the state in the period between 1850 and 1860, as the deep South's greatest railroad center.[8] Before she finished, Sallie recorded her moonlit return to Atlanta in the spring of 1865 and how she carefully avoided falling into uncovered wells among the piles of bricks and burned wood of the ruined city.

Between those moments, Sallie remembered the parades, the picnics,

---

[7]Harry Wright Newman, *The Maryland Semmes and Kindred Families* (Baltimore: Maryland Historical Society, 1956), 70-71, 76, 82.

[8]Ralph Benjamin Singer, "Confederate Atlanta," (Ph.D. diss., University of Georgia, 1973), 12-13. In 1860 Savannah and Augusta were the only Georgia cities larger than Atlanta.

the hospitals, the shellings, the wounded, and the visiting dignitaries. Atlanta's population during those years swelled with munitions workers, refugees, and wounded, each person with a particular part in the city's tragic Civil War story. Although Atlanta paled in importance to some of the South's other munitions centers, the Confederacy's failure to save "the Gate City of the South," despite herculean efforts at its defense, opened to invasion the self-sustaining heartland of the Confederacy and signaled the eventual defeat of the southern nation. The fall of Atlanta gave badly needed support to President Lincoln's bid for re-election and the continuance of the war to Union victory.

Sallie wrote of many major historical events that made up the story of this "Gibraltar of the Confederacy:" the hanging of the federal saboteurs known as the Andrews Raiders, the parade for Confederate hero General John H. Morgan, and the elaborate funeral given for Confederate General Leonidas Polk. Her memoirs provide almost all the information that survives on the Atlanta Female Institute; the private life of later Georgia Republican Governor Benjamin Conley; the Georgia riots at the end of the war; and General Bragg's headquarters on the eve of the Battle of Lookout Mountain.

Even when her accounts of such activities as working with the relief societies appears superficial, she still gave extremely rare details of Civil War life, such as the use of white turbans to denote social status among slave women. Other book-length memoirs of the Civil War often exaggerated or defended the author's role in major events. In the few instances in her memoirs where Sallie herself appeared as the major figure, she still wrote as an observer and seldom with self promotion. Her detailed writing, combined with her skills as a story teller, gave a sense of the author's world as she saw it.

Her story does not lack spectacle. Sallie's descriptions of the Atlanta Female Institute's May Festival, with her as the queen, makes the ceremony come to life. The reader visualizes the crowd at the Athenaeum jumping to their feet to yell "Never!" with Sergeant Fishback, when he answered the question of if his company would ever surrender its colors. Sallie wrote with high drama of fleeing to a waiting train when her family, visiting the Confederate army, encountered the federal attack on Lookout Mountain, Tennessee, the opening event in the campaign that ultimately led to the capture and destruction of Sallie's Atlanta. With similar depth of emotion, Sallie wrote of the circumstances surrounding the death of her younger sister and protégé, Gussie, from typhoid fever. Clayton family members and friends dodged shells to inter Gussie in the family garden as the Battle of Atlanta raged around the city cemetery, within sight of the Clayton house.

Sallie recorded that particular tale from second hand information, as she at that time lived on the Conley plantation, what she described as an artificial, almost surrealistic, idealistic caricature of the realities of southern plantation life. Similarly, while in Alabama, she witnessed the launching of a Confederate gun boat, a romantic, nationalistic, but false image that contradicted the truth of a crumbling agricultural nation being overwhelmed by a vastly technologically-superior foe. Shortly afterward, reality returned as she rode to her family on a rickety train on tracks being repaired after a federal raid. She rode her train into the night, evading the enemy troops who had brought an end to her plantation world and her Confederacy, real and artificial.

Such deep irony abounds in her writings. Like so many writers of Victorian era memoirs, Sallie frequently seems to hurry past some events without detail or precision. However, her reminiscences also contain cryptic representations of complexities more fully explained here in the annotation of the memoirs. Sallie's account of the siege of Atlanta provides many examples of the importance of her accounts. When her teacher asked, Sallie successfully drew the lines of the combating armies on the school blackboard—an example of how the approaching fighting became so common a part of the lives of civilian Atlantans that even a school girl knew the locations of the opposing forces. When federal shells reached the Clayton home, Sallie's mother became expert in crossing the streets during the pauses between the federal artillery salvos. The only victims of the shelling in the Clayton household, however, proved to be two slave children, persons that the Union soldiers fought to free.

For safety from the cannon, the Claytons moved to the Georgia Railroad Bank, a stone building. It had been the place of business for the head of the household until financial problems brought on by the war forced the bank to close. The building now served as a refuge from the siege of the city. Sallie's family finally joined the stampede of Atlantans, black and white, rich and poor, fleeing the doomed city, as the Confederate press proclaimed General John Bell Hood's disastrous attacks on the federal forces around Atlanta as great "victories" and predicted the eminent defeat of General Sherman's armies. These news stories circulated as the triumphant Yankees entered Atlanta. Then, in November, as one of their last actions before abandoning the city they had suffered so to win, the federals blew up the remaining buildings of military use to the rebels, including the Georgia Railroad Bank building that had been the Claytons's haven.

Sallie's memoirs, no matter how valuable for such anecdotes and details of life in Civil War Atlanta, must be read with a special understanding of the background and the prejudices of the author. Her reminiscences, especially when read in parts rather than as a whole, mislead the reader about her family's place in southern society. From Sallie's descriptions of making homespun dresses and knitting for the soldiers, the reader might incorrectly imagine Sallie belonged to a family representative of most of the Georgians of the period. Although Sallie wrote of daily visits to help at the Confederate hospitals, a slave actually carried her tray of food for the wounded. That the servants appeared only occasionally in the memoirs, and very seldom by name, only reflected that Sallie took them for granted. A teenager from a typical Georgia family of Atlanta, or elsewhere, would not have had slaves or servants to forget. Even during the hard times and shortages of war-time Atlanta, one survivor would remember that the spirits among Atlanta's upper class rose with rumors of the Claytons planning a party to include the war time luxury of sardines![9]

Sallie Clayton's writings represent more than a memoir of the lost antebellum city of Atlanta but documentation of the transition of life for many southern women from Georgia's long pioneer period to the modern world. During the war, Sallie and her sisters learned sewing and knitting out of the wartime necessity. Her grandmothers learned those skills as part of their expected roles in everyday life in an earlier Georgia. Similarly, Sallie wrote at length of how families like hers, with inherited rather than purchased slaves, taught their own children to be self-sufficient and able to perform all household tasks in order to manage household slaves better. She and her sisters also received their training, as well as an indoctrination in southern nationalism, in the Cass County female academy taught by Reverend C. W. Howard. The war reduced the Claytons' fortunes and by October 1865 they only owned the Atlanta house where Sallie's sister remained buried in the flower garden. The Clayton girls then worked as school teachers. However, in 1870, the family still depended upon four live-

---

[9]MS 291F, memoirs of Kate Hester Robson, Atlanta Historical Society.

in servants to maintain their large but all adult household.[10]

Similarly, Sallie wore homespun and knitted socks, at least at the beginning, as a show of Confederate patriotism rather than economic need. She belonged to the upper class of a second category of American feminism, a new generation of women of the household and not of the frontier that had more aptly described even her wealthy mother and grandmothers. Sallie's struggles to find teachers in such subjects as French and higher mathematics reflected the planter ideals of woman educated to be prized as spouses by men of her class. A classic education, by the time Sallie became a teenager, served in the Old South as almost the only female avenue to archiving or maintaining class as politics, business, and professions remained almost exclusively male avenues of advancement and status. Her accounts of punishments at the Atlanta Female Institute provides a classic example of the type of formal discipline imposed on the southern belle. She and her sisters also did not have large numbers of children as did their female ancestors (Sallie had only one child). While her ancestors' priority had been settling and populating a wilderness, Sallie by contrast worried over finding a French teacher. Similarly, her father and his brothers, during her youth, moved from a life of a planter-politician typical of their class, to careers in business and government more suitable to the new age. When Sallie and her family left their Kingston plantation in 1861, they unknowingly left their planter lives behind for future careers in postwar Atlanta as businessmen, journalists, and bankers.

A comfortable household of antebellum southern nationalism, followed by radical change, produced Sallie's sentimental prejudice for the "Lost

---

[10]Edgar W. Knight, ed., *A Documentary History of Education in the South Before 1860* 5 vols. (Chapel Hill: University of North Carolina Press, 1990), 5:451; Anne Semmes to Raphael Semmes, 1 October 1865, Raphael Semmes Papers, Alabama Department of Archives and History; and Ninth Census of the United States (1870), Fulton County, microcopy M593, 344, National Archives, Washington, DC. For the status of women in the Old South see Eleanor Miot Boatwright, *The Status of Women in Georgia, 1783-1860* (Brooklyn NY: Carlson Publishing, 1994); Jane Turner Censer, *North Carolina Planters and Their Children, 1800-1860* (Baton Rouge: Louisiana State University Press, 1984); and Elizabeth Fox-Genovese, *Within the Plantation Household: Black and White Women of the Old South* (Chapel Hill: University of North Carolina Press, 1988). William Wirt Clayton began rebuilding his fortunes almost as the war ended. By 1866, he worked as treasurer for the Western & Atlantic Railroad. The following year he organized the state sponsored purchase and distribution of corn to the needy. William W. Clayton file, File II Names, RG 4-2-46, Georgia Department of Archives and History.

Cause" of the Confederacy. Similarly, her background gave her contradictory views on race and slavery, reproduced here as she wrote them. While she referred to the slaves as happy, healthy, and contented, her family feared slave revolts following the news of Lincoln's election. She did not mention that her neighbors even lynched one slave. Her family and other Cass County planters left their plantations to overseers and fled to the security of urban Atlanta. When the federal army threatened North Georgia, these planters moved their slaves to Southwest Georgia to keep them from escaping to the Union lines. Even there, Sallie's mother feared for the safety of her daughters from the allegedly happy and contented slaves, as described in the letters reproduced here in an appendix.

Plantation mistresses, like Sallie's mother, owed more to slavery than anyone else. Their fiscal well being and social status came from the "peculiar institution." However, they harbored ambivalent feelings as reflected in the writings of Sallie and her mother. Mrs. Clayton bemoaned the end of slavery but also feared harm to her daughters from her slaves. She, like so many other people of her class, failed to see the African-Americans as human beings, with conscience, self respect, and integrity. The former slaves usually continued, in freedom, as families that structurally mirrored those of the white southerners, and with the same mutual support, loyalty, sense of community, and love.

References to being a woman in Civil War Georgia also appear indirectly in Sallie's memoirs. She made a comparison of "the bad treatment" of slaves to the difficulties of "any other state of life—marriage, parentage, etc., etc." Details of Sallie's life as a woman in this memoir come by way of inferences. Hospital officials barred her and other unmarried women from working in the wards but allowed her adolescent sister, Gussie, to visit with the sick and wounded men. Waltzes, polkas, and other dances served as calisthenic exercises for women at the Atlanta Female Institute but Atlanta society frowned on dancing between men and women. She wrote of her enormous embarrassment on receiving the good-natured taunts of a regiment of Confederate cavalry. Sallie wrote of her training in all domestic chores, unintentionally describing the duties expected of women in Civil War Atlanta. However, Sallie never discussed such sexual matters as the prostitution, so obvious at the Athenaeum Theater that she visited so often and the miscegenation that diarist Mary Chesnut reported as so common among planter men of Sallie's class.[11]

However, she freely wrote of military matters. Sallie and the other students of the Atlanta Female Institute practiced military drills and successfully competed in marching against a Confederate cavalry company. She described a teacher sympathetic to the students as a spy in the enemy camp. Throughout the memoirs, Sallie referred to retreat, assuming a new position, showing the white feather, and other military phrases that entered her vocabulary and remained in her writings more than forty years after the Civil War. She wrote of war not only because of the support of her class for the war effort but, as one Atlantan wrote in June 1864, the war and Atlanta had become one:

> If the war continues four years longer, it seems to me those who escape deaths from bullets or pestilence must die of excitement, for there you see nothing but war. You eat war; you hear war; you talk nothing but war; and when you retire to your bed you dream of war. You wake tired of war but the despot has you by the throat, with a thousand bayonets bristling round you, and you must fight or do worse.[12]

Sallie's memoirs appear virtually identical to the model Victorian memoir described in Anne C. Rose's *Victorian America and the Civil War*. Sallie shared almost all of the common traits of Rose's Victorian memoirists: a youth during the Civil War with a successful but amateur politician father, in a household deeply concerned with politics. Sallie's work also coincided with Rose's model of the Victorian memoir as an unpublished thesis to prove, optimistically, that the author's experiences and sacrifices served a purpose that justified the whole-hearted support of such a costly cause. Such a manuscript helped the writer to achieve a private closure, redemption, revenge, retrospection, or therapy but "pruned of horrors" and complicated qualifications.[13] Such a memoir did not serve as an objective history. She protected her selected memories from reality and saved herself

---

[11]Robert Gibbons, "Life at the Crossroads of the Confederacy: Atlanta, 1861-1865," *Atlanta Historical Journal* 23/2 (1979): 39, 42.

[12]*Louisville* (KY) *Daily Press & Times*, 28 June 1864, 1, c. 4.

[13]Anne C. Rose, *Victorian America and the Civil War* (Cambridge: Cambridge University Press, 1992), 245.

from becoming alienated from those memories by sharing her story. Sarah Morgan and Mary Chesnut similarly wrote memoirs of their respective Confederate lives that saw print only after their deaths. They even destroyed parts of the diaries upon which they based their memoirs. No record of Sallie having a diary survives but she did selectively destroy at least some private papers.

The specific theme of Sallie's memoirs also varied little from other writers of her class, time, and place. George C. Rable, in writing of southern women in the Civil War, described an almost fanatical female devotion to the Confederate cause created both by the sacrifices made on the home front and the isolation from such causes of the southern defeat as the hard realities of the battlefield and the incompetence of the Confederate government. Supporters of what became the "Lost Cause" never realistically evaluated the war. They laid blame for the defeat to a greater unknown purpose.[14]

The letters of Sallie's mother, reproduced here as an appendix, especially match Rable's stereotype of the female Confederate patriot and served as a model for Sallie's memoirs. Even after Atlanta fell and her oldest son walked on crutches from a battle wound, Sallie's mother anguished not over the waste and the defeat of the southern cause but over the fact that the majority of the southern soldiers had abandoned the fight. She pleaded to reunite her family, even though most of them (including Sallie) suffered from sickness, so that they might be together at the end of their world. Mother Clayton despaired for the "Lost Cause"—even before it finally became lost. Sallie's memoirs greatly expand on those letters and add the Victorian vindication that Anne C. Rose discovered as so common in the other memoirs of the period.

Sallie, like so many members of the planter class, for decades increasingly believed their own self-serving propaganda about slavery. After emancipation, few realities of the Old South remained to conflict with the traditional planter rhetoric. By the 1880s, such romantic memories of the Confederacy, unchallenged by the facts, became popularly accepted national history. The rhetoric and the legend found literary expression in the memoirs of many southern women, such as Sallie, in the early decades of the twentieth century. Historian William Garrett Piston points out that the majority of the literature in the South on the war, during Sallie's

---

[14]Rable, *Civil Wars*, 144-151.

lifetime, came from such women. They became the staunchest defenders of the memory of the Old South, as their mothers had supported of the southern nation.[15]

These reminiscences of Sallie Clayton, therefore, for all of their value in providing rare and even unique information on the Civil War South, only give a very select view of her adventures in Atlanta and elsewhere. Her prejudices account for the absence of any real mention of the problems of shortages, inflation, and profiteering that had made more than twenty Atlantans the then enormous sum of over $100,000 by November 1862.[16] Contemporary accounts of visits to Atlanta as early as 1862 conflict with her memoirs by picturing a city where poor soldiers' families obtained food from wealthy speculators only at grossly-inflated prices. Poor men, while forced into the Confederate service by the draft, complained bitterly of the politically powerful buying substitutes or otherwise obtaining exemptions from military service. By the autumn of 1862, only six months after the war had begun, Atlanta's newspapers already reported the desperate efforts of the army to obtain shoes locally and carried pleas for clothes for the local regiments serving in Virginia. A female Atlanta Unionist wrote a memoir of the other women of Atlanta—not those of Sallie's wealthy upper class:

> Many a woman walks eight or ten miles to town to get sewing; they often have no shoes, or only those made of cloth "pitched within & without"—and rarely ever wear stockings—for the simple reason they have none. The dresses of these country women are sometimes made of flour sacks dyed with bark; gingham "Sunbonnets" were long ago dispensed with,—and those made of straw or the long leaved pine take their place...They said their rich neighbors persuaded their husbands to volunteer in the first of the war, promising that their families should never suffer. But the promise was forgotten, & the little sewing they could get hardly

---

[15]Catherine Clinton, *Tara Revisted: Women, War, & The Plantation Legend* (New York: Abbeville Press, 1995), 13-14, 107-188; Boatwright, *The Status of Women in Georgia*, 5-24; and William Garrett Piston, *Lee's Tarnished Lieutenant: James Longstreet and His Place in Southern History* (Athens: University of Georgia Press, 1987), 113-116.

[16]Grigsby H. Wooten, Jr., "New City of the South: Atlanta, 1843-1873," (Ph. D. diss., John Hopkins University, 1973), 47.

kept them alive.[17]

Sallie omitted mention of these women although at that time more than two hundred destitute Atlanta families of the soldiers received relief from the State of Georgia. Overall, Georgia had 84,119 "war indigents" by 1864, one-seventh of the state's total white population in 1860. At the war's end, Atlanta alone reportedly had more than eight thousand destitute civilians while the war resulted in Georgia having thirty-six thousand more women, many of them destitute, than men.[18] No mention appeared in her memoirs of food prices soaring in the winter of 1863 to flour at $35 per barrel, shoes for $500 per pair, and eggs to $1 per dozen. At the same time, the value of the Confederate currency declined so rapidly that Atlantans bought books and other non-perishables to quickly dispose of their inflating money.[19] Almost the only wartime profiteering Sallie mentioned involved the selling of leeches to the hospitals and frogs to the Atlanta Hotel by her younger brother and his playmate.

The hotels where Sallie began her narrative, "never anything to brag about," according to one Atlantan, served as symbols of these stories that

---

[17]Cyrena Bailey Stone, Miss Abbey's Diary, MS 1000, Hargrett Rare Book and Manuscripts Library, University of Georgia Libraries; Mills B. Lane, ed. *Times That Prove People's Principles: Civil War in Georgia* (Savannah: Beehive Press, 1993), 83, 127-128; Annie M. Schor to John Kimberly, 27 May 1862, MS 398, John Kimberly Papers, Southern Historical Collection, University of North Carolina at Chapel Hill; *Southern Confederacy* (Atlanta), 30 October 1862, 3, c. 4, 5 November 1862, 2, c. 2, 20 November 1862, 2, c. 2; *The Commonwealth* (Atlanta), 4 December 1862, 1, c. 4; Clinton, *Tara Revisited*, 151-152; and Singer, "Confederate Atlanta," 126-127. By the summer of 1864, however, even Atlanta men who had hired substitutes were drafted. Males too old or too young for conscription in Georgia, reportedly, were deported to South Carolina and other states where their ages met the requirements for service. *Louisville* (KY) *Daily Press & Times*, 28 June 1964, 1, c. 5.

[18]*Southern Confederacy* (Atlanta), 25 March 1863, 3, c. 4; Clinton, *Tara Revisited*, 166; and Salem Dutcher, *Memorial History of Augusta* (New York: D. Mason, 1890; reprint, Spartanburg SC: The Reprint Company, 1980) 182. For an account of private and public efforts for families of soldiers in Civil War Atlanta, including by Atlanta's black community, see Gibbons, "Life at the Crossroads of the Confederacy," 24-25, 37.

[19]Carter, *Siege of Atlanta*, 74, 92. Francis Lawley blamed the food shortages in Atlanta on the failures of the Confederacy's railroads. Francis Lawley, *Francis Lawley Covers the Confederacy*, ed. William Stanley Hoole (Tuscaloosa: Confederate Publishing Company, 1964), 44.

she did not tell.[20] As the war continued, the informant explained, the hotels no longer furnished guests with sheets, towels, or soap, all of which the soldiers had taken. Meals consisted of merely bacon and corn bread with rye substituted for coffee. However, the cost of room and board soared to between thirty and forty dollars per day. By the time of the federal siege, the hotels served as Confederate hospitals, their yards so covered with wounded that Atlantans walked blocks to avoid the park by the train depot which the hotels faced.

Sallie's life contrasted with the experiences of the majority of Atlantans in many other ways. Unlike her middle class contemporary, Lucy Harvie Hull, Sallie's family likely bought goods from stores and refrained from purchasing meats and produce from the "Crackers" or poor, yellow-skinned, rural Georgians in the covered wagons that passed through the streets of Atlanta. Even that access to food for Atlanta's starving families declined as food seizures by the Confederate army frightened the independent farmers out of the city. Lucy remembered wishing for a hundred dollars to buy candy, only to have her father angrily hand her the money and challenge her to find a stick of candy in Confederate Atlanta for even that price.[21]

The suffering of Atlanta's women took many such particular turns, as the war progressed, that Sallie omits in her memoirs. A writer to a newspaper complained that the some two thousand jobs the war brought to Atlanta's women too often went first to the wealthy families and not for the city's hundreds of needy women. When the women of the Atlanta Hospital Association tried to sell sugar to finance an "invalid ladies" home, the Confederate army impressed the sugar.[22] On 18 March 1863, a mob of desperate wives of soldiers looted Atlanta stores.[23] A northern sympathizer

---

[20]*Louisville* (KY) *Daily Press & Times*, 28 June 1864, 1, c. 5. Sidney Andrews wrote that Atlanta had no hotel better than fifth rate and that even the boarding houses were better accommodations. Sidney Andrews, *The South Since the Civil War: As Shown by Fourteen Weeks of Travel and Observation in Georgia and the Carolinas* (Boston: Ticknor and Fields, 1866), 342.

[21]Autobiography of Lucy Hull Baldwin, MS 849, Southern Historical Collection, University of North Carolina at Chapel Hill.

[22]Singer, "Confederate Atlanta," 193-195; *Daily Intelligencer* (Atlanta), 30 October 1862, 3, c. 1; Rable, *Civil Wars*, 137; and Lee Kennett, *Marching Through Georgia: The Story of Soldiers and Civilians During the Atlanta Campaign* (New York: HarperCollins, 1995), 114.

[23]*Southern Confederacy* (Atlanta) 25 March 1863, 3, c. 4; Clinton, *Tara Revisited*, 152; and Gibbons, "Life at the Crossroads of the Confederacy," 41. Similar bread riots also occurred in at least three other Confederate states that month. See Emory M. Thomas, *The*

from Confederate Atlanta wrote in June 1864 that without the sacrifices of the women of Atlanta and the South in caring for the hospitalized soldiers "the rebellion would have broken down ere this" but added,

> While many [persons] have thus been laboring, others, in Atlanta in particular, have been riding in their four thousand dollar carriages, dressed in thousand dollar silks and two thousand dollar cloaks, and at night attending the theatre or joining in the dance for John Morgan or some other hero.[24]

Sallie and her family rode in such carriages while the husbands and fathers of other families died for their cause on battlefields and in the nearby Atlanta hospitals. Other Atlantans looted, fled, or grew rich off the imperiled city. A "Vigilance Committee" formed in Atlanta at the City Hall in August 1863 to slow further depreciation of the Confederate currency by preventing persons from selling out their property and fleeing to the federal lines. During the winter of 1863-1864, Confederate inflation and the usurping of wood by the Atlanta Arsenal made the effects of the record cold weather far worse for most of the city's population. Families like the Claytons moved their livestock indoors to protect the animals not only from the savage cold but also from starving neighbors. During the federal siege of the city in the summer of 1864, the Clayton family used their connections to remove their property and themselves from the city by train. Sallie neglected to mention the panic that spread among the poor refugee supporters of the Confederacy abandoned by the fleeing speculators and wealthy families like hers.[25] Similarly Sallie Clayton ignored the realities of the Confederates burning scarce war-time housing; Atlantans using the federal bombardment to rob other Atlantans; streets infested with white orphans and runaways committing robberies; and Confederate soldiers

---

Confederacy as a Revolutionary Experience (Englewood Cliffs NJ: Prentice-Hall, 1971), 103; James C. Bonner, *Milledgeville: Georgia's Antebellum Capital* (Athens: University of Georgia Press, 1988), 162-163; and Huldah Briant to Mr. MV. C. B., 17 April 1863, Huldah Annie Briant Papers, William R. Perkins Library, Duke University.

[24]*Nashville* (TN) *Daily Times & Press*, 28 June 1864, 1, c. 4.

[25]Southern Confederacy (Atlanta), 16 August 1863, 6, c. 2; Charles Henry Smith, *Bill Arp, So Called. A Side Show of the Southern Side of the War* (New York: Metropolitan Record Office, 1866), 98-103; Singer, "Confederate Atlanta," 205, 221; and J. Cutler Andrews, *The South Reports the Civil War* (Pittsburgh: University of Pittsburgh Press, 1985), 442-443.

looting Atlanta in their evacuation of the city.[26]

Class and status even existed among the refugees. In the last days of the war, black and white families of Augusta starved and froze as the mayor pleaded in the newspaper for food for the needy refugees and returning soldiers.[27] The Claytons were also there but they suffered only because their furnace malfunctioned and because even they now had to sit and wait to make purchases. They worried over waking the cook, not where their next meal would come from. At that time, tens of thousands of Georgia's soldiers lacked any communication with their starving families. Sallie's father and her uncle Philip Clayton, however, each weighing in the "neighborhood" of three hundred pounds, made only their legally required appearances each day at the militia camp near their comfortable homes.

Sallie, more than just avoiding this less noble side of the Civil War in Atlanta and Augusta, also omitted anything or anyone in opposition to her almost blind devotion to the "Lost Cause" of southern nationalism and the slave-planter system. Her uncle and namesake, provided but one of many examples. Despite all that her family owed Benjamin Conley (including the roof over their heads in Augusta), she hardly mentioned him at all. She recounted his opposition to secession only when she told of the federal atrocities committed against him. Sallie makes no mention of how Conley and his friend Republican Governor Rufus Bulloch, endorsed the petition to Congress by her father William W. Clayton to have his citizenship restored after the war. Conley's plantation in Montgomery, by contrast, received several paragraphs of description in the memoirs. Likely she omitted a discussion of her uncle because he soon moved to Atlanta to became one of the leaders in the federal reconstruction of Georgia that finally ended her antebellum world. A so-called "scalawag," he eventually served as Georgia's last Reconstruction and last Republican governor.[28]

---

[26]Singer, "Confederate Atlanta," 230, 255. The Confederate army did distribute to the civilians 550,000 pounds of meal that could not be removed before the evacuation. Benedict J. Semmes to Jorantha Semmes, 4 September 1864, MS 2333, Benedict J. Semmes Papers, Southern Historical Collection, University of North Carolina at Chapel Hill.

[27]*Daily Chronicle & Sentinel* (Augusta), 26 April 1865, 3, c. 2. For conditions in Civil War Augusta see Lee Ann White, *The Civil War as a Crisis in Gender: Augusta, Georgia, 1860–1890* (Athens: University of Georgia Press, 1995).

[28]Her full name was Sarah "Sallie" Conley Clayton, later Mrs. Benjamin Elliot Crane. She was named for her uncle and aunt Benjamin and Sarah Semmes Conley. Although Conley served as a northern born Republican governor in Reconstruction Georgia and

Similarly, she did not include in her account certain other relatives of prominence. Her account of her Uncle Philip Clayton's illustrious political career omits his final years as a Republican political appointee of President Grant. Her aunt's father-in-law, William King, supported the Union and even served as an envoy to Georgia's Confederate governor for King's old friend General Sherman. Sallie mentioned the husbands of several women, but not the name of the federal officer who married her close friend Maggie Pool. Cyrena Stone, a female Atlanta Unionist, wrote that families like the Claytons fled the federal army to keep daughters from marrying Yankee soldiers and officers but that these marriages frequently happened anyway.[29] Sallie remained silent on that subject.

Similarly Sallie wrote of her older brother's wound at the Battle of Cold Harbor, followed by a brief and exaggerated account of that Confederate victory, but she did not mention his subsequent desertion. She weaved a powerful image of the Confederate army's arrival in Atlanta—telling how the soldiers slept on streets and porches—but she omitted any account of how many of those same Rebels roamed the streets drunk, terrorizing the unprepared citizenry.[30] Spreading from the Confederate soldiers recuperating in the city's makeshift hospitals, typhoid, smallpox, and other diseases raged among Atlanta's civilians, black and white, rich and poor—including the Claytons. Sallie's memoirs of the Atlanta hospitals described the efforts by women, such as Martha Winship, to ease the suffering of the soldiers but not of the medical shortages and widespread medical incompetence of the hospital staffs. No mention appears of how drug addiction became a major cause of death for veterans for many years afterward from the overdoses prescribed by the doctors.[31] White women volunteers, like Sallie, worked in the hospitals not just to support the Confederate cause but also because the

---

founded the notorious political machine known as the "Augusta Ring," the Augusta City Council in 1886 marked his passing with a tribute to his honesty and integrity. James F. Cook, "Benjamin Conley," in *Dictionary of Georgia Biography*, eds. Coleman and Gurr, 215-216; and Edward J. Cashin, *The Story of Augusta* (Augusta: Richmond County Board of Education, 1980), 133, 139.

[29]*Montgomery* (AL) *Daily Mail*, 30 September 1864, 1, c. 3; and Cyrena Bailey Stone, Miss Abbey's Diary, MS 1000, Hargrett Rare Book and Manuscripts Library, University of Georgia Libraries.

[30]*Southern Confederacy* (Atlanta), 18 June 1864, 1, c. 1.

[31]H. H. Cunningham, *Doctors in Gray: The Confederate Medical Service* (Baton Rouge: Louisiana State University Press, 1958), 60, 254; and Joe Taylor, "Atlanta Mortality Trends: 1853-1873," *Atlanta Historical Bulletin* 20 (1976): 17-20.

slave owners feared exposing valuable slaves to diseases from the sick soldiers literally dying for that same slave economy.[32]

Sallie, in her account of sister Gussie's death from typhoid likely contracted from aiding those sick soldiers, failed to add that as Gussie passed away, so too did her Atlanta—but not in a way that conformed with a heroic Victorian image. The Confederate army marched by the Clayton house in the moonlight to their desperate and forlorn attack on the besieging federal army, while men and women looted the stores and other Atlantans clogged the roads leading south with their wagons of booty and goods. As Don H. Doyle wrote, "Atlanta felt what Sherman called 'the hand of war' with greater fury than any other southern city—perhaps more than any American city ever."[33]

Contrary to popular myth, federal General William T. Sherman only ordered selected Atlanta buildings of military value burned. Some of the city even survived the war due to to the actions of the federal soldiers. Atlanta fell victim to the military actions of both armies. The rebuilding and postwar expansion of Atlanta demolished the remaining traces of the antebellum city that Sallie knew. By the time she wrote her memoirs, after 1896, the Atlanta of her youth existed only in memories and photographs.

What survives of Sallie's memoirs contains little of what happened in those some thirty intervening years. The Claytons regained some of the wealth they had known before the war. On 21 February 1867, Sallie married wealthy ex-Confederate officer Benjamin Elliot Crane (1835-1885), a successful wholesale grocer and cotton factor. Crane served as president of the Atlanta Chamber of Commerce and commissioner for constructing the present state capitol building.[34] They built a large home at 59 (later 85)

---

[32]Singer, "Confederate Atlanta," 205.

[33]*Nashville* (TN) *Daily Times & True Union*, 30 August 1864, 1, c. 6; and Don H. Doyle, *New Men, New Cities, New South: Atlanta, Nashville, Charleston, Mobile, 1860-1910* (Chapel Hill: University of North Carolina Press, 1990), 31.

[34]Sallie Clayton marriage license, MS 518, Nicolson Family Papers Collection, Atlanta Historical Society; Compiled Service Records of Confederate Soldiers of Georgia, microcopy M266, reel 582, National Archives, Washington, DC; Georgia vol. 13, 77, R. G. Dun Collection of Credit Reports, Baker Library, Harvard Graduate School of Business Adminstration; *Brief Biographies of the Members of the Constitutional Convention July 11, 1877* (Atlanta: The Constitution Publishing Company, 1877), 77-79; *The National Cyclopedia of American Biography* 63 vols, 12:379 (New York: James T. White & Company, 1904), 379; Benjamin E. Crane, File II Names, RG 4-2-46, Georgia Department of Archives and History; and Walter G. Cooper, *Official History of Fulton County* (Atlanta: self published, 1933), 869.

Washington Street in 1884. Following her husband's death in 1885, Sallie expanded her active career in civic and church affairs. She bought property next door to her daughter's house on Piedmont Avenue and Sixth Street but sold that lot in 1895 and soon afterwards went to live with her daughter and son-in-law. In 1919, when the State of Georgia removed the $1,500 and above property ownership restrictions on Confederate pensions, Sallie received a widow's stipend.

Declining health in her later years confined Sallie to living in her daughter's home, where she spent much of her time reading.[35] By 1896, she served as a prime source for Clayton family history and genealogy. Starting in 1909, the Atlanta Pioneer Women's Society began recording Atlanta's oral history. Sallie joined as a charter member but unlike her aunt, Augusta Clayton King, and her neighbor, Anne Austell, Sallie never fulfilled this organization's requirement for membership of writing her testimony to publish in the Atlanta newspapers.[36] Her omission appears particularly odd as many of her close relatives managed the city's major newspapers, the *Atlanta Journal* and the *Atlanta Constitution*.[37] Sallie likely felt that what she wanted to write went beyond an article and that her adventures were too incredible for some readers to accept.

Benjamin Crane's wealth was listed in 1870 at the then considerable sums of $10,000 in real estate and $25,000 in personal property. Ninth Census of the United States (1870), Fulton County, 327, microcopy M593, reel 151, National Archives, Washington, DC.

[35]Confederate Pensions, Fulton County, Georgia Department of Archives and History; and Sarah C. Crane obituaries, Lucian Lamar Knight Scrapbooks, vol. 13, 20, Georgia Department of Archives and History. Knight was at that time Georgia's most prominent historian. His inclusion of Sallie's obituaries in his scrapbook suggests that he interviewed her for such works as his *History of Fulton County*. The Nicolson House, now the Shellmont Bed and Breakfast Lodge, where Sallie undoubtedly wrote her memoirs, still stands at 821 Piedmont Avenue in Atlanta. See Isabelle Gournay, *AIA Guide to the Architecture of Atlanta* (Athens: University of Georgia Press, 1993), 106.

[36]Lily E. Morehouse to Mrs. Walthour, 26 April 1896, MS 518, Nicolson Family Papers Collection, Atlanta Historical Society; Atlanta Pioneer Women's Society Papers Collection, MS 391, Atlanta Historical Society; and D. Louise Cook, ed., *Guide to the Manuscript Collections of the Atlanta Historical Society* (Atlanta: Atlanta Historical Society, 1976), 11.

[37]Sallie's brother-in-law, E. F. Hoge, founded the *Atlanta Journal* where her brother Smith Clayton became one of the South's leading reporters. Their aunt, Augusta King Clayton, edited the women's page of the *Atlanta Constitution* for over twenty years. Ms. King's son-in-law was Henry Grady, the famous *Atlanta Constitution* editor and writer for whom Grady County, Georgia is named.

After a sudden illness, Sallie Clayton Crane died on 5 February 1922.[38] By 17 February 1942, her daughter, Caroline Crane (Mrs. William Perrin Nicolson), had given what survived of Sallie's manuscripts to Sallie's nephew, the Reverend William Clayton Torrence, secretary and director of the Virginia Historical Society.[39] He used a magnifying glass to read Sallie's small handwriting, transcribing all but the last part of the main manuscript and some variations of the main manuscript in three wire-bound notebooks. Torrence had his cousin, Mrs. Caro C. Irwin Kirby (Sallie's niece by her sister Caroline Maria Clayton) of Dallas, Texas, make a typescript of most of his transcriptions and provided Sallie's daughter, Caroline, with a carbon copy of the typescript.

Torrence found the manuscript "extremely interesting and *fascinating*."[40] He allowed Earl Schenck Miers to use the Clayton memoirs in *The General Who Marched to Hell* (1951) but Torrence never finished having the memoirs transcribed and typed.[41] Why Torrence, editor of such works as the *Magazine of Virginia History* and *The Edward Pleasants Valentine Papers*, never published his aunt's memoirs remains a mystery.

From the description of the Clayton memoirs given in the Miers book, this editor wrote to the Virginia Historical Society for information on where the memoir might be found. E. Lee Shepard, the senior archivist, and his

---

[38]Death certificate of Sarah C. Crane, Vital Records Service, Georgia Department of Human Resources.

[39]William Clayton Torrence was Sallie's nephew by her sister Katherine Winter Clayton (Mrs. John Torrence). Torrence served as corresponding secretary and director of the Virginia Historical Society from 1940 until his death in 1953. Claud Franklin Clayton, *Family Notes and Recollections* (Knoxville TN: self published, 1959), 75-76; and Virginius Cornick Hall, Jr., *Portraits in the Collection of the Virginia Historical Society: A Catalogue* (Charlottesville: University of Virginia, 1981), 243-244. Born and raised in Atlanta in the house where Sallie and her family lived during the Civil War, Clayton Torrence wrote in Sallie's copy of his 1906 genealogy *Rootes of Rosewall* that she gave him his first family data. A copy of this book is in the Rootes Family Vertical File in the Search Room of the Georgia Department of Archives and History.

[40]Torrence to Carrie Nicolson, 4 October 1941 and 18 February 1942, MS 518, Nicolson Family Papers Collection, Atlanta Historical Society. Mrs. Nicolson's daughter-in-law, Mrs. William P. Nicolson II, gave the carbon copy of the memoirs to the Atlanta Historical Society. In the unprocessed Clayton Torrence papers of the Historical Society of Virginia there is an inscription on a piece of cardboard that proves that the memoirs were given to Torrence by Sallie's daughter and not by Sallie herself.

[41]Torrence wrote lists of subjects on Sallie's memoirs as if organizing Sallie's memoirs for publication.

staff (with flashlight in hand) located the memoirs, the incomplete typescript, and some related letters in a collection of Torrence's unprocessed papers, stored in an unlit back room at the Virginia Historical Society. The printed guide to the manuscript collections of the Atlanta Historical Society identified the carbon copy of the incomplete typescript of the memoirs donated to the Atlanta Historical Society, along with letters from Torrence to Sallie's daughter about the typescript.[42] Samuel Carter III quoted from this carbon copy in his *The Siege of Atlanta, 1864* (1973) and Ralph Benjamin Singer used it as a source in his dissertation "Confederate Atlanta" (1973). A quotation from Sallie's memoirs appears in *Atlanta*, a volume in the Time-Life series *Voices of the Civil War* (1997).

Margaret Mitchell, however, likely did not read Sallie Clayton's memoirs. In some of her correspondence, Mitchell declined to even dignify her work as an historical novel although she based her fiction around easily identifiable members of her family including her famous cousin Martha Anne Holliday, who lived until 1939.[43] In wealth and prominence, the Claytons exceeded the status attributed to the fictional O'Haras and Wilkeses of the novel *Gone With the Wind*, and also of novelist Margaret Mitchell's Fitzgerald ancestors upon whom the O'Haras were at least loosely based.[44] The real life Sallie Clayton and the fictional Scarlett O'Hara would have been almost the same age during the Civil War and would have been at least acquainted as volunteer workers in the city's Confederate hospitals. Scarlett loved Ashley Wilkes, a major of Cobb's Confederate Legion. Sallie

---

[42]Cook, ed., *Guide to the Manuscript Collections of the Atlanta Historical Society*, 133. Since the guide was published, the carbon copy of the typescript of the Clayton memoirs has been transferred to the Nicolson Family Papers Collection.

[43]Martha Anne Holliday earned fame as the lost love of her famous gambler/brawler cousin, John Henry "Doc" Holliday. See David O'Connell, *The Irish Roots of Margaret Mitchell's Gone With the Wind* (Decatur GA: Claves & Perry, 1996). For other claims of historical accuracy by Margaret Mitchell and comparisons of the novel with documented scholarship see Albert Castel, " 'I Didn't Want to Get Caught Out': *Gone With the Wind* as History," *Blue & Gray Magazine* (July 1986): 3, 36-40.

[44]The 1860 federal census of Cass County, Georgia credited William Wirt Clayton with real estate worth $17,000 and personal property worth $46,000. The latter included fifty slaves on his Cass County plantation. The Fitzgeralds of Clayton County, by contrast, had only thirty-five slaves. Eighth Census of the United States, Clayton County, Population Schedule, microcopy M653, reel 114, 795, National Archives, Washington, DC; Slave Schedule, microcopy M653, reel 143, 367, National Archives, Washington, DC; and Anne Edwards, *Road to Tara: The Life of Margaret Mitchell* (New Haven: Ticknor & Fields, 1983), 26-29. Also see O'Connell, *The Irish Roots of Margaret Mitchell's Gone With the Wind.*

Clayton married a man she remembered as a real major of that same famous unit. Coincidentally, the mythical characters of *Gone With the Wind* and their real life counterparts in Margaret Mitchell's family tree lived in Clayton County, named for the real Sallie Clayton's grandfather. Margaret Mitchell (Mrs. John Marsh) is buried in Atlanta's Oakland Cemetery, a few feet from the grave of Sallie Clayton (Mrs. Benjamin Crane).

Sallie's memoirs both challenge and support the authenticity of the novel and the movie *Gone With the Wind*. As implied in Sallie's memoirs, Civil War Atlanta's "Puritanical" society frowned on dancing between men and women, contrary to the image portrayed in *Gone With the Wind*. Similarly, Sallie and others wrote of the cots and other furniture at the car shed used as the Atlanta Receiving Hospital, all noticeably missing in the movie *Gone With the Wind*. However, the movie's dramatic depiction of the seemingly endless numbers of wounded at the car shed agrees with her memoirs. Sallie Clayton wrote of the use of white turbans or bandanas as special symbols of authority among African-American women house servants, a detail also mentioned repeatedly in the novel *Gone With the Wind* but seemingly nowhere else. Margaret Mitchell's description of Civil War Atlanta includes references to the speculation, prostitution, and other dark qualities of the city that Sallie failed to discuss in her memoirs. However, Mitchell's explanation of the limited role of unmarried women in the city's hospitals does not exactly match that written by Sallie Clayton, once an unmarried female volunteer in those hospitals. Sallie criticized the children of the slave owning planter who buys rather than inherits his slaves and allows slaves to do tasks that he, self-conscious about his new high social status, refuses to have his children perform. She might have described the fictional O'Haras.

However, any contribution from Sallie Clayton to *Gone With the Wind* appears, at best, indirect. Margaret Mitchell likely never even met Sarah "Sallie" Clayton (Mrs. Benjamin Elliot Crane). Mitchell entered Atlanta society in 1920-1921, after Sallie had become virtually home bound by poor health, prior to her death in February 1922. Margaret Mitchell reportedly wrote *Gone With the Wind* between December 1922 and 1926. Nothing that this editor located about the novel and its author mentions Sallie.[45] Had

[45]Elizabeth I. Hanson, *Margaret Mitchell* (Chapel Hill: University of North Carolina Press, 1991), 26, 48-49. Other Mitchell biographical works consulted include Darden Asbury Pyron, *Southern Daughter: The Life of Margaret Mitchell* (Oxford: Oxford University Press,

Sallie and Margaret met, Sallie Clayton would have been only one of several Atlantans still living in the 1920s with memories from which Mitchell's research might have been drawn. Sallie's memoirs remained in the possession of Sallie's daughter, Caroline Crane (Mrs. William Perrin Nicolson), until 1942. *Gone With the Wind* historian Debra Freer points out that in the small and closed society of upper class white Atlantans, relatively close neighbors, like Carolyn Nicolson and Margaret Mitchell, almost certainly knew of each other, at least socially. However, they did not know each other well as late as 1938, after the publication of Mitchell's novel, although Sallie's granddaughter Carolyn later became a good friend of Margaret's husband.[46]

A case can be made for the historical details of Civil War Atlanta in *Gone With the Wind* being the results of the research of Atlanta historians Stephens Mitchell (Margaret Mitchell's brother) and her friend Wilbur G. Kurtz. The latter also served as a technical advisor in the making of the movie *Gone With the Wind*. How much of his exhaustive research came from any acquaintance with Sallie Clayton or Sallie's memoirs remains unknown. He started interviewing Atlantans for details of the city's past as early as 1903 and as a permanent Atlanta resident starting in 1911.[47]

The memoir of Sarah Conley Clayton (Mrs. Benjamin Elliot Crane), published here for the first time, comes from her original manuscripts—written in pencil in a very small handwriting and on deteriorating scraps of paper—in the unprocessed Clayton Torrence Papers of the Historical Society of Virginia. The pieces of the memoirs, sometimes incomplete, vary widely in length from a single page to complete chapters.

1991); Edwards, *Road to Tara*; Richard Harwell, *Gone With the Wind: As Book and Film* (Columbia: University of South Carolina Press, 1983); Bruce Clayton, "Dixie's Daughter: The Life of Margaret Mitchell," *Georgia Historical Quarterly* 77 (1993): 393-409; and Margaret Mitchell, *Margaret Mitchell's "Gone With the Wind Letters"*, ed. Richard Harwell (New York: Collier MacMillan Publishers, 1976).

46 William Perrin Nicolson Jr. to Mrs. John Marsh, 24 March 1938, folder 60:8, and John R. Marsh to Carolyn Nicolson, March 24, 1950, folder 60:4, MS 9005, Margaret Mitchell Marsh Collection, Hargret Rare Book and Manuscripts Library, University of Georgia Libraries.

47 Richard Barksdale Harwell, "Technical Advisor: The Making of Gone With the Wind The Hollywood Journals of Wilbur G. Kurtz," *Atlanta Historical Journal* 22 (1978): 8-11. A search of the papers of Wilbur Kurtz at the Atlanta Historical Society failed to document any contact with Sallie Clayton.

No chapter headings or plan for a finished book survive.[48] The present editor arranged the surviving parts by subject and assigned to them chapter headings.

Sallie's exceptionally literate writing required few editorial intrusions in the text. Where required, to correct spellings or provide clarification, editing appears in square brackets "[]." Additional information on clarifications appears in the annotations, as do words or passages added by Sallie that no longer have any intelligible context in the manuscript. Annotation also indicates the end of each fragment. Several parts of the manuscript have different drafts and sometimes the same text appears in different parts of the manuscript. The editor has combined the different drafts, with Sallie's original words preserved, changing sentence structure only when necessary. All details from all of the drafts appears here. Duplicate text was only eliminated only when possible without changing context or meaning, and as indicated by the annotation. All editorial changes are noted in the annotations. Canceled type is used to indicate words that Sallie crossed out.

Other annotations explain confusing text or identify persons, places, and events. Every attempt has been made to identify anyone mentioned in the memoirs, except for the persons appearing only on lists of names. Full identifications appear only with the first mention of each person or place. Not every person could be identified. Sallie's younger contemporary, Lucy Hull, wrote, "it was said that no one was ever born in Atlanta, but everyone moved there from somewhere else."[49] Atlanta during the Civil War had a transient population of all classes, rendering even city directories, census records, newspapers, and county records of limited value in making identifications.

---

[48]Clayton Torrence to Carrie Nicolson, 4 October 1942, MS 518, Nicolson Family Papers Collection. Atlanta Historical Society.

[49]Autobiography of Lucy Hull Baldwin, MS 849, Southern Historical Collection, University of North Carolina at Chapel Hill.

1

WAR COMES TO GEORGIA

IN PASSING TO AND FROM AUGUSTA TO MY HOME ON A LARGE PLANTATION around Kingston.[1] I had sometimes spent a night at the Atlanta Hotel,[2] but I was here so short a time during the day that I had little opportunity of seeing much of the place before we came to make it our home in December 1860.

---

[1]William W. Clayton's holdings in Bartow County included Kingston and several hundred acres to the east of the town. When Sallie lived there, Kingston was a cotton boom town with forty businesses and a population of twelve hundred people by 1852. During the Civil War, the town served as a major Confederate hospital that treated some ten thousand soldiers; and as a source of saltpeter for the Confederate Ordnance Bureau. Ironically, the Barnsley family, Clayton neighbors in Bartow County, likely served as models for characters in Margaret Mitchell's novel *Gone With the Wind*. "Kingston Tells Tales of Past But Predictions not New," unidentified newspaper clipping in Kingston files, Special Collections Bartow County Public Library, Cartersville; Bartow County Deed Book P (1861-1867), 369, 370, 446, microfilm reel 153/13, Georgia Department of Archives and History, Bartow County Courthouse, Cartersville, GA; Craighton Dominey, "Northwest Georgia's Ghost Town," *Georgia Journal* 16/4 (July/August 1996): 5, 7; and Don O'Briant, *Looking for Tara: The Gone With the Wind Guide to Margaret Mitchell's Atlanta* (Atlanta: Longstreet Press, 1994), 28-30. Captured Confederate map no. N-221-8 in RG 77 of the National Archives shows the location of the Clayton home and mill. A photograph of Kingston in 1864 appears on page 695 of William C. Davis and Bell I. Wiley, *Civil War Times Illustrated Photographic History of the Civil War Vicksburg to Appomattox* (New York: Black Dog & Leventhal, 1994). Sallie writes later in the manuscript that the plantation was named for the nearby Two Run Creek, which in the language of the Cherokee Indians, the former residents, is "Tala-Tana-rah." Also see William Clayton-Torrence, *Rootes of Rosewall* (n.p., n.d.), 75. In the unprocessed papers of Clayton Torrence at the Virginia Historical Society can be found the composition book of Caro Clayton and in it notes on where the Clayton family lived from 1859 to 1862: "June 10, 1859 left Augusta 12 o'clock at night for Kingston"; "June 10, 1860 at Tula La Narah, Georgia [the Claytons's Bartow County plantation]"; "June 10, 1861 in Atlanta, Ga.; and June 10, 1862 in Atlanta, Ga."

[2]The Atlanta Hotel was built in 1846. Atlanta's first brick building, it stood two stories and had entrances on Pryor and Wall streets. The hotel was among the buildings destroyed when Atlanta was burned in November 1864. Franklin Garrett wrote of the Atlanta Hotel, "Its broad rambling galleries, in the antebellum style, stood as a prophetic monument of the city that was to be." Franklin Garrett, *Atlanta and Environs* 3 vols. (New York: Lewis Historical Publishing Company, 1954) 1:236.

The Atlanta Hotel appears as Sallie Clayton knew it in this Civil War photograph. (Courtesy Atlanta Historical Society)

The Spring Bank School from George White, *Historical Collections of Georgia* (1854).

In the fall of 1860 I was here for a day in attendance on the State Fair of that year.[3] I came as a pupil of Spring Bank school, near Kingston, taught by our neighbors and friends Misses Jane and Lila Howard under the supervision of their father, the Reverend Charles Wallace Howard.

Now there is nothing very remarkable in a body of school girls[4] attending a fair with several teachers, but this was unusual in that to show our patriotism at that critical time, we were all clad in homespun dresses made by our own hands, the girls, with two or three exceptions, all being under sixteen years of age. We were a proud set, and were confident of being the first to appear in Georgia cotton; so in our simply made blue and

---

[3]The annual fair of the Southern Central Agricultural Society was first held in Atlanta in 1850 and permanently located in the city starting in 1857. The fair grounds, later a Confederate hospital, included three major buildings, one for "Ladies' work," one for mechanical arts, and one for plants. James Michael Russell, *Atlanta 1847-1890: City Building in the Old South and the New* (Baton Rouge: Louisiana State University Press, 1988), 52-53. Although Sallie makes no mention of it, Cass County (later renamed Bartow County), where the Spring Bank students came, also had a fair in September 1860. Lucy Cunyus, *History of Bartow County Formerly Cass* (Cartersville GA: Tribune, 1933; reprint, Easley SC: Southern Historical Press, 1996), 182.

[4]The original manuscript of Sallie's memoirs includes a list that she made of the students, probably from memory, at the Spring Bank School in Cass County in 1860: Mary Tinsley, Savannah; Anne Winter, Savannah; Rossie Wade, Savannah; Gertrude Butler, Rome; Virginia Ware, Rome; Georgia Ware, Rome; Sydney Carr, Rome; Anna Spurlock, Rome; Lizzie Neal, Warrenton; Laura Neal, Warrenton; Anna Battle, Warrenton; Con Reese, Americus; Anna Griffin; Fannie Bullock; Laura Williams; Mary Williams; Mollie Sanford, near Sparta; Camilla Sanford, near Sparta; Harriet Lane, near Sparta; Cornelia Redmond, Augusta; Mellie Redmond, Augusta; Julia Roper, South Carolina; Rebecca Mayson, near Kingston; Lizzie Mayson, near Kingston; Loula Mayson, near Kingston; Mary Roper, near Kingston; George Johnson, Kingston; Laura Johnson, Kingston; Sallie Clayton, near Kingston; Caro Clayton, near Kingston; Gussie Clayton, near Kingston; Fannie Howard, near Kingston; Sallie Howard, near Kingston; Mattie Wimberly, Savannah; Emma Stapler, Valdosta; Nellie Wyche, Valdosta or Florida. The unprocessed Clayton Torrence papers at the Virginia Historical Society contains the composition books of Caro and Julia Clayton that include autographs by their school mates. Caro's composition book also includes a list of the faculty of the Spring Bank School in 1860: Reverend C. W. Howard, president and principal of Latin; Miss Jane W. Howard, Principal Teacher and Instructress in French and German; Miss Lila Howard, Principal of Preparatory Department; Miss Fannie Howard, Principal of French and Fancy Work; and Miss Henriette Muhr (?), Instructress in Music.

white and brown checks, with all eyes upon us we walked proudly from the Union Depot out to the grounds on Fair Street near the cemetery.[5]

It is needless to say we took a prize though we were just a little bit crest fallen to find one other, not a school girl but a young lady, also wearing homespun, which was a much more showy, pretentious one than ours. In her dress, a clear, bright blue was the predominating color; a narrow buff stripe, with probably a red and white thread running through it, alternated with the blue about every half inch. It was made quite stylishly, as I remember; more of a riding habit, a pretty skirt and tight coat piped with buff and ornamented with numerous buttons. We understood that she herself had woven the material. Both dress and wearer looked remarkably well and richly deserved the premium that was awarded them.

When war became a reality as time passed and it grew harder to get materials for dressing, the ladies adopted homespun for the winter to save their better dresses, and there was soon great improvement in the patterns for weaving. They were no longer confined to checks and stripes but were made to resemble other materials, especially Irish poplin. Many ladies on the plantations and throughout the country learned to spin.

The only thing to mar the pleasure of the day was the running away of a horse attached to a buggy in which one of the young men was driving with Miss Anna Barnard, now Mrs. Hunt.[6] Both were thrown out and the young lady was so seriously hurt that she lay in an unconscious state for nine or ten days.

---

[5]The homespun dresses, however, proved to be a costly symbol of southern independence because they washed so poorly. George C. Rable, *Civil Wars: Women and the Crisis of Southern Nationalism* (Urbana: University of Illinois Press, 1989), 95. The Union depot stood near the corner of Pryor and Alabama streets in what is today Underground Atlanta. Fair Street is now Memorial Drive and the cemetery referred to is Oakland Cemetery. The walk that they describe must have covered close to two miles and would have passed the city hall-court house, where the present state capitol building now stands, across the street from the house where Sallie lived during the early years of the Civil War. The Union depot was regarded as the center of Civil War Atlanta.

[6]Anna Morgan Barnard, b. 15 December 1836 d. Atlanta 3 January 1910, married William H. Hunt in LaGrange, Georgia on 16 February 1871. Sallie might have added that Anna's son William married Sallie's niece Eloise Clayton. Jeannette Holland Austin, *Georgia Obituaries (1905-1910)* (n.p., n.d.) 193; family chart by William Barnard Hunt in the possession of Elizabeth Ford; and *Atlanta Constitution*, 4 January 1910, 4, c. 7. This passage in Sallie's memoirs reads as if written before Mrs. Hunt died.

Soon after our return to Kingston there were rumors of an insurrection (among the slaves) which caused excitement and alarm throughout the entire neighborhood. All men were called upon to do patrol duty; while women and children, sometimes several families in one house, were huddled together, more for sympathy than protection. My mother's[7] room had several smaller ones opening into it and one or two nights the other rooms of the house were left vacant while the overseer's family and ourselves, seventeen people, were crowded together in these rooms. There was very little sleeping and we gladly hailed the morning.

One evening in the beginning of the trouble several of us had to be at the school a mile and a half from us, for a concert, and going through a certain part of the woods our terror was so great that we crouched in the bottom of the carriage like frightened hares, though we had the driver and one or two others he had brought along with him for protection.

There was probably not the slightest foundation for those rumors, they were usually gotten up by people who did not own a slave and who wanted to bring trouble between whites and blacks.[8] But I tell it that you may know something of what [rumors] were passing through in those days. After it was

---

[7]Caroline Maria Semmes (Mrs. William Wirt Clayton), b. Washington, Georgia 8 October 1819 d. Atlanta, 4 April 1893, was the daughter of Andrew Green Simpson Semmes and his second wife Mary Robertson. William Wirt Clayton Bible in the possession of Gordon Ford of Forest Park, GA.

[8]Fear of slave revolts became obsessive among southerners in Georgia and throughout the Confederacy, from Lincoln's election to immediately after the war. The 1860 panic in Georgia resulted from reports of mysterious fires in Texas. At that time, another group of slaves allegedly plotted to burn Dalton, Georgia and then steal a train with which to flee to Marietta, Georgia and freedom. Clarence L. Mohr, *On the Threshold of Freedom: Masters and Slaves in Civil War Georgia* (Athens: University of Georgia Press, 1986), 20-40; David Stroud, *Flames and Vengeance: The East Texas Fires and the Presidential Election of 1860* (Carrollton TX: Alliance Press, 1997), 108; Donald L. Grant, *The Way It Was in the South: The Black Experience in Georgia* (Seraucus: Birch Lane Press, 1993), 51; and Thomas Conn Bryan, *Confederate Georgia* (Athens: University of Georgia Press, 1953), 127. Sallie implies elsewhere in her memoirs that many of the Cass County families moved to Atlanta in 1860 from fear of slave revolts by the field hands. Her father and many of her Atlanta neighbors moved their slaves to southwest Georgia to prevent liberation by the federal army. Mohr, *On the Threshold of Freedom*, 103. However, as shown by the letters of Sallie's mother, reproduced here in the appendix, even there the planters did not feel their families would be safe from liberated former slaves.

all over and quiet was once more restored, a friend, Mr. Charley Goulding,[9] gave me a memento of the occasion, a little book he had carved from soft stone with the words cut into the front cover: "History of the Insurrection, 1860."[10]

Those of us who had heard of the great uprising in Virginia which occurred long years before this and was called "Nat Turner's Insurrection" were spared additional terror by our ignorance of all particulars. For owing to the great effort at that time to keep everything in connection with it as quiet as possible few details were known beyond the scene of its enacting. Consequently, it was not until of late years a full account was given to the public in this part of the country.[11]

The misses Howard gave their long vacation in the winter and after the close of school in November [1860] I went to Sparta [Georgia] with one of the girls for a visit of a few weeks until the other members of my family were ready for me to join them in Atlanta about the middle of December. There

---

[9]Charles Howard Goulding, b. circa 1835 d. Richmond, Virginia, 30 August 1862, was the nephew of Reverend Charles Howard and the son of Reverend Francis Robert Goulding (1811-1881). The latter authored *The Young Marooners*, operated a boys boarding school in Cass County, and, reportedly, built the first sewing machine. Charles Goulding died of sickness while serving in the 8th Georgia Confederate Volunteer Infantry Regiment. Eighth Census of the United States (1860), Cass County, microcopy M653, reel 114, 705, National Archives, Washington, DC; Etowah Valley Historical Society, *Historic Bartow County 1828-1866* (Cartersville: self published, n.d.), 27; Robert M. Willingham, Jr., "Francis Robert Goulding," in *Dictionary of Georgia Biography*, Coleman and Gurr, eds. (Athens: University of Georgia Press, 1983), 360; and Compiled Service Records of Confederate Soldiers from Georgia, microcopy M266, reel 228, National Archives, Washington, DC. The Francis Goulding house in Kingston still stands, just north of where the Claytons had lived. Martha Mullinax, interview by the author, 25 January 1997.

[10]Sallie does not mention that the following May a slave was hanged in Kingston, Cass County, on charges of inciting a slave revolt. A white man accused of aiding in the slave revolt also faced execution. Fears of slave revolts in Georgia persisted throughout the war but especially in southwest Georgia, where her family and other slave owners moved their slaves to prevent the liberation of the slaves by the proximity of the federal army. Bryan, *Confederate Georgia*, 127; *Daily Intelligencer* (Atlanta), 10 May 1861, 3, c. 4; and *Augusta Daily Constitutionalist* (GA), 31 August 1864, 3, c. 2-3.

[11]Nat Turner, b. 2 October 1800 d. 11 November 1831, an educated black minister and slave, led some seventy slaves in a spree of killing whites in Southampton County, Virginia in August 1831. Turner and sixteen of his followers were later executed. For the history of this incident see Frank Roy Johnson, *The Nat Turner Slave Insurrection* (Murfreesboro NC: Johnson Publishing Co., 1966) and Henry Irving Tragle, ed., *The Southampton Slave Revolt of 1831* (Amherst: University of Massachusetts Press, 1971).

was some mistake about the day of my starting [for Atlanta] and I reached Atlanta twenty-four hours in advance of the others [in my family] and had to spend the time at the Atlanta Hotel which stood where the Kimball House was built afterwards and faced the railroad with an entrance for ladies on Pryor Street. My father and the proprietor, Dr. Thompson,[12] were good friends, and the former was a guest of the hotel at the time,[13] so though he could not stay with me on account of having to be out attending to business I did not have that altogether desolate feeling experienced by so many young travelers when they first find themselves alone.

The home that had been rented for us was where the Angier house now is, and the lot extended from the corner of Washington Street to Doctor Baird's house, where old Trinity Church (Methodist) stood then, and back to Mr. Coker's on Washington Street, which was then Major Yancey's home. The Street which our house faced was in those days Mitchell Street.[14]

---

[12]Dr. Joseph Thompson, b. 29 September 1797 d. 21 August 1885, was one of the first citizens of Atlanta and president of the city's medical college. He was remembered for his sense of humor and for standing as security for many strangers attempting to cash checks with cashier William W. Clayton (Sallie's father) at the Georgia Railroad Bank. Frequently those checks proved to be worthless. His wife was a friend of the famous Confederate diarest Mary Chesnut. Nellie Peters Black, *Richard Peters: His Ancestors and Descendants 1810-1889* (Atlanta: Foote & Davies Company, 1904), 104-11; Garrett, *Atlanta and Environs*, 1:237, 324; and Mary Chesnut, *The Private Mary Chesnut: The Unpublished Civil War Diaries*, eds. C. Vann Woodward and Elisabeth Muhlenfeld (New York: Oxford University Press, 1984), 41. A picture of Thompson appears opposite page 104 of Black, *Richard Peters*.

[13]The 1859-1860 city directory for Atlanta listed W. W. Clayton's residence as the Atlanta Hotel. C. S. Williams, *Williams' Atlanta Directory For 1859-60* (Atlanta: M. Lynch, 1859), 63.

[14]Sallie's family lived at the house of Dr. N. L. Angier, on the south side of the corner of Mitchell and Washington streets, what would later be 38 Mitchell Street. The house at that time faced the Atlanta City Hall/Fulton County Court House. During the federal occupation, Union General John M. Schofield used the house as a headquarters. A. A. Hoehling, *Last Train from Atlanta* (New York: Bonanza Books, 1958) map after 96. A photograph of this house appears in Norman Shavin, *Whatever Became of Atlanta?* (n.p., n.d.), 8. Today the site of Sallie's house is covered by a state office building, across the street from the state capitol building that Sallie's husband, Benjamin Elliot Crane, helped to build. At the time that she wrote these memoirs, the section of Mitchell Street that passed beside the state capitol building was called Capitol Square. Some time after the publication of the 1930 Atlanta city directory, that part of the street reverted back to being part of Mitchell Street, as it had been during the Civil War and is today.

The next morning while I was sitting alone in the parlor (of the hotel) looking out of the window and wondering whether I could find the place, a fine-looking young man entered the room and coming directly to me introduced himself as Mr. Harvey Thompson.[15] He remained a few minutes only and left some papers and magazines to help me while away the time. This was my first Atlanta acquaintance. He was the son of the proprietor of the Atlanta Hotel and Mrs. Richard Peters' eldest brother.[16]

After getting into our new home we found ourselves delightfully situated. Besides being in a desirable house, on a large lot, we had the advantage of the open square of the City Hall[17] just opposite and were in convenient distance to churches, schools and stores.[18]

In addition to the Yanceys[19] as neighbors we were on a line with the first Trinity Church, Mr. and Mrs. B. B. Crew, and Mr. and Mrs. William Solomon and family.[20] The latter had been our neighbors in Cass County, afterwards Bartow, having lived for a long time on a plantation between Kingston and Cassville, not more than a mile or two from us. A few weeks later Mr. and Mrs. John Neal with their family moved into their new

---

[15]George Harvey Thompson, b. 16 January 1838 d. 18 December 1864, was the first captain of the Gate City Guards of Atlanta. Black, *Richard Peters*, 112; and Garrett, *Atlanta and Environs*, 1:110.

[16]Richard Peters, b. 10 November 1810 d. 6 February 1889, was a civil engineer and agriculturalist who helped to pioneer the railroads that were the reason for Atlanta's existence. Peters took credit for inventing the name "Atlanta." He married Mary Jane Thompson, daughter of Dr. Joseph Thompson, on 18 February 1848. For the history of Peters and of the Thompsons, see Black, *Richard Peters*.

[17]The Atlanta City Hall/Fulton County Court House stood on the site of the present Georgia state capitol building. A picture of the old city hall taken from the Clayton home appears in Shavin, *Whatever Became of Atlanta?*, 7.

[18]A map of this neighborhood during the Civil War by Atlanta historian Wilbur Kurtz follows page 96 of Hoehling, *Last Train From Atlanta*.

[19]She refers here to the family of Benjamin Cudsworth Yancey, of whom she wrote more in chapter 6.

[20]See Eighth Census of the United States (1860), Fulton County, microcopy M653, reel 122, 756, National Archives, Washington, DC. B. B. Crews should have been James R. Crew. He later played an important role in helping to evacuate civilians from Atlanta during the federal occupation. V. T. Barnwell, *Barnwell's Atlanta City Director and Stranger's Guide* (Atlanta: Intelligencer Book and Job Office, 1867), 29; and MS 130, box 37, folder 12, Wilbur Kurtz Collection, Atlanta Historical Society.

house[21] which had just been built for them on the corner of Washington and Mitchell streets where the present Girls High School stands. Farther out Washington Street were Mrs. Robinson, afterwards Mrs. Bell, and her mother, Mrs. Hathaway,[22] Mr. and Mrs. Dabney, a little later Doctor and Mrs. E. N. Calhoun, Mr. and Mrs. L. B. Richards, Mr. and Mrs. James Clark, Mr. and Mrs. Sidney Root, Mr. and Mrs. Zimmerman and others.[23] At the extreme end of the Street in a beautiful grove lived Mr. and Mrs. James Ormond.[24]

We lived near five churches. Trinity Methodist was on Mitchell Street next door to us and diagonally across from us in Washington Street, was the Second Baptist—then noted for its lovely choir composed of Mr. and Mrs. L. P. Richards, Mr. and Mrs. West, and Mr. Sidney Root, the tenor. This church had no organ and the choir simply led the congregation in singing, not elaborate music, but appropriate hymns, albeit simple tunes in which all

---

[21]The John Neal house stood where the present Atlanta city hall now stands on Washington Street. The Neal house was used by General Sherman as a headquarters during the federal occupation of Atlanta. Wilbur Kurtz Collection, MS 130, box 36, folder 3, Atlanta Historical Society. A photograph of the house, probably made from Sallie's yard, appears in Shavin, *Whatever Became of Atlanta?*, 7.

[22]The widow Mrs. H. Hathaway and her daughter the widow Mrs. M. A. Robinson are listed in Eighth Census of the United States (1860), Fulton County, microcopy M653, reel 122, 756, National Archives, Washington, DC.

[23]Families like Sallie's frequently moved during the war years, as reflected in Sallie's memoirs, and Atlanta always had a very transient population of all classes, making identifications of people, even through city directories, tax digests, and censuses, difficult. The L. B. Richards referred to here must have been J. J. Richards, bookseller, living next door to James Clark, as shown on p. 761 of the 1860 federal census of Fulton County. The Rootes are recorded on page 768. Dr. E. N. Calhoun ran a boarding house, listed in the census on p. 751. Mr. Zimmerman was Richard Parks Zimmerman and Mr. Dabney was former state senator William H. Dabney whose house on Washington Street was used by federal General Slocum as a headquarters. Fulton County Index to Grantees (1854-1871), microfilm reel 151/62, Georgia Department of Archives and History; and Barnwell, *Barnwell's Atlanta*, 28.

[24]James Ormond, b. Leith, Scotland 7 May 1815 d. 14 December 1892, was a wealthy merchant who came to Atlanta in 1858. Garrett Necrology, reel 33, frame 236, Atlanta Historical Society. The text that follows is combined from two different versions of the same incidents by Sallie. The two versions do not conflict but each contains some details not found in the other.

could unite. Next the Central Presbyterian, St. Philip's Episcopal, and at the corner of Hunter and Loyd streets the Catholic Church.[25]

Three excellent schools were also our neighbors. Mrs. Wright's on Fair Street,[26] where Mr. Patillo's[27] home was afterwards built, Mr. Davis'[28] in the basement of the Second Baptist Church,[29] Misses Brown and Hamilton's in the basement of the Central Presbyterian Church.[30] The first and last were for girls and the second for boys.

The churches in which these three schools were held were nice brick buildings with excellent basements above ground for Sunday School. They were not so wide as the new buildings put up afterwards, and this allowed room on both sides for quite broad, paved walks, the length of the lots. So there was plenty of light and ventilation to the basements, and room for the scholars to move about in the open air a little, owing [to the] recesses.

---

[25]Torrence notes here that the Roman Catholic church is the Church of Immaculate Conception. For other accounts of Atlanta's Civil War churches see *Southern Confederacy* (Atlanta),, 8 September 1861, 3, c. 1, and 24 March 1863, 2, c. 3-4; and Christina M. McCoy, "The Ante-Bellum Churches of Atlanta," (Masters Thesis, Georgia State University, 1996).

[26]Now Memorial Drive.

[27]Torrence identifies him as Henry P. Patillo but he must have been Methodist minister and insurance agent William Pulaski Pattillo, b. Harris County, Georgia 27 January 1837 d. Atlanta 12 April 1909. Harold Lawrence, *Methodist Preachers in Georgia 1783-1900* (Tignall GA: self published, 1984), 413; Garrett Necrology, microfilm reel 16, frame 433, Atlanta Historical Society; and Fulton County Deed Book L (1868-1869), 17, microfilm reel 100/65, Georgia Department of Archives and History.

[28]She refers to Thomas W. Davis. See Williams, *Williams' City Directory*, 73. In a variant draft of this part of the text, Sallie also mentioned the boys school of her neighbor, Mr. A. N. Wilson of Tennessee, at the corner of Peachtree and North Pryor streets. He had operated a classical academy and fought unsuccessfully for a public school for Atlanta, modeled on that of Providence, Rhode Island. Russell, *Atlanta 1847-1890*, 64. Sallie might have also mentioned the City Hall Female Seminary that was operated by J. W. Miller and his wife Mary in the basement of the Central Presbyterian Church, almost next door to where Sallie and her family lived on the corner of Mitchell and Washington streets; and John C. McDaniel's boys school on Houston Street, near the Atlanta Female Institute. *Southern Confederacy* (Atlanta), 10 January 1862, 3, c. 1-2, and 8 April 1864, 2, c. 5.

[29]The Second Baptist Church of Atlanta, established 1 September 1854, stood on the corner of Washington and Mitchell streets, across the street from where Sallie and her family lived, on the same intersection. Garrett, *Atlanta and Environs*, 1:374.

[30]See chapter 2. Sallie made a note in another variation of this part of the text that Brown and Hamilton later "bought a home on Pryor Street near Mr. Rawson's, and taught there." Also see the memoirs of Leila Larendon (Mrs. V. P.) Sisson, MS 391, Atlanta Pioneer Women's Society Papers Collection, Atlanta Historical Society.

At the Central Presbyterian Church where several of us were entered as pupils the space on the right, as the church faces Washington Street, was very serviceable to us in many ways. The principal one of which was, in allowing room for us to form a semi-circle around our little friend Willie Williams, while he read to us the war news in the mornings before we were called into school by the ringing of the bell.

Mr. Jim Williams lived in the brick cottage next door to the church with his wife and three little boys, Willie, Claud and Tommie[31] and it was our delight to have Willie read to us. With great dignity the little fellow, then about five years old only, would seat himself on the top of the middle fence, and reading as well as any grown man, he would entertain us as long as we had time to listen. How we did enjoy it and how glad we were that his father, Mr. Jim Williams, lived next door, so we could be sure of our reader every morning.

Of the many things happening at this time I have little recollection of when Mr. [Jefferson] Davis passed through Atlanta on his way to Montgomery [to assume the presidency of the Confederate States of America].[32] It was in the morning when I was probably in school and at that time I think we were enjoying some of the advantages of city life in the form of a contagious affliction, of which we had fifteen cases of measles. Consequently, we were not seen outside of the house for several weeks.

When Mr. [Alexander H.] Stephens [the Confederacy's vice president] was on his way from Alabama to Charleston, he stopped in the afternoon and we stood quite near him on the side porch of the Atlanta Hotel, facing Pryor Street while he made a speech.[33]

---

[31]The 1858 city directory of Atlanta listed James E. Williams as a commercial merchant. In the 1860 census, he is recorded as age thirty-four and born in Tennessee with his wife S. E. Williams, age twenty-six; son William T., age six; Etheldred, age four; and son Thomas, age two. Williams, *Williams' City Directory*, 146; and Eighth Census of the United States (1860), Fulton County, microcopy M653, reel 122, 756, National Archives, Washington, DC.

[32]This visit by Jefferson Davis occurred on 16 February 1861. A reception for the new president was held at the Trout House Hotel. Garrett, *Atlanta and Environs*, 1:496-497; and Ralph Benjamin Singer, "Confederate Atlanta," (Ph.D. diss., University of Georgia, 1973), 67-8.

[33]This visit of Georgian Alexander H. Stephens occurred on 12 March 1861. He was actually on his way to Savannah, not Charleston. At that time, Atlanta was making an unsuccessful bid to become the capital of the Confederacy. Garrett, *Atlanta and Environs*, 1:497; *Southern Confederacy* (Atlanta), 2 May 1861, 2, c. 1-2; and Singer, "Confederate

Long years after, in the early seventies [27 May 1871], I stood on the upper porch of the Kimball House,[34] facing the same Street and heard Mr. Davis speak.[35] Besides the pleasure of seeing him, everybody had a hearty laugh at one of the incidents of the evening. It was a dark night, there was not light enough from the one or two lanterns held for the people in the Street to see his features and someone called out "Hold that light up to his face!" This was immediately done and the reply came, "I'm satisfied, the same old postage stamp!"[36]

I remember how particularly cordial was the greeting of Mr. Davis to Mr. Fisher, Father of Mr. Harry Fisher, and to my mother. The former told

---

Atlanta," 65-67, 69. One of Atlanta's first major political events had occurred on the same piazza of the Atlanta Hotel in 1848 when this same Alexander H. Stephens was nearly knifed to death after striking his political enemy Judge Francis Cone. Sarah Huff, *My 80 Years in Atlanta* (Atlanta: n.p., 1937), 46, and Thomas E. Schott, *Alexander H. Stephens of Georgia* (Baton Rouge: Louisiana State University Press, 1988), 92-93. Despite this incident, Stephens was still able to attend a political rally at the Walton Spring. Pioneer Citizens' Society of Atlanta, *Pioneer Citizens' History of Atlanta 1833-1902* (Atlanta: Byrd Publishing, 1902), 159.

[34]H. I. Kimball built the Kimball House Hotel, on the site of the Atlanta Hotel (destroyed in 1864), in 1870. At that time, the Kimball House was the largest hotel in the South. Garrett, *Atlanta and Environs* 1:835-836. A photograph of the Kimball House is in ibid, 876.

[35]She refers to his visit of 27 May 1871 and not to his famous last visit to Atlanta in 1886. In his speech from the Kimball House in 1871, the former Confederate president remarked that when he first visited Atlanta [in 1861?], it was in the woods and that the next time it was in ruins [May 1865]. *Atlanta Constitution*, 28 May 1871, 3, c. 2; and Noah Andre Trudeau, *Out of the Storm: The End of the Civil War, April-June 1865* (Boston: Little, Brown & Co., 1994), 296.

[36]This common joke in the South refers to Davis's well known likeness on the Confederacy's postage stamps. See, for example, the article reproduced in Dunbar Rowland, ed., *Jefferson Davis Constitutionalist: His Letters, Papers and Speeches* 10 vols. (Jackson: Mississippi Department of Archives and History, 1923) 9:438.

him he had once had the pleasure of shaking the hand of LaFayette,[37] and of the latter he had heard through friends and felt that he knew her.

It seemed to me that before we were well settled war excitement was at its height. South Carolina had seceded, quickly followed by several other states; military companies were diligently drilling, new ones were being rapidly formed; sounds of the fife and the drum and bands playing martial music filled the air. There were frequent political meetings, the making and presentation of flags; ladies forming societies. Everything seemed to be preparing for active service; and on all sides the cockade was visible.[38]

The first entertainment that I remember for raising funds to help the Cause was a large fair held in the City Hall. Then Captain W. H. Barnes formed his celebrated concert company, "The Atlanta Amateurs," and was soon giving performances for the benefit of the different military organizations.[39]

---

[37]Marie Joseph Paul Yves Roch Gilbert du Motier, Marquis de Lafayette, b. Le Puy, France, 6 September 1757 d. Paris, 20 May 1834, was a leader in the American and the French revolutions. He toured Georgia and America in 1824-1825. Sam Scott, "Lafayette," in *The American Revolution 1775-1783: An Encyclopedia*, ed. Richard L. Blanco (New York: Garland Publishing, 1993), 896-902. Mr. Fisher points out the irony that he had shaken hands with LaFayette and also with the leader of the Confederate revolution, Jefferson Davis. This Mr. Fisher likely would be W. H. Fisher, born c. 1801 in Connecticut, the father of Harris Fisher, born c. 1853 in South Carolina. Ninth Census of the United States (1870), Fulton County, microcopy M593, reel 151, 199, National Archives, Washington, DC; and Garrett Necrology, reel 7, frame 597, Atlanta Historical Society.

[38]Mrs. R. M. Massey remembered that so much enthusiasm for the war was in the air that even her young son was drilling the family's slaves. Memoirs of Mrs. R. M. Massey, Atlanta Pioneer Women's Society Papers Collection, Atlanta Historical Society.

[39]Actually William H. Barnes's Atlanta Amateurs, a male and female dramatic and concert company, was formed in May 1859. They performed plays and concerts across Georgia for all types of local Confederate charities. In June 1861, Atlanta's Soldiers Relief Association even gave a benefit on behalf of the Atlanta Amateurs. Garrett, *Atlanta and Environs*, 1:456; *Southern Confederacy* (Atlanta), 19 June 1861, 3, c. 1; *Daily Intelligencer* (Atlanta), 29 May 1861, 2, c. 2, 11 May 1863, 2, c. 6; Gibbons, "Life at the Crossroads of the Confederacy: Atlanta, 1861-1865," *Atlanta Historical Journal* 23/2 (1979): 21-22, 27-28; and Caro Yancey to Benjamin C. Yancey, 6 September 1861, Benjamin Cudsworth Yancey Papers, MS 2594, Southern Historical Press, University of North Carolina at Chapel Hill. An invitation to Sallie to attend an Atlanta Amateurs Concert on 13 May 1864 is among the Nicolson Family Papers Collection of the Atlanta Historical Society, MS 518 and copies of programs of the Atlanta Amateurs appears in Mary A. H. Gay, *Life in Dixie During the War*, 1897 (Atlanta: C. P. Byrd, 1897; reprint, Decatur: DeKalb County Historical Society, 1979), 37-41. The Boston Anthenaeum has a copy of *Original Songs of the Atlanta Amateurs* (Atlanta: Atlanta Intelligencer Print, 1861).

I don't know that I can recall many of the names of those who did such faithful, noble and helpful work, though I do remember that among the ladies were first and foremost Misses Julia and Frank Whitney, then Mrs. Boyd, Mrs. Farrar, Miss Gamling, with many others, both ladies and gentlemen, and especially two little girls, Betty Sasseen and Jennie Sims.

Mr. Barnes' company was composed of local talent; but others than members often helped, and later when ladies of other places had to seek Atlanta as a safer point than their own homes, many of them did what they could to help him and the Cause.

Then there was an exhibition of tableaux in the theater, "The Athenaeum"[40] on Decatur Street, just opposite the present Kimball House, mainly gotten up by Mrs. Perino Brown.[41] Mr. W. P. Howard suggested one scene he thought would be amusing, and called it "The Young Ladies with the Blues." When the curtain raised, instead of seeing doleful and melancholy countenances, a number of young ladies and girls, with happiness upon their faces were seen arranged in graceful groups about the stage with members of our youngest military company whose name was "The Fulton Blues." This military company was composed of those under age for active service, called "The Fulton Blues" and their uniform was a comparatively dark blue trimmed with a lighter shade of the same color.

At that time someone, whose name cannot be recalled, had a large singing class in Atlanta, and he gave one of the first concerts, which was

---

[40]The Athenaeum, Atlanta's first theater, was built by James Etheldred Williams on Decatur Street at the intersection known as Five Points in 1855. It had a row of white fluted columns above the ground floor. During the war, various entertainments were held there including a history of the opening of the war and the firing on Fort Sumter, performed by robots; a play of the history of the Crimean War by the Inkman Zouaves; and shows by the blind musical mimic Blind Tom. Garrett points to the rural nature of pre-Civil War Atlanta by the fact that the first floor of the theater was used for grain storage. It was also used as an auction house, including for the sale of slaves. Meta Barker, "Some High Lights of the Old Atlanta Stage," *Atlanta Historical Bulletin* ½ (1928): 33; Gibbons, "Life at the Crossroads of the Confederacy," 27; *The Commonwealth* (Atlanta), 12 November 1862, 2, c. 5, 14 November 1862, 2, c. 5, 18 November 1862, 2, c. 4; *Southern Confederacy* (Atlanta), 15 March 1864, 2, c. 6; and Garrett, *Atlanta and Environs*, 1:375. A lithograph showing the Athenaeum appears in Shavin, *Whatever Became of Atlanta?*, 22 and a photograph is in Walter G. Cooper, *Official History of Fulton County* (Atlanta: self published, 1934), 181.

[41]Georgia McKeen, b. Georgia c. 1833, d. Atlanta, May 1888, was the wife of Atlanta banker Perino Brown. Garrett Necrology, reel 34, frame 382, Atlanta Historical Society; Eighth Census of the United States (1860), Fulton County, microcopy M653, reel 122, 862, National Archives, Washington, DC; and Garrett, *Atlanta and Environs*, 2:554.

beautiful in arrangement, as well as music. The class did not come and go, but remained on the stage the entire evening, and was large enough to fill every part of it, all standing. The music was principally chorus, with a few solos and duets. One of the latter was "Gypsy Countess," sung by Misses Rosa Wright and Gussie Clayton,[42] in costume.

The singers of solos and duets were not arranged, as one might think, in the front row for convenience, but when their names were announced came from different parts of the stage through the crowd. One little girl in singing a solo began her song at the back of the stage and sang as she worked her way through the crowd around her to a full view of the audience. It was all very pretty and everyone seemed delighted.

The first [military] company to leave Atlanta for active service was the Gate City Guards[43] under the command of Captain William Efford [sic, Ezzard].[44] They were sent first to Pensacola[45] and after this to West Virginia, reaching the latter point in good time to share in the frightful experiences of some of our forces at Laurel Hill. A short time, I think the morning of the day before they were to go, the company was presented with a beautiful flag by Miss Anna Handliter.[46] The morning of their departure a very large crowd gathered at the depot to bid them "Godspeed." Among the number were all the collegiate members of the only large school in town, "The Atlanta Female Institute," situated on Ellis Street, and each young lady was

---

[42]Gussie Clayton was Sallie's sister Augusta King Clayton, b. near Athens, Georgia 13 April 1849 d. Atlanta 22 July 1864. Torrence, *Rootes of Rosewall*, 78.

[43]Company F, 1st (Ramsay's) Georgia Confederate Volunteer Infantry Regiment. Garrett, *Atlanta and Environs*, 1:500.

[44]William L. Ezzard. Garrett, *Atlanta and Environs*, 1:508.

[45]The federal garrison at Pensacola, Florida was besieged by the Confederacy until May of 1862, when the Rebels abandoned Pensacola. Mark M. Boatner III, *The Civil War Dictionary* (New York: Vintage Books, 1987), 641.

[46]Garrett identifies her as Miss Josephine Etta Hanleiter (later Mrs. Henry Gullatt), daughter of newspaper publisher Cornelius Redding Hanleiter, and describes the flag presentation as being at the train depot on the morning of the company's departure for Pensacola. Garrett, *Atlanta and Environs*, 1:508; and Elma S. Kurtz, "War Diary of Cornelius R. Hanleiter," *Atlanta Historical Bulletin* 14/3 (1969): 11. She had presented the Gate City Guards with a flag in 1859 modeled after the Stars and Stripes. In 1861, the new flag that she presented them was based upon the Confederacy's stars and bars. Pioneer Citizens', *Pioneer Citizens' History*, 160-161.

escorted by a member of our young military company, composed of those under age for active service,[47] "The Fulton Blues."

Companies from all parts of the state began to pass through Atlanta and sometimes one or more would be in camp here for a few days. The camping ground was in Walton Spring,[48] somewhere out Spring Street or rather west of it.

The Atlanta companies followed each other ("to the front") in quick succession. Among them were the Fulton Dragoons, Davis Infantry, Atlanta Grays, Georgia Volunteers, Atlanta Cadets, Irish Volunteers, Stevens [sic, Stephens'] Rifles, Steuben Yaegers and others.[49]

---

[47]Sallie might have mentioned that one of the speeches given was by one of Sallie's classmates at the Atlanta Female Institute, Sallie Avery, later the wife of Sallie's friend, Confederate general and Georgia governor Clement A. Evans. The young women of the Atlanta Female Institute presented each member of the Gate City Guards with a small Confederate flag. Garrett, *Atlanta and Environs*, 1:508; and Gibbons, "Life at the Crossroads of the Confederacy," 17.

[48]Walton Spring was a popular resort in early Atlanta that was sometimes used for May Day Festivals. The resort was operated at the corner of Spring and Walton streets by city councilman Anderson W. Walton and had Atlanta's only ice cream parlor. The resort originally consisted of a four room frame dwelling, a kitchen, a smoke house, a servant's cabin, a stable, and a carriage house. The spring, now gone, was large enough that it was used for baptisms. Spring Street is named for the Walton Spring and Walton Street for the spring's owner. Garrett, *Atlanta and Environs*, 1:271, 795; and memoirs of Lucy H. Kirklighter, Mrs. G. J. Foreacre, and W. H. Venable, MS 391, Atlanta Pioneer Women's Society Papers Collection, Atlanta Historical Society. The Confederate barracks in Atlanta were built on Peachtree Street, near the Walton Spring. Barnwell, *Barnwell's Atlanta*, 25; and Doreen McMahon, "Pleasure Spots of Old Atlanta," *Atlanta Historical Bulletin* 7/29 (1944): 231.

[49]Official designations of these units are: Fulton Dragoons, Company G, Cobb's Legion; Davis Infantry, Company K, 7th Georgia Infantry Regiment; Atlanta Grays, Company F, 8th Georgia Infantry; Georgia Volunteers, Company B, 7th Georgia Infantry; Irish Volunteers (sic, Jackson Guards) Co. B, 19th Georgia Infantry; and Stephens Rifles, Company C, 9th Georgia Cavalry. Garrett, *Atlanta and Environs*, 1:500; Charles Edgeworth Jones, *Georgia in the War 1861-1865: A Compendium of Georgia Participants* (Atlanta: Foote & Davies, 1909), 141, 153; and Lillian Henderson, *Roster of the Confederate Soldiers of Georgia 1861-1865* 2/6 (Hapeville GA: Longino & Porter, 1958), 205. Other Atlanta companies included the Continental Volunteers (Captain Seago), Lee's Volunteers (Captain G. W. Lee), the Atlanta Volunteers (Captain Woodall), and the Lewis & Philips Rifles (Captain Kendrick). *Southern Confederacy* (Atlanta), 29 June 1861, 3, c. 1. The German Steuben Yaegers appear to have been a home defense unit that never formally entered the Confederate army. Gibbons, "Life at the Crossroads of the Confederacy," 20; and *Southern Confederacy* (Atlanta), 26 April 1861, 3, c. 1. There were other Atlanta local defense units, such as the Silver Grays, composed of men over the age of regular service; the Atlanta Volunteers; the Ordnance

While the different flag presentations, which were sometimes made in open air, and at others in the Athenaeum, were all pretty, one especially so was that made to the Atlanta Grays, the chief feature of the evening being the presentation by Colonel Mark A. Cooper[50] (father of the captain, Thomas L. Cooper) of a copy of the New Testament to each man in the company, and that to the Davis Infantry at which was sung (to the tune of "Columbia") a farewell composed for the occasion by Captain W. H. Barnes.[51]

But the most impressive flag presentation that I saw was the one made to Captain Foreacre's company, "The Georgia Volunteers,"[52] on the evening before their departure for the front. The beautiful flag was made and presented by Miss Caro Yancey,[53] daughter of Colonel B. F. Yancey, and niece of the Hon. William L. Yancey[54] who came so near being the president of the Confederacy. This presentation was made in the Athenaeum, as had been also the two above-mentioned, during one of Captain Barnes' concerts.

Guards (115 boys too young for regular service); and the Raid Repellers. Singer, "Confederate Atlanta," 70-71; Gibbons, "Life at the Crossroads of the Confederacy," 24; and *Southern Confederacy* (Atlanta), 27 May 1863, 1, c. 1.

[50]Mark Anthony Cooper, b. 20 April 1800 d. 17 March 1885, was a former congressman and an industrialist who operated the Etowah manufacturing village in Cass County, near where Sallie had lived. James Dorsey, "Mark Anthony Cooper," in *Dictionary of Georgia Biography*, eds. Kenneth Coleman and Stephen Gurr (Athens: University of Georgia Press, 1983), 217-218. He had to defend himself against charges of being a speculator of questionable ethics, even though two of his sons died fighting for the Confederacy. *Southern Confederacy* (Atlanta), 15 September 1861, 3, c. 1, 27 December 1861, 2, c. 1, and 4 May 1863, 1, c. 2-3.

[51]For an account of this flag presentation see *Southern Confederacy* (Atlanta), 4 June 1861, 3, c. 1-2.

[52]Foreacre's company was actually the Confederate Volunteers. *Southern Confederacy* (Atlanta), 29 June 1861, 3, c. 1.

[53]Caroline Yancey, later Mrs. Hugh Nesbitt Harris of Athens, was the only child of Benjamin Cudsworth Yancey (1817-1891) by his first wife Laura Hines (d. 1844). She died 30 October 1905. James W. Patton and Clyde Edward Pitts, *The Benjamin Cudsworth Yancey Papers in the Southern Historical Collection of the University of North Carolina Library* (Chapel Hill: Southern Historical Collection, 1967), 7, 9; and Charlotte Thomas Marshall, *Oconee Hill Cemetery* (Athens: Athens Historical Society, 1971), 2.

[54]William Lowndes Yancey, b. 1814 d. 1863, was a former United States senator and soon after a Confederate States Senator from Alabama. Stewart Sifakis, *Who Was Who in the Confederacy* (New York: Facts on File, 1988), 313.

The evening was lovely and the theatre was very (crowded—a better word). Usually when a captain received a flag, after an appropriate reply of thanks to the young lady presenting it, he turned and placed it in the hands of the color bearer who received it in silence. But not so that evening; for when Captain Foreacre[55] finished his reply to Miss Yancey's pretty speech, he addressed the color bearer, calling him by name, Sergeant Fishback,[56] and after a few remarks closed by saying that in committing the flag to his keeping he felt sure it was in safe hands, admonished him to guard it with his life; and then after a short pause as he transferred the flag to the sergeant's hands, he added in particularly earnest and impressive manner—"And never allow its folds to trail in the dust."

Sergeant Fishback not only took the flag, but slowly, with emphatic pause after each word, in a loud bass voice, that increased in volume with every utterance, and resounded through the entire hall, he exclaimed—"Never! Never! Never!!!" The house went wild and could be quieted only by the loud playing of the orchestra until they could begin the music for a favorite chorus!

The fulfillment of Sergeant Fishback's promises was verified; that flag never went down, and after the surrender of the Confederate forces in 1865 it was returned to Miss Yancey.[57]

It seemed to me the ladies were on hand on all occasions. The [railroad] station was crowded with them at the coming and going of every train; sometimes to meet or say farewell to friends and relatives, all recognizing in every soldier a father, husband, brother and son, and all were anxious to aid each one of them in some way.

---

[55]Greenberry Jones Foreacre, b. Rainsborough, Ohio 19 February 1828 d. Newark, Ohio 16 December 1886, was Atlanta agent for the Macon & Western Railroad. After a serious wound at the First Battle of Manassas that ultimately took his life, Colonel Foreacre served as Confederate Provost Marshal in Atlanta. Garrett, *Atlanta and Environs*, 1:500; and Mrs. Delia Foreacre Sneed, "Sketch of G. J. Foreacre," Foreacre Willett Papers, MS 89, and memoirs of Mrs. G. J. Foreacre, MS 391, Atlanta Pioneer Women's Society Papers Collection, Atlanta Historical Society.

[56]Fourth Sergeant William G. Fishback. Garrett, *Atlanta and Environs*, 1:500.

[57]Sergeant Fishback, however, did not return the colors as he was discharged with a disability two months later, on 31 May 1861. Henderson, *Roster of the Confederate Soldiers of Georgia*, 1:844.

It was not long before the "Ladies Sewing Society" under Mrs. Willis Westmoreland,[58] as president, was well under way and a great deal of work was done. They held their meetings in the City Hall at first, then rented a room on the north side of Decatur Street, near Ivy, where numbers would meet for sewing, rolling bandages, and scraping lint. If more were needed than our room would accommodate we would be called out again to the City Hall. Now this is as I remember it, though I am not sure the room on Decatur Street did not belong to the Hospital Association instead of the Sewing Society; but no matter, we all worked in both.

A little later a large recruiting camp was opened at Big Shanty, now Kennesaw,[59] which was visited by citizens from Atlanta from time to time who always carried for the soldiers as many good things to eat as they could. Our first visit was on the occasion of a dress parade, I think it must have been. We went with Misses Neal, whose brother, Captain James Neal, afterwards colonel of the Nineteenth Georgia Regiment and killed at the Battle of Petersburg in 1865,[60] was there with his company, The Irish Volunteers;[61] and Captain John Keely[62] his lieutenant. The Volunteers were

---

[58]Mariah Jourdan Westmoreland formed, in her home, an organization for making bandages and lint for the volunteers at Pensacola. Garrett, *Atlanta and Environs*, 1:508.

[59]She is describing Camp McDonald, Georgia's largest Confederate training camp or camp of instruction, near the present city of Kennesaw. It was a popular place for friends and relatives to visit soldiers. William S. Smedlund, *Camp Fires of Georgia's Troops, 1861-1865* (Lithonia: self published, 1994), 201-205; and Bryan, *Confederate Georgia*, 190-191.

[60]James Henry Neal, as colonel of the 19th Georgia, died in the arms of Captain (formerly his lieutenant) John Keely at the Battle of Bentonville, NC in March 1865. Neal is buried in Oakland Cemetery in Atlanta. Henderson, *Roster of the Confederate Soldiers of Georgia*, 2:705.

[61]Neal's company was the Jackson Guards (Company B, 19th Georgia Volunteer Infantry Regiment). However, the Jackson Guards was formed before the war as the Irish Volunteers. Pioneer Citizens', *Pioneer Citizens' History*, 43. The 19th Georgia Infantry Regiment was famous for having large numbers of Irishmen in its ranks and several Atlanta newspapers carried an appeal by local Irishman O. A. Lochrane for Irishmen in the South to fight for the Confederacy. Ella May Thornton, "Captain John Keely An Informal Reminiscence," *Atlanta Historical Bulletin* 4 (1939): 74; and *Southern Confederacy* (Atlanta), 9 May 1861, 2, c. 5.

[62]John P. Keely, b. Newtonberry, Ireland 1839 d. Atlanta 1888, served with distinction throughout the Civil War, achieving the rank of captain before a leg wound late in the war took him out of the fighting. He never completely recovered although he became a successful Atlanta businessman after the war. Henderson, *Roster of the Confederate Soldiers of Georgia*, 2:706; Thornton, "Captain John Keely," 73-76; and Cooper, *Official History of Fulton County*, 854-55. A photograph of Keely appears in ibid, 308. The Atlanta Historical Society has

beautifully uniformed in dark green with gold trimmings and large dark hats with drooping white plumes and were an exceedingly fine-looking body of men.

We were entertained at Captain Neal's tent and among the pleasures of the day was that of hearing the lovely voice of Lieutenant Keely in several beautiful songs. Handsome at all times, he was at that time unusually so in his becoming uniform; far too handsome for the enemy or anyone else to shoot at; yet [not] long afterwards it was found that before the day was over, before he had even seen an engagement, his heart had been pierced by the blue eyes of his captain's sister, Miss Ella Neal.[63]

The first thing that happened in our midst to give us a realization of the sad things of war was the hanging of seven bridge burners who were with Andrews in the capture of the engine "General" at Big Shanty, now Kennesaw, in 1862. No connection with any federal command could be proved, consequently they were regarded as spies. The execution took place below Oakland Cemetery as it was then [Spring of 1862] but the addition to the cemetery in 1866 embraced the spot, which is said to have been at or near, where the Confederate Monument now stands.[64]

---

excerpts from his Civil War diary and letters. D. Louise Cook, ed., *Guide to the Manuscript Collections of the Atlanta Historical Society* (Atlanta: Atlanta Historical Society, 1976), 67-68.

[63]Keely was renowned for his singing voice and his good looks. He married Ella Neal on 3 November 1869. Sallie's son-in-law, William P. Nicolson, would be one of Ella's pall bearers. Thornton, "Captain John Keely," 74-75; and Fulton County Marriage Book C (1866-1873), 321, microfilm reel 110/67, Georgia Department of Archives and History.

[64]Sallie is describing the execution of seven federal saboteurs who, under the orders of Union General O. B. Mitchell, attempted to burn the bridges of the Confederacy's Western & Atlantic Railroad on 12 April 1862. The saboteurs captured the locomotive the *General* but were prevented from accomplishing their mission in what became known as the "Great Locomotive Chase." For the history of this episode see Henry H. Kurtz Jr, "Hijack of a Locomotive: The Andrews Raid Revisited," *Atlanta History* 34 (1990): 5-14 and Stephen Davis, "The Conductor versus the Foreman: William Fuller, Anthony Murphy, and the Pursuit of the Andrews Raiders," *Atlanta History* 34 (1990): 38-54. For the location of the executions of 18 June 1862 see Garrett, *Atlanta and Environs*, 1:523-524.

Smith and Tom Clayton[65] with two cousins, Tom and Andrew Semmes,[66] ranging in ages from eight to ten years, were exceedingly anxious to be present at the hanging, and all of us entreated those in authority not to permit such a thing. However, it was decided to let them have their wish, hoping it would be a lesson to them and that they would never want to see another execution. To dissuade, we tried to explain how the sight might remain a lasting mental picture, that might probably never leave them; but, they turned deaf ears to all that was said and away they went.

When the men, who were all hanged at the same time from a long beam were led on the scaffold the two Toms couldn't stand any more; they turned their backs, closed their eyes, and, I think, their ears. The two others (Smith Clayton and Andrew Semmes) looked on and saw the springing of the trap which left seven men dangling in the air until the ropes holding two broke and let their burdens fall, which required a second hanging of the two unfortunate men.

That night the two little fellows who hadn't been able to look on the dreadful sight had no trouble in sleeping. The others also went to bed and to sleep; but, maybe towards midnight, they would send up howls that were loud enough to have brought out the entire police department. One poor little fellow insisted that all seven of the men were sitting on the foot of his bed. No one could comfort them and it was ever so long before they could be sufficiently made to sleep. However, the desired effect was produced, for the sight of that hanging caused a complete loss of taste for executions, and woeful sights were likewise avoided.

These boys, active, industrious, full of life, wanting continual occupation, very much to our amusement, carried on a brisk business in leeches and green frogs. The first sold to physicians as fast as they could catch

---

[65]Smith and Tom were her brothers Augustin Smith Clayton, b. 9 December 1850 d. 24 April 1916, later a respected Atlanta journalist; and Thomas Andrew Clayton, b. 22 August 1852 d. 21 October 1911, later sextant of Atlanta's Oakland Cemetery and an employee of the Southern Railway. Torrence, *Rootes of Rosewall*, 77-78; and Garrett Necrology, reel 18, frame 10, and reel 20, frame 253, Atlanta Historical Society.

[66]Andrew Green and Thomas Hemphill Semmes were twins, b. 19 November 1852 at Wynston, near Columbus, Georgia, the sons of Confederate General Paul Jones and Emily J. Hemphill Semmes. General Semmes, mortally wounded at the Battle of Gettysburg, was the brother of Sallie's mother Caroline Maria Semmes Clayton. Harry Wright Newman, *The Maryland Semmes and Kindred Families* (Baltimore: Maryland Historical Society, 1956), 88-89.

them; the latter were for the Atlanta Hotel, and were kept in large tubs of water in the well-house until they could be delivered. In the meantime the boys would give them some exercise by bringing them into the house and running after those who were afraid of them. I would escape because I had shown an interest in their stock in trade by visiting the ponds and letting them show me how the frog protects the eye under water by drawing down an inner, thin, and transparent eyelid.

One day they found me sitting in a room alone reading and I must acknowledge that it was with no degree of comfort that I looked up and saw the quartet, and counted two frogs to the boy, and my relief was very great on hearing one of the little Semmes boys say: "Oh! that's Cousin Sallie; we won't trouble her; she comes out and looks at our frogs." Up to that time my visits to the well-house had been without design; but I am not altogether sure they were afterwards.

In the spring of 1861 before leaving for the army became[67] general the young ladies and gentlemen attended a few parties and picnics. That year the latter were given principally at Ormond's grove[68] at the end of Washington Street and at Williams' mill.[69] A favorite amusement of a few of the youngest set was to go out early in the morning to a mineral spring near the Macon depot.[70] Among the boys and young men who usually went with us here and elsewhere were Phil Sims, Willie Clayton, Edgar Thomp-

---

[67]The rest of this chapter comes from another fragment of the Clayton memoirs.

[68]Sallie refers here to the "beautiful grove" of Mr. and Mrs. James Ormond that she mentioned earlier in the chapter.

[69]Williams' or Durand's Mill was on the south side of Peachtree Creek, across from the mouth of the North Branch of Peachtree Creek, in land lot 49 of Fulton County's 17th District and near the present Seaboard Railroad Bridge. It was owned by furniture maker and saw mill operator Frederick A. Williams of Atlanta, b. 1817 d. Atlanta 1883, the son of prominent businessman Ammi Williams. Robert N. Scott, comp., *The War of the Rebellion: a Compilation of the Official Records of the Union and Confederate Armies* (Washington, DC: United States Government Printing Office, 1890-1908) Series I, vol. 38, pt. i, 137, pt. v, 231; George B. Davis, Leslie J. Perry, and Joseph W. Kirkley, *Atlas to Accompany the Official Records of the Union and Confederate Armies* (Washington, DC: United States Government Printing Office, 1891) plate XLVII, map 5; Franklin Garrett to author, 2 September 1994; and Sextant Registers, volume II, 66, Oakland Cemetery, Atlanta.

[70]The stone depot of the Macon & Western Railroad was built on what is now Pryor Street in 1846. Garrett, *Atlanta and Environs*, 1:235. The spring behind the depot was considered to be the center of Atlanta and the beginning of the Ocmulgee River. J. Cutler Andrews, *The South Reports the Civil War* (Pittsburgh: University of Pittsburgh Press, 1985), 430.

son, Alton Angier, Tom Ware, Marcellus Markham, Ed Holland, Joe Thompson, Tom Walker, Frank Stovall, George Hammond, and Euclid Young. Some of these went also with the full grown young ladies. There were a few small buildings in the immediate neighborhood of the spring and one large one that was kept by a young man as a place of amusement and refreshment for he also kept a stock of sweetmeats and served ice cream. Though we went early, if it were Saturday or a holiday, we sometimes stayed late, and we frequently sat in this saloon to rest, or to get out of the sun.

One morning in the absence of the proprietor, everything was closed, but thinking we were there so often that we were almost at home, and nothing would be thought of it, one of the young men climbed through a window and opened the door to let us in, and while we were having a good time the householder appeared. He was so indignant at the liberty that had been taken that he threatened to have the entire crowd arrested. We were badly frightened till the young men succeeded in pacifying him.

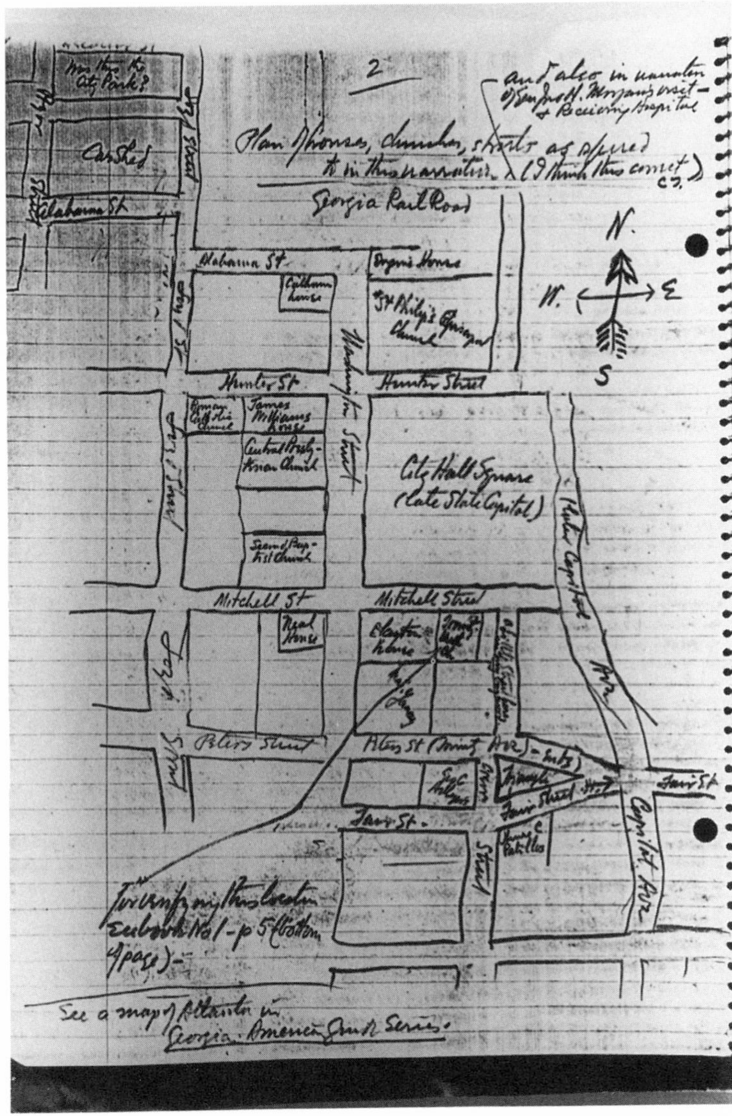

Clayton Torrence's drawing of the neighborhood of Atlanta where Sallie Clayton lived early in the Civil War. The "City Hall Square" in the drawing is today the site of the Georgia State Capitol building. (Courtesy Historical Society of Virginia)

Sarah "Sallie" Conley Clayton (Mrs. Benjamin Elliot Crane). (Courtesy Atlanta Historical Society)

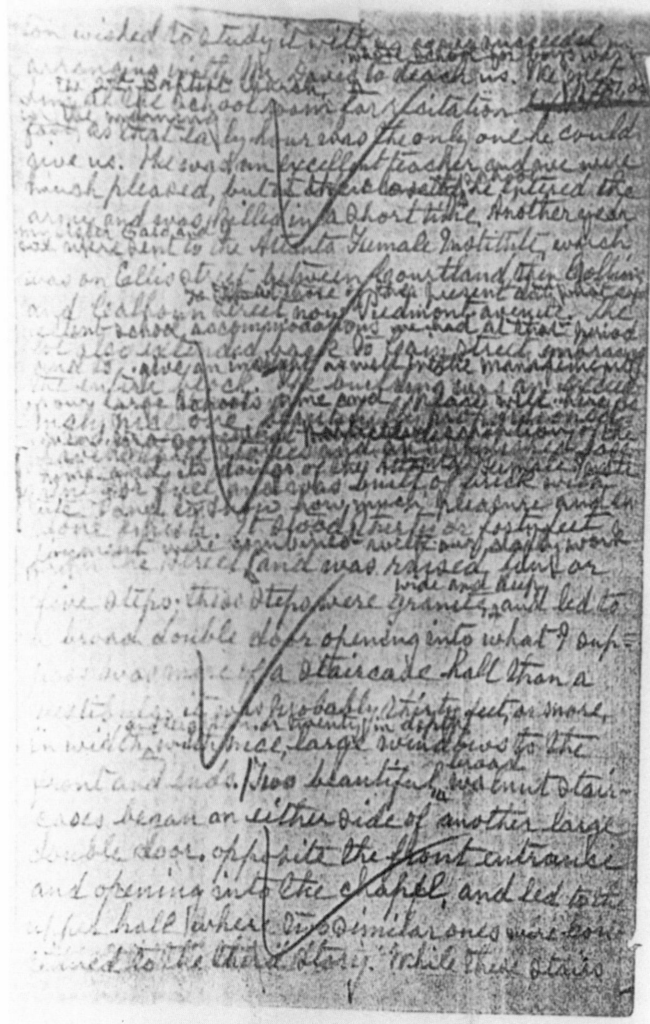

[illegible] wished to study it with us [illegible] arranging with Mr. [illegible] to teach us. We met in the Baptist Church [illegible] at the school room for recitation [illegible] as that early hour was the only one he could give us. He was an excellent teacher and we were much pleased, but at the close of the session he entered the army and was killed in a short time. Another year my sister Sallie and I were sent to the Atlanta Female Institute, which was on Collins street between Courtland and then [illegible] and Calhoun street, now Piedmont avenue. The [illegible] school accommodations we had at that period [illegible] It stood thirty or forty feet from the street and was raised [illegible] or five steps; these steps were granite, wide and deep, and led to a broad double door opening into what I suppose was more of a staircase hall than a vestibule. It was probably thirty feet or more in width and twenty in depth, with three large windows to the front and sides. Two beautiful broad walnut staircases began on either side of another large double door, opposite the front entrance and opening into the chapel, and led to the upper hall where two similar ones were continued to the third story. While these stairs

A page from the original memoirs of Sarah "Sallie" Conley Clayton. (Courtesy Historical Society of Virginia)

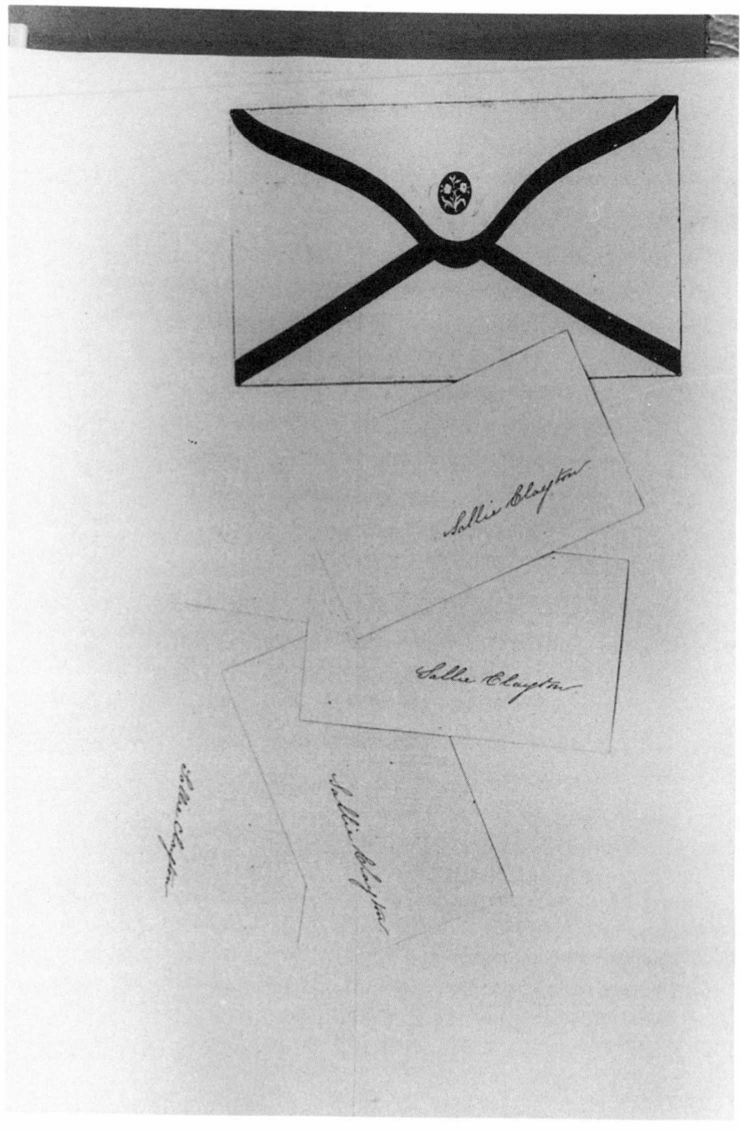

Sallie's Civil War calling cards. (Courtesy Atlanta Historical Society)

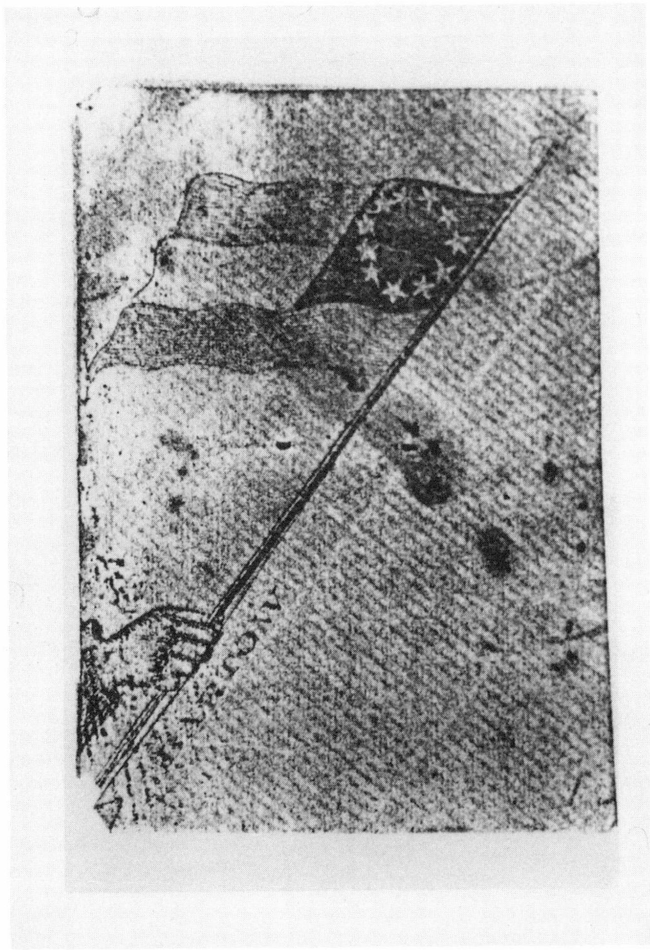

This card, with an illustration of a Confederate flag, belonged to Sallie Clayton. On the back she wrote: "This little flag I have held very dear having worn it in my hat during the trying days of civil strife in the United States of America." (Nicolson Family Collection, MS 518, Series I, Box 5, Atlanta Historical Society)

The Atlanta Female Institute is the domed building on the horizon, to the right of center in this Civil War drawing of Atlanta. (Courtesy Atlanta Historical Society)

2

THE ATLANTA FEMALE INSTITUTE[1]

AT THE SCHOOL OF MISSES BROWN[2] AND HAMILTON[3] NO HIGHER BRANCHES of mathematics than arithmetic were taught and no languages. We could get along without the first, and the modern languages for awhile, but we were anxious to continue our Latin and Miss Hamilton, the junior teacher wished to study it also; so we succeeded in arranging with Mr. Davis,[4] who had a boys' school, to give us an hour before opening his school. We recited this lesson before breakfast. Our recitation [period] was from a quarter to seven to a quarter to eight o'clock in the morning, as that early hour was the only one he could give us. Mr. Davis proved to be a superior teacher and we were very much pleased especially as we thought the question of our being taught Latin was settled. At the close of school, however, he entered the army and was killed in a short time.[5]

In the Spring of the next year, 1862, my sister Caro[6] and I were sent to

---

[1]This chapter is compiled from seven separate fragments of the manuscript. Two versions of the fragment used for the beginning of this chapter survive. The more complete version is used here. The two fragments contain the same information, differing only in wording. For additional information on female academies in the Old South see Christie Anne Farnham, *The Education of the Southern Belle: Higher Education and Student Socialization in the Antebellum South* (New York: New York University Press, 1994) and Eleanor Miot Boatwright, *The Status of Women in Georgia, 1783-1860* (Brooklyn NY: Carlson Publishing, 1994).

[2]Miss Brown was from Columbus, Georgia and set up a school for boys and girls under age fifteen in the basement of the Second Baptist Church. *Southern Confederacy* (Atlanta), 9 January 1862, 2, c. 4. No reference to her first name or background have been found. The failure of the census taker in Muscogee County (Columbus) to note occupations of adult women makes even tentative identification impossible.

[3]Miss A. E. Hamilton ran a select school in Atlanta. *Atlanta Daily Intelligencer*, 2 August 1860, 2, c. 4.

[4]She refers to Thomas W. Davis. See C. S. Williams, *Williams' Atlanta Directory For 1859-60* (Atlanta: M. Lynch, 1859), 73.

[5]Captain Thomas W. Davis of the 42nd Georgia Volunteer Infantry Regiment died of disease at Vicksburg, Mississippi, 18 July 1863. Lillian Henderson, *Roster of the Confederate Soldiers of Georgia 1861-1865* 6 vols. (Hapeville GA: Longino & Porter, 1958) 4:606.

[6]Caroline Maria Clayton, b. Athens, Georgia 14 January 1847 d. Atlanta 25 July 1876, married William George Irwin on 21 February 1871. Torrence, *Rootes of Rosewall*, 78.

the only large school in the place, the Atlanta Female Institute,[7] which was on Ellis Street, between Courtland, then Collins Street, and Calhoun Street, now Piedmont Avenue. The lot also extended back to Cain Street, thus embracing the entire block. This part of the square was very much lower than the front, and that being the case, we had room enough under the rear of the house, without any trouble of digging, for a nicely walled, but unfinished basement for fuel.

In the middle of the lot facing Ellis Street, about forty or fifty feet from the Street, stood the building of brick, pointed with white, and finished with stone. It was raised four or five steps; these steps were granite, wide and deep, and led to a broad double opening into what I suppose was more of a staircase hall than a vestibule; it was probably thirty feet, or more, in width and ten or twenty in depth, with nice, large windows to the front and ends. Besides the broad entrance door there were two single doors in back, one on either side of the rostrum. It was exceedingly nice: beautifully proportioned, and with high ceiling, many tall and broad windows.[8] There was plenty of light and ventilation. There was nothing on the first floor but a very large chapel, except a hall across the front in which were built two beautiful walnut stair cases, broad and easy of ascent, one on either side of

---

[7]The Atlanta Female Institute began as a private stock company in 1859 largely financed by $4,000 in city bonds, allegedly as a conspiracy to defeat the movement for public schools in Atlanta. The building opened in 1860 and remained a school until made into a Confederate hospital in July 1863. The institute held a "grand levee" in December 1861 that gave Atlanta's young men a chance to socialize with the school's students. Professor J. R. Mayson, a Methodist minister and the principal, reopened the school at the John Neal house, on the corner of Washington and Mitchell streets, across the Street from where Sallie Clayton and her family lived. The school closed during the summer of 1864 for vacation. It never reopened. In the fall, Atlanta fell to the federal army and the Neal house became General Sherman's headquarters. Wallace P. Reed, *History of Atlanta, Georgia* (Syracuse, New York: D. Mason & Co., 1889), 318-319; *Southern Confederacy* (Atlanta), 6 December 1861, 3, c. 3; James Michael Russell, *Atlanta 1847-1890: City Building in the Old South and the New* (Baton Rouge: Louisiana State University Press, 1988), 64; and Franklin Garrett, *Atlanta and Environs* 3 vols. (New York: Lewis Historical Publishing Company, 1954) 1:456-457. After the war, the site of the original Atlanta Female Institute was sold to Mayson in lieu of debts owed by the institute to him. Fulton County Deed Book K (1867-1868), 438-439, microfilm reel 100/64, Georgia Department of Archives and History.

[8]Two Civil War panoramic views of Atlanta include the Atlanta Female Institute and its cupola just to the right of the center of the horizon. Garrett, *Atlanta and Environs*, 1:574; and Norman Shavin and Bruce Galphin, *Atlanta: Triumph of a People* 2nd ed. (Atlanta: Capricorn Corporation, 1985), 58. The Atlanta Female Institute, as the Confederacy's Institute Hospital, appears in the novel and the movie *Gone With the Wind*.

the double door leading into the chapel, and under each stair case was a large cloak room. The chapel itself had the usual furniture of a stage, with its desk and chairs, a piano just below in front of it, and plenty of long movable seats. On the second floor was a broad hall and four spacious recitation rooms. In the third story were eight music rooms, four on each side, separated by narrow halls from a large inner room, with a good sized library just back of it, and opening into it, fitted with nice walnut bookcases built in one end, a library table, and comfortable seats. It [the library] was the only room carpeted and I think the windows were curtained. This large room [the third floor inner room, not the library,] was a noticeable feature of the building in that it was without windows. In the third story, in the center, was a hall for the meetings of our literary society, The Isabella Society it was called, and lighted entirely from above, something I had never seen before. [The third floor's] four music rooms, each furnished with a piano and chairs, [were] on each side of the society hall and separated from it by passage ways five or six feet wide, with windows in the rear end.[9]

The faculty consisted of seven. Mr. James R. Mayson,[10] president; Mr. W. P. Howard,[11] Mrs. Bessant, Miss Sudie Means (afterwards Mrs. Henry

---

[9]This description of the Atlanta Female Institute was compiled by combining the details from two drafts written by Sallie. Clayton Torrence wrote here, at the end of the typescript of this fragment, "This completes a page: but evidently there was more to be written into this manuscript." However, the continuity of thought in this next fragment suggests that these two parts were originally combined.

[10]James R. Mayson, b. near what became Atlanta 11 October 1827 d. Atlanta 29 August 1893, was a graduate of Emory College and a Methodist minister. Harold Lawrence, *Methodist Preachers in Georgia 1783-1900* (Duluth, Georgia: self published, 1984), 362.

[11]Clayton Torrence made a note on the typescript that Howard was later a Confederate general. Actually, Howard served as a general in the Georgia militia, beginning 1 May 1861. He led the Confederate reoccupation of Atlanta after the federal evacuation of the ruined city in November 1864. Howard prepared a detailed report and map of the devastation for Georgia Governor Joseph E. Brown. Louise Frederick Hays, "Adjutant General's Office Book of Commissions Military Records 1861-1865 Volume B—49" (unpublished typescript, Atlanta: Georgia Department of Archives and History, 1939), 118; *Southern Confederacy* (Atlanta), 25 December 1861, 3, c. 1-2; and *Macon Daily Telegraph and Confederate* (GA), 10 December 1864, 2, c. 2. Professor W. Pinckney Howard was one of the most prominent music teachers in the United States having been president of the National Music Convention at the Smithsonian Institute in 1858. He moved to Atlanta from Randolph County, Georgia after 1860. In the years immediately after the Civil War, he toured the world with the mimic Thomas "Blind Tom" Betune before becoming professor of Music at the Atlanta Classical College. In the early days of the war, he earned notoriety for pulling a knife on guards in Virginia to obtain arms needed by his brother's company. He died in

Capers), Miss Jennie Clayton (daughter of Mr. John Clayton, a merchant, of Atlanta), Miss Correy, and Miss Davis, the two latter were music teachers. The number of trustees was a hundred, and sometimes more.

At first the school hours were from half-past eight, or nine o'clock to twelve in the morning; and from one to half-past four, or five o'clock in the afternoon. Later there was a change to one session and we were dismissed at two o'clock. This was generally liked better on account of not having so much walking to do, if for no other reason, for at the mid-day hour we went home for lunch, and that gave most of us a walk of five miles a day. There were no Street cars or pavements[12] and it was never known at what moment a cow would dispute the passage of a Street with us; so walking was not altogether one of the pleasentest [sic] things we could do.

The school was open at all times to visitors, and one afternoon in the Spring, when so many soldiers were passing through an entire military company called. A few weeks before Mr. Howard, who expected very soon to enter the cavalry service himself,[13] had been practicing his class, the sophomore, in that drill, and when the young men found it out, as they were cavalrymen, they proposed a drilling match, the challenge was readily accepted. By seating the spectators on one side of the large chapel plenty of space was left for those who were drilled. After we finished, judgment was in favor of the young ladies, though the best men of the company had been chosen to represent it in the match. One of the young men gained the

---

Athens, Alabama on 4 August 1868. Garrett Necrology, microfilm reel 6, frames 369-370, Atlanta Historical Society; *Southern Confederacy* (Atlanta), 29 June 1861, 2, c. 2; Eighth Census of the United States (1860), Randolph County, microcopy M653, reel 135, 576, National Archives, Washington, DC; Henry Kyd Douglas, *I Rode With Stonewall* (Chapel Hill: University of North Carolina Press, 1959), 373; and Garrett, *Atlanta and Environs*, 1:437, 797.

[12]Mrs. Frank P. Rice would remember that only Whitehall Street in Civil War Atlanta had paved side walks and they were paved in stone. Memoirs of Mrs. Frank P. Rice, Atlanta Pioneer Women's Society Papers Collection, Atlanta Historical Society; and Pioneer Citizens' Society of Atlanta, *Pioneer Citizens' History of Atlanta 1833-1902* (Atlanta: Byrd Publishing, 1902), 43. A southern editor lyrically reported that the sidewalks of the hurried, rowdy city of Atlanta were paved in goober-shells and apple peelings, while the actors at the theater were nightly joined by their audiences in the plays. Andrews, *The South Reports the Civil War*, 430-431.

[13]Sallie apparently does not refer here to W. Pinckney Howard but to his brother, Rufus A. Howard. *Southern Confederacy* (Atlanta), 29 June 1861, 2, c. 2. Also see note 20 below.

applause of the assembly by dancing a sailor's horn pipe[14] for us.

On reaching the school in the morning we assembled in the chapel for roll call and a short religious service, at which there was always singing. Then someone of the pupils, though usually Mr. Howard, would play a march on the piano, while we formed double columns on opposite sides of the hall, and after marching, and counter-marching, these columns, crossed each other at the broad door and ascended the stairs on either side to the recitation rooms above.

The last hour in the afternoon was given to calisthenic exercise, but waltzes, polkas, the Schotische and the May-pole were used also, though only under the above name.[15] After the change to one session these exercises were left out and the last hour we met again in the chapel at one o'clock for an hour's singing. The closing time was always announced, and rising to form our line, we sang the last of on our outward march. To prevent confusion, or breaking the double line, as we marched out after dismissal, each girl carried her books and bonnet with her into chapel.

At that time girls didn't wear hats to school, and their bonnets were of all sizes, shapes and material; some were corded thickly and flared; some were stiffened with paste-board; some with thin wooden slats; and then there was the shaker bonnet woven of straw, and shaped something like a large, narrow sugar scoop, drawn over the face. The bonnet itself came to the neck in the back and a deep cape of beige, dark blue, brown or green color, pleated on with a heading. The binding and a quilting across the top about midway between back and front were of the same color. These bonnets were not very closely woven, and when they were first used some wearers got freckles almost as large as okra seeds on their face from the sun's peeping at them through the cracks, but, mothers were soon wise enough to line them with the same color as the trimming.

A funny thing happened one day about the singing. Mr. Howard, who was an excellent musician, taught us and we hadn't been doing satisfactory work, which discouraged him. So, on that day, instead of joining us in

---

[14] A sailor's horn pipe is an English folk dance named for an obsolete musical instrument. Lewis Mulford Adams, ed., *Webster's Unified Dictionary and Encyclopedia* (New York: H. S. Stuttman Co., 1961), 2053.

[15] She means that dancing as anything but classroom exercise by young women was not considered proper. Atlanta society frowned upon a woman even attending a dance. *Southern Confederacy* (Atlanta), 24 March 1863, 2, c. 3.

chapel, the members of the faculty stood outside the door talking the matter over with our leader. Inside a hundred and thirty-five to fifty girls were waiting, but no teacher came. Then they began to sing; and sang song after song without any notice being taken of them; so, very naturally concluding it to be a case of desertion they struck up a song that had been composed by Mr. Howard for the children, and often, for their pleasure sung as the closing piece, "Let's Go Home to Dinner," and began to march out, when they were stopped and detained awhile for a short lecture, though it was acknowledged their singing had been better than for a long time before.

The rules of the school were not very many or stringent. Two were made for the safety of the pupils, to wit: we were not to go to the cupola, or to slide down the railing of the stairs. The latter was a great temptation, even to the larger girls[16] for they could begin at the top of the third story and come down to the chapel door. Of course nobody would undertake this while any of the teachers were on the ground, but, instead of having a janitor to attend to the building, the girls themselves did it and a number of them from the different classes were appointed once or twice a week, to come after school hours and do the sweeping. They were called the sweeping brigade, and thinking it no harm to combine a little pleasure with work, one or more would sometimes take a trip on those winding rails. I do not know that these prohibitions were in effect when one afternoon one of the little girls had a fall of about fifteen feet and was very badly hurt. That happened before I went there.

Two other rules savored of cruelty. We were not to eat apples that grew on a number of trees in the front yard, or to get sweet gum from several trees in the corner of the lot at Collins (now Courtland avenue) and Cain streets, where Mr. Snook[17] afterwards built his home.[18]

In those days there was no manufactured chewing gum all came from

---

[16]Sallie made an annotation here: "The stairs were built here in such a way that there was a broad graceful curve of the rail at the bend forming an almost circular wall, enough for anything to fall through, therefore, very dangerous, notwithstanding the delight of being able to stand at the top of the third story, and slide down to the chapel door."

[17]Clayton Torrence identified him as P. H. Snook. Peyton H. Snook, age twenty-nine and born in Virginia, lived in Atlanta in 1870. He was an Atlanta furniture dealer. Bradley W. Steuart, *Georgia 1870 Census Index* (Bountiful UT: Precision Indexing, 1990), 2765; and Franklin Garrett to author, 13 December 1993.

[18]Clayton Torrence made the note here: "Think of bars of any sort raised between school girls, sweet gum and green apples!"

trees and was called "sweet-gum," but, no matter where it came from, or what it was called, we were not to use it.

My introduction to this rule was one morning very soon after I became a pupil in this school. I was with a class that had come down to chapel for recitation, as was our custom every morning in order to make room for another teacher to have her pupils in our classroom.

One of the little girls ran in and said to the teacher that someone wanted to speak to me in the front hall. As I passed out of the door a slender, pretty girl hurried to meet me, and putting something into my hand, she said in a rapid, tragic, whisper, "Maggie Poole[19] is my name. I heard you liked sweet gum and I ran downstairs to bring you a piece. But don't let the teachers see you with it, for if you chew it they'll take twenty off your deportment." Before I could catch my breath, she had disappeared up the steps and left me standing with the contraband goods in my hand.

At first I didn't know exactly what to do, for I had never, so far broken a rule anywhere, having always found we could have fun enough without getting ourselves into trouble. Fortunately in those days our dresses afforded deep pockets; so, without losing time, into one with which I was supplied, went the sweet gum, and I returned to class.

And how about the apples? Did we fall? Yes, as thick as leaves; more than a hundred of us! Not deliberately or intentionally, for the school was composed of a remarkably good set of girls, but in this way. A few days before we were to be dismissed for the summer holidays, two girls saw some of the apples fall and understood Mr. Howard to say, as there were only two or three, they might take them. The mistake they made was in not enjoying their find then and there. Too generous for that, they went around giving everybody they met a taste, and apple tasting became so general that others thought that permission to get them under the trees extended to all. I do

---

[19]Margaret J. Pool was listed in the 1860 federal census of Black Hall District, Fulton County, as a wealthy thirteen year old orphan living in the household of E. M. Taliaferro. Eighth Census of the United States (1860), Fulton County, microcopy M653, reel 122, 938, National Archives, Washington, DC. Ten years earlier, she was living in the household of E. M. and June Pool, presumably her parents, in Fayette County, Georgia. She married Major William H. Smythe, a federal officer who came to Atlanta immediately after the war. Rhea Cumming Otto, *1850 Census of Georgia (Fayette County)* (Savannah: self published, 1983), 51; Memoirs of Mrs. Lewis H. Clark, Atlanta Pioneer Women's Society Papers Collection, Atlanta Historical Society; and Garrett Necrology, microfilm reel 13, frame 226-227, Atlanta Historical Society.

not know that any were pulled.

While all this was going on there were a few comments from the teachers, and the president said to several: "Girls, you are going to hear more of these apples before the day is over." And sure enough, after school, instead of marching out as usual, it was announced from the rostrum that all girls who had not pulled, eaten or tasted, an apple were dismissed, the others would please remain. Less than a dozen girls rose and began to straggle out, and even of this small number some were recalled when witnesses called their names, and raised a cry of guilty. At first the culprits enjoyed it, knowing they had not done anything wrong, and thinking perhaps there were enough of us to make any offense somewhat respectable, but the teachers were taking the matter most seriously. They began what we girls called a pow-wow that lasted until the afternoon was far gone. A great many of the offenders attempted to explain how they had been caught, but they were promptly silenced by hearing "That's enough; we don't want to hear any more from you. Take your seat."

After that all the talking came from the stage; we could listen only without the privilege of replying. This state of things had gone on a long time when suddenly Mr. Howard proposed that the entire crowd should be suspended. We were getting very tired, to say nothing of being hungry, and, Maggie Poole, always full of fun, unable to restrain herself at this, jumped to her feet and called out "Second the motion!" Many others rose and followed her example so that it took the faculty fully fifteen minutes to get us sufficiently quiet to resume the fight upon us. It was all of half past four o'clock when we wended our way home, stopping at the gate of every "Innocent" wherever we found one waiting to hear the result of our detention.

It was with somewhat a feeling of regret with me that we couldn't say suspension was the decision, for I had been appointed to read the salutary at the closing exercises, and knowledge of that fact was not altogether inductive to my happiness.

We thought we were about through with the whole thing, but the following morning the lecturing was resumed, and continued until one would have thought that apple business was as serious as the original pulling and tasting of similar fruit in the Garden of Eden.

After different ones had taken a part in lecturing us Mr. Howard's brother, Mr. Rufus Howard,[20] rose and began to speak. This amused us very much, for he had been coming to the school only a short while to get a little training, as it were, in the art of teaching, in order to take his brother's place, to allow the latter to enter the army, so we couldn't help wondering what he had to do with the matter.

Well, he spoke and spoke and spoke, just like somebody wound up who couldn't stop himself. And, after all of this, we had to forgive him when we found he was an enemy in the camp. For when some of the young ladies afterwards called him to account for having half killed us with such a long speech, it turned out he was on our side. He declared it was to kill time only; that he found if the speaking was finished by a certain hour, we were all to be sent to the recitation room for lessons; and thinking that was something we didn't want, he determined to save us if he could.

The lessons wouldn't have amounted to very much anyway, for the next night, or on the one following, the closing exercises took place and we were overjoyed to know we would hear no more of eating apples for at least a long season.

The graduates for the year 1862, were Miss Emma Latimer, valedictorian, Misses Imogene Hoyle, Sallie Avary, and Anna Bomar; and though of a lower class the salutatory was read by me.

So full a description of the Atlanta Female Institute is given for several reasons: First, it always is well that succeeding generations should know somewhat of schools and their management of earlier periods than their own: Then to let it be seen how much pleasure and enjoyment were combined with our daily work following so closely upon the time when so little regard was paid to even the rights and comfort of pupils, and none whatever to relaxation and diversion. And especially to show that in those days we had this school building which would have been a credit to a larger place than Atlanta then was, though she numbered at the time fully fifteen thousand, and probably more, in population.[21]

---

[20]Rufus A. Howard, b. Troup County, Georgia 22 August 1831 d. Atlanta 13 July 1900. Garrett Necrology, microfilm reel 12, frames 717-719, and reel 33, frame 325, Atlanta Historical Society.

[21]The population of Atlanta, as given in the 1859 state census, numbered 11,500 and insurance agent C. C. Hine reported 11,000 that same year. However, the 1860 Federal census counted only 7,741 people in Atlanta. Williams, *Williams' Atlanta Directory*, 11; Robert S. Davis, Jr., ed., "Georgia Cities on the Eve of the Civil War: The Insurance Reports of C. C. Hines," *Atlanta History* 31 (1987): 51; and Garrett, *Atlanta and Environs*, 1:488.

Then also this school building became the successive home of gladness and sorrow to a greater extent than any other building that I know of in the place. It became likewise through sheltering the sick and wounded, among us one of the historical points in our city. With as much done for the welfare and pleasure of the pupils [sic? wounded soldiers?] as any one could expect or wish.

It was a most fascinating school, almost too much so for study, as the average school girl views it. No building in the place could have been the scene of more joy and happiness from its opening day in 1860, to the close in 1863. Then it was taken for a hospital, and all this was followed by an equal amount of suffering, sorrow, sickness and death. For some of us saw the building filled with cots, and on each cot a sick or wounded soldier. We even looked upon the dead laid temporarily in the basement; and the basement itself was the "Dead House."

To those of us who had known its happy days the change was so like a play. First, the ringing down the curtain on a picture of Life, and Joy, and Mirth, and raising it again to present one of Gloom and Sorrow, Suffering and Death.

And what was the fate of the building? One would have thought that after such valuable services in these two noble and important lines, this house deserved not preservation alone, but a place of honor. But, when the town fell into the hands of the enemy, there was no time for thoughts like these. Even had they been willing to indulge the community in any such sentiment, it was entirely out of the question with them, especially as the high point the building occupied[22] could be made so serviceable for their own protection. So, without hesitation, they not only took its life, but even denied it the spot on which it had stood as a place of burial. For, in 1865, those who passed that way saw that it had been razed to the ground and a

---

During the war, Atlanta's population swelled from the addition of refugees and Confederate ordnance workers. Z. A. Rice estimated that by the summer of 1864 Atlanta had a population of more than twenty thousand people. *Macon* (GA) *Daily Telegraph and Confederate*, 29 November 1864, 1, c. 3; and *Nashville* (TN) *Daily Times & True Union*, 3 August 1864, 2, c. 2. Federal estimates that Atlanta had a population, with the Confederate army, of 180,000 in 1864 must be grossly inflated.

[22]Although the Atlanta Female Institute did not survive, even as a memory, the hill where it stood retained the name of "College Hill." Garrett, *Atlanta and Environs*, 1:457. Today the Radisson Hotel occupies this site.

large fort had been built on the site.[23]

During the summer of 1862 the young ladies had a very pleasant society for improvement in music gotten up by Misses Mary and Pauline Semmes,[24] who were then in Atlanta as refugees. Musical gentlemen were also admitted as members, and a few school girls. The society met for the first time at Mrs. Westmoreland's,[25] and afterwards was invited to meet at the homes of different ladies, some of whom were Mrs. Si Robson, Mrs. Clayton, Mrs. Shackleford, Mrs. Semmes,[26] who lived in the late Mrs. Duncan's house on Peachtree Street, which belonged at that time to Mrs. Semmes' brother in law, General Lucius J. Gartrell.[27] After the completion of Mrs.

---

[23]This fragment of the manuscript ends here. A panoramic view of Atlanta made from the cupola of the Female Institute during the federal occupation of Atlanta in 1864 is on page 54 of Shavin and Galphin, *Atlanta: Triumph of a People*. Federal troops demolished the building to provide bricks for winter quarters. Macon (GA) *Daily Telegraph and Confederate*, 10 December 1864, 2, c. 2. V. T. Barnwell, however, claimed that the Female Institute burned during the destruction of the Confederate manufactories by General Sherman's army. V. T. Barnwell, *Barnwell's Atlanta City Directory and Stranger's Guide* (Atlanta: Intelligencer Book and Job Office, 1867), 30. The Union army did fortify a section of Atlanta as a defense against a Confederate attack that never came. However, that line of forts ran far to the south of the Atlanta Female Institute. George B. Davis, Leslie J. Perry, and Joseph W. Kirkley, *Atlas to Accompany the Official Records of the Union and Confederate Armies* (Washington, DC: United States Government Printing Office, 1891) plate LXXXVIII, map 1; and Lee Kennett, *Marching Through Georgia: The Story of Soldiers and Civilians During the Atlanta Campaign* (New York: HarperCollins, 1995), 207.

[24]They were Sallie's first cousins and the daughters of Confederate General Paul Jones Semmes, later mortally wounded at the Battle of Gettysburg. Harry Wright Newman, *The Maryland Semmes and Kindred Families* (Baltimore: Maryland Historical Society, 1956), 88.

[25]Mariah Elizabeth Jourdan Westmoreland, b. 1840, the daughter of prominent politician Dr. Warren Jourdan of LaGrange and early cook book author Mary Thornton, was the wife of Dr. Willis F. Westmoreland. She wrote "The Soldier's Wife" and "The Soldier's Trials," plays performed at the Atlanta Athenaeum on behalf of the wives and children of the Confederate soldiers. With Madeline V. Bryan, she made the first public symbol of Confederate authority in Atlanta, the revenue flag for the Customs House. Although pregnant, she refugeed to Milner, Georgia during the siege of Atlanta. Memoirs of Mrs. R. M. Massey, Atlanta Pioneer Women's Society Papers Collection, Atlanta Historical Society.

[26]Clayton Torrence makes the note here "she was Emily Hemphill, wife of Gen. Paul J. Semmes, CSA, (who died from a mortal wound received on the second day at Gettysburg) and brother of Mrs. Caroline (Semmes) Clayton, mother of Mrs. Crane. Gen. L. J. Gartrell's wife was a Hemphill, sister of Mrs. Semmes."

[27]Lucius Jeremiah Gartrell, b. Wilkes County, Georgia, 7 January 1821, d. Atlanta, 7 April 1891, served as a Confederate general and congressman. Jon L. Wakelyn, *Biographical Dictionary of the Confederacy* (Westport CT: Greenwood Press, 1977), 199.

Solomon's new house, the old [Harry][28] Jackson home in Capitol Square, she insisted that the society make use of her parlors at any and all times, offering as a special inducement a new grand piano. There were a number of exceedingly pleasant meetings in her house.

The entertainments were called musicales. There was no regular hour, or time of day, appointed for the meetings until just before they were to occur; then it would be decided whether the time should be morning, afternoon or evening.[29]

In the latter part of April [1861] while the two ends of the Republic were preparing to do battle the one end to the other, our school resolved itself into a monarchy and chose a sovereign: in other words, preparations were begun for a May party.[30] These parties were of two kinds, alike in some respects and very different in others. For instance, the Woodland May Party was always given in the country and entirely by boys, who made all the arrangements themselves except preparing the refreshments.

First, on one side of the play ground chosen a bower of green bushes and leaves was built in which we placed a throne covered with green and ornamented with garlands of various flowers. The throne was usually raised a step or two from the ground. A large pole made of a smooth young tree, stripped of its bark, was planted in the center of a large circle marked off especially for it; then under some tree, with extending branches, an egg shell was suspended from one of the limbs by a thread, or string, long enough to give full play. Sometimes there was a May pole with garlands of flowers fastened by one end to the top and extending to the ground, but somewhat longer to give the dancers surrounding it room to plait them around the pole as they circled it in their merry-making.

The boys even made one or two long narrow tables somewhere to one side, out of the way, and all the ladies had to do was to put the linen on, decorate them with vines and flowers and cover them with the feast.

After the guests had all arrived and were seated around the large circles that held the pole and suspended eggshell, the order of exercises was for the

---

[28]This note was made by Clayton Torrence.

[29]This sentence ends this fragment of the manuscript. This organization was remembered by Mrs. R. M. Massey as the Amateur Musical Club. Memoirs of Mrs. R. M. Massey, Atlanta Pioneer Women's Society Collection, MS 391, Atlanta Historical Society.

[30]For additional information on May parties, as held at southern female academies, see Farnham, *The Education of the Southern Belle*, 168-171.

different boys to climb the pole, which was kept very wet to make it slick and slippery, and bring down a crown of flowers resting on the top. Those who could not climb had their trials at the swinging egg-shell. Each must be blindfolded and furnished with a long stick, he was near the eggshell which he must try to strike and break; a wreath also awaited his success.

They alternated in their trials and the winner, bearing the wreath, would kneel before the lady of his choice and first lay it at her feet, then rising he would crown and conduct her to the throne.

The queen selected two maids of honor to stand the one on either side, and then as her subjects passed before the throne each made obeisance to the newly crowned sovereign, after which there was a general merry-making and feasting. The usual time for the Woodland May party was in the afternoon.

In the City May party which was always given by a school, those taking special part were selected or chosen. They were drilled in marches, choruses, songs and speeches appropriate to each part taken, and dresses suitable for each must be prepared. This last was by no means a small undertaking, for a great many spangles were used, and in those days each spangle had to be cut and applied by hand.

The performance which was somewhat on the order of a play was always presented in a public hall and always in the evening. Afterwards the chairs, or benches, used by the audiences were moved out of the way for dancing, but there was no feast.

In our school the children were greatly in the majority and I was very much of a favorite with them. When the party was proposed and the selection of a queen was being considered, they did not altogether understand about the nomination of candidates for election so, without waiting for that they began calling my name from all parts of the room at such a rate that they paid me the compliment of my life in acclaiming me queen. To carry out the form the teachers took a vote and my election was pronounced unanimous.

Miss Lydia Brown, a young sister of our senior teacher, composed and drilled us in our speeches; and Mr. Carl Harmsen[31] took charge of the

---

[31]She probably refers here to music professor Ludwig Harmsen, d. Minneapolis, Minnesota 23 September 1915, rather than to his brother, German-born bookkeeper Carl Harmsen. Garrett Necrology, microfilm reel 20, frames 7-8, and reel 11, frame 18, Atlanta Historical Society.

music.

The performance was given in the City Hall.[32] A stage large enough for our use, about a third of the width of the room, was built in one end of the hall, and to prevent any look of bareness it was made a recess stage, it had an arched crimson cover, the floor and two or three steps built at the front of the stage, were covered with a red and black carpet; the sides and back were also curtained with heavy material of crimson; these were hung with garlands of flowers and all made a pretty setting for the bright costumes of the players. Curtains were extended on the right from the front corner of the stage to the side wall to form a large dressing room. A throne raised one or two steps and having a pretty canopy over it, was placed at the farthest end of the recess. When all was ready, at a given signal, the singing of a chorus was begun and we marched out into the hall and entered the stage from the front. The royal robe was white tartan, thickly spangled with gold stars half an inch in size, the train was not very long, but the sleeves were, for they were made in a fashion prevailing at the time: open flowing, wide and long, down to the hem of the dress, and called "Angel-Sleeves."

The crown was a gilt creation and was something gorgeous. The dresses of the others were all white and spangled with either gold or silver, except that of Winter and she wore also a frosted wreath. The little boys, numbering five or six, were dressed in black velvet and colored suits. The maids of honor were Misses Ivy Rushton and Caro Clayton,[33] who stood beside the throne. After the coronation there was a pretty chorus and then [there] approached the different seasons with little girls representing the months of each, and bearing gifts appropriate to their name. Mary Grant (a cousin of Mrs. Dickson) was Spring, Mary Eaton was Summer, Sallie Glenn was Autumn, and Sallie Spear was Winter. There was a crown bearer, a scepter bearer, a cushion bearer (for the City queen must kneel for her coronation), train bearers and pages.

The little ones who had no special offices but were flowers and butterflies marched up in a graduated line, the smallest coming last, to pay their respects to the queen. Affie Cassin and Walter Taylor, between four

---

[32]This building was also the Fulton County Court House and stood across the street from the corner of Mitchell and Washington streets, where Sallie was living at the time. The city hall building was torn down in 1884, to be replaced five years later by the present state capitol building. Norman Shavin, *Whatever Became of Atlanta?* (n.p., n.d.), 6.

[33]Sallie's sister Caroline. See note 6 above.

and five years of age, came up together. I think they were cupids, though they looked like cherubs. Last of all came Miss Fannie Brown, three years old. With sparkling eyes and brilliant wings, she was a neat representation of a baby butter-fly.

After the short speeches of the different ones, songs and the queen's address, we left the stage to mingle with the crowd. But the audience had been so pleased with our play, which was really very pretty, and not too long, that they began to clamor for a repetition, and the consequence was we were soon recalled to the dressing room and marched out for a second performance.

Before this we attended a number of these pretty festivals, but in so far as I know that City May party of 1861 was the last of its kind. I have never heard of one since.[34]

MAY CELEBRATION

Flora (Mary Cushing)
her nymphs Lou Barnes, Ola Brown, Rossie Hubbard, Julia Taylor, Julie Rushton, Mattie Dabney, Lettie Grant, Pauline Howard, Nora Robinson
Maids of honor Caro Clayton, Mary Grant, Evey Rushton

Queen Sallie Clayton
Cupid Walter Taylor
Cupid's attendants Joy (Julian Purse), Beauty (Arthur Harden), Youth (Tommie Clayton), Garland Bearer (M. Eaton), Friendship (Fannie Brown), Crown Bearer (Gussie Clayton), Septer Bearer (C. Brown)

Attendants Trust (Willie Eaton), Youth (Willie Ruston), Purity (Eliza Luckie), Hope (Hannah Calhoun)

Seasons Spring (Myra Grant), her attendant (J. Darby), Summer (Abel Gilmer), her attendant (A. Winship), Autumn (Sallie Glenn), her attendant (Fannie Tyner), Winter (Sallie Spear), her attendant (C.

[34]This fragment of the manuscript ends with this sentence. On May Day 1861, the Atlanta Female Institute had a "Floral Festival," including a floral re-enactment of the bombardment of Fort Sumter. Gibbons, "Life at the Crossroads of the Confederacy: Atlanta, 1861-1865," *Atlanta Historical Journal* 23/2 (1979): 21.

Overby)

Enter Flora saying—

Let us strew the earth with flowers
For our beauteous Queen of May
Bring the freshest from my bower
Yet she is more fair than they.
Enter Nymphs with their baskets strewing flowers.

Singing—

Yes we'll scatter the bright blossoms
Glad our Lady to obey
For we think there's none so lovely
As our chosen Queen of May.
When her morning face we meet
Tis radiant with smiles of love
We'll strew bright flowers for her feet
And wish her blessings from above.
Though she is tall she never has scorned
To help the children in their play;
To make their tasks seem easier
By her kind and gentle way.
And now we're the Nymphs of Flora
On this bright and sunny day,
Gladly do we sprinkle flowers
For our sweet, loved Queen of May.

Enter Maids of Honor & Queen. Flora salutes ******* (Queen) Saying-[35] . . . about her. Garland Bearer turns aside. Crown [Bear]er advances and kneeling, presents the crown. Say-

Maidens! here I bear a crown
That 'mid Flora's gems was found

---

[35]Note by Torrence: "were there formerly pages 3 and 4 now missing from this manuscript? The matter following immediately follows in the manuscript as now preserved."

Trimmed with buds and blooms today
Waiting to deck our queen of May.
Place it on her gentle brow
May she reign for aye, as now,
With Hope and Love and Friendship round her
Just as this Summer day has found her.
Maids of honor then take the crown and as they place it upon the head of the Queen the whole band shout:

> "Yes crown our Queen of May! Long live our
> Queen of May."

While this is being done Crown bearer retires to one side and Scepter bear[er] advances kneeling as she presents the Scepter, saying—

Take it Lady, wield it o'er us
For we know thy temper well
And in kindness thou will rule us
Waving thus a flowery spell
May thy gentle reign be long and happy
Not only now, but through life's pathway
Wheresoe'er its windings would.
bearer withdraws. Spring advances with her . . . of buds which her attendant carries, saying-
Fair young buds of every hue,
Modest in their coats of green
(From hill and dale I've called for yo[u]
Oh! accept them Lady Queen)
Called to life by breath of Spring
Nought more precious could I bring

Summer-
I've kissed the buds in my passing by
And bid them open each starry eye,
And here full blown and of every shade
I've gathered them up from hill and glade
Here are those of sunshine and those of shade.

Accept the offering by Summer made.

Autumn—

When buds and flowers have passed away
With their delicate shades and tinting gay
The fruits of Autumn fill each stand
All over the bright luxurious land.
And these are the choicest I offer to the[e]
Delicious and sweet may the banquet be.

Winter—

I've iced the cakes and frosted the w[ine?]
To cool the palate and clear the mi[nd]
And I think 'mid these wreaths that your. . .
My vends are not the worst you'll find;
May each season its beauties & dainties. . .
To meet thee and bless thee everywhere—

[A section of this fragment is missing.]

[C]ome Lady and each maiden
[To] my grove of blooming shade
[Wi]th its leaflets fragrance laden
[I] reign this fairy glade
Gladly, gladly for your pleasure
May it flow without alloy
It will, for selfishness is banished
I only wait to see your joy.

Flora retires to one side, her nymphs arrange themselves along the front of the bower

Maids of honor to Flora:
Thank thee, thank thee gentle Goddess
We will ne'er forget thy grace
While the greatest favor given
Is, that thou adornst the place—

Maids of honor then conduct the Queen to the throne where she takes her seat, while Love & his attendants arrange themselves on the left hand. Friendship and here on the right. Hope in front. Garland Bearer advances, kneeling before the throne presents a garland saying—

> Accept this garland lady fair,
> Over thy heart its beauties bear
> May no sorrow enter there
> Queen bends graciously forward to receive it, while its bearer, assisted by the maids of honor, place. . . .[36]

[The following list of the students of the Atlanta Female Institute was prepared separately by Sallie Clayton.]

Atlanta Female Institute

Emma Latimer	Jennie Sims	Young lady 22 yrs. old
Anna Bomar	Alvarine Hoyle	Gussie Hoge
Sallie Avary	Gussie Neal	Fannie Skinner
Imogene Hoyle	Sallie Pope	Two other Fords
Helen Howard	Julia Wilson	Corinne Caldwell
Ella Neal	Mary Reeves	. . . Glass
Maggie Poole	Eunice Berry	Mary Harwell [Yarnell? Garrell? Hole in manuscript]
Almeda McConnell	Camella Caldwell	Della Verderig
Mittie Ruckey	Ella Jones	Ellen Richards
Amorette Foster	Laura Strickland	Maria Cumming
Mollie Gardner	Mary Wilson	Anna Montgomery
Mattie Watkins	Sallie Clayton	Lottie Young
Kate Chivers	Caro Clayton	Camelia Redmond
Cynthia Kellog	Mary Patton	Margie Swann
Floyd Glass	Ella Ezzard	Anna—, cousin to Mary Poullain
India Law	Georgia Mims	Lizzie Gardner
Anna Cozart	Mattie Gardner	Belle Crane
Cordelia Sasseen	Clara Watkins	
Bettie Sasseen	Mattie Ford	
Susie Sims	Eugene Skinner	

[36]This fragment of the manuscript ends here.

Anna Ford
Lizzie Osborne [?]
Emile Mustin
Clara Oakman
Annie Bessant
. . . Pitman
Ruth Hollingsworth
Leslie Hayden
Evie Hayden
Lil Holroyd
Nannie Judson
Lizzie Judson
Mamie Judson
Ida Pittman
Eva Guttman
Tookie Platt
Marie Hungerford
Marie Poulaine
Sophy Stovall
Rosa Cooper
Lou Cotting
Sallie Clayton
Caro Clayton
Marion Richards
Alice Adam
Margie Adam
Loulie Adam
Fannie Poole
Josie McArthur [?]
Abbie Pope
Lizzie Smith
Mattie Bruckner
Rebecca Calhoun
Anna [?] Foster
Eva Patton
Gussie Pope
Ida Einstein
Sallie Foster
Georgia Williams
Allie Williams
Valentia Turner
Margaret Camp
Hattie Griffin
Julia Miller
Pet Kinchley
Johnnie Reese
Colburn Rhind
Willie Turner
Fannie Hatch
Tallulah Gartrell
Mildred Toliver
Cora Clanton
Fannie Oakman
Eugenia Skinner
Fannie Skinner
Mary Richman
Cleo Bignion [?]
Julia Dawson

This photograph of the Atlanta City Hall/Fulton County Court House was made during the federal occupation of Atlanta in the fall of 1864. The photograph was made from the yard of what had been the Clayton home on Mitchell Street. (Courtesy Atlanta Historical Society)

3

ATLANTA AT WAR

THE STREETS WERE MORE THAN EVER CROWDED WITH VEHICLES OF ALL kinds and sometimes a passing wagon train would be so long and interfere with crossing with the Street that we, who were still in school, would have to go a long way from our accustomed route to reach our destination. The most trying experience I had on the Street was one morning when I had to go to school alone. Just as I started from home a regiment of cavalry was passing out Marietta Street and I was in time to meet the first company. For a wonder no one else was on the sidewalk, and I suppose the opportunity for a little fun was more than they could resist, for the soldiers began to call good morning to me, and then, not only to compliment me in the highest terms, but to claim me as a personal property in terms equally endearing, and laugh, Oh! so heartily while I was trying not to be offended and to conceal my embarrassment as best I could, just as though the crimson hue of my face did not show that every remark was having telling effect. I tried to hope they would soon pass and there would be an end to it all.[1]

The first company passed, but it was a mistake about its ending, for the second took it up and then the third; and still a long block to go without a Street into which a turn could be made, for Bridge Street (afterwards called Broad) had not then been opened to the north side of Marietta Street. When a look down towards Peachtree Street showed the remaining seven companies that must be met, with probably the same greetings, it made me almost frantic, and then and there my mind was very soon made up that a retreat would have to be called.

Well, the shouts and laughter that went up when this resolve was put into execution was enough to have put to flight one braver than I, but my determination was that they should not make me run no matter how much

---

[1]Ironically, a similar incident happened to author Margaret Mitchell as a six year old. She rode with a group of Confederate cavalrymen, many decades after the war, from whom she learned stories of the war and "a salty vocabulary that later served her well as a female journalist." Don O'Briant, *Looking for Tara: The Gone With the Wind Guide to Margaret Mitchell's Atlanta* (Atlanta: Longstreet Press, 1994), 2.

I felt like it. Yet, I acknowledge it was with the utmost difficulty that a dignified pace was maintained until I was safely in the house. And even then, until the last company had passed, they continued their calls, though dividing them with my sister Mary[2] who was standing. . . .[3]

It seemed to me the ladies were on hand on all occasions. The station was crowded with them at the coming and going of every train, sometimes to meet or to say farewell to friends and relatives; all recognizing in every soldier a father, husband, brother or son and all were anxious to aid each one of them in some way.

The only time any of us ran into danger at the car shed, as the station was called, was one afternoon when the Louisiana Zouaves[4] were expected, and then fortunately there was not a great many present, they had probably been advised not to go.

I was there with a cousin, Lucy Clayton,[5] and while we were intently watching the train roll in, by the time Whitehall Street was reached, the soldiers, in their picturesque costumes of red trousers made in full bloomer style to the knee where their white stockings reached, bright blue cut-away jackets over full white shirts, long sashes of red, or blue and white caught together at the ends with tassels, and turbans of red and white with pendants finished with tassels,[6] began to jump, or swing themselves off the cars like so many monkeys and just as the train came under the shed some of them began to shoot off pistols or whatever firearms they had.

---

[2]Mary was Mary Semmes Clayton, b. Athens 16 January 1842 d. Atlanta 31 July 1899, who married Cary Wood Henderson 3 October 1871. William Clayton Torrence, *Rootes of Rosewall* (n.p., 1906), 77.

[3]The fragment of the manuscript ends with this sentence unfinished.

[4]She refers here to the 1st Louisiana Zouave Infantry Battalion. Arthur W. Bergeron Jr., *Guide to Louisiana Confederate Military Units 1861-1865* (Baton Rouge: Louisiana State University Press, 1989), 152-154.

[5]Lucy Cary Clayton, b. 19 December 1842, the daughter of George Rootes and Ann R. Harris Clayton, married Reverend B. F. Larrabee. Torrence, *Rootes of Rosewall*, 69.

[6]Zouaves, on both sides in the Civil War, were largely defined as having uniforms adopted from the costumes of Algerian mercenaries of the French Army. Contrary to popular myth, these Civil War units never abandoned their outlandish costumes for regulation uniforms. The Louisiana Zouave uniform was inspired by a troop of actors in New Orleans. Patricia L. Faust, ed., *Historical Times Illustrated Encyclopedia of the Civil War* (New York: Harper & Row, 1986), 850; and John D. Winters, *The Civil War in Louisiana* (Baton Rouge: Louisiana State University Press, 1963), 16-17. Photographs of Zouave uniforms, some in color, appear in William C. Davis, *Memorabilia of the Civil War* (New York: Mallard Press, 1991), 6-7, 12, 14, 16-17.

For all who had time to laugh, it was amusing to see the crowd taking care of itself. The place was closed in less time than it takes to tell it. Lucy and I couldn't get out immediately and we were trying to hide behind something that would protect us from the bullets when Mr. R. F. Maddox[7] came to our rescue. He couldn't help getting after us a little for coming into such danger, as though we knew there was going to be any; the truth was he was about as badly frightened as we were, but we forgave him inasmuch as he was so kind as to take us to the hotel Washington Hall,[8] at the corner of Loyd Street [now Central Avenue] and the railroad where he left us with an order to go home.

After I got to my home the feeling of security wasn't very much greater for the command was shut up in the City Hall just opposite to us, which was where the present capitol stands. This was a strong brick building but was only two stories high[9] and the men had no trouble in forming human ladders so they could come and go at pleasure. There was a strong guard around the square on which the hall stood but I don't know how successful they were in keeping them in the enclosure![10]

It was not long before the Ladies' Sewing Society under Mrs. Willis Westmoreland as president was well under way and a great deal of work was

---

[7]Robert Foster Maddox of Putnam County, b. LaGrange, Georgia 3 January 1829 d. Atlanta 6 June 1899, was colonel of the 42nd Georgia Volunteer Infantry Regiment. Lillian Henderson, *Roster of the Confederate Soldiers of Georgia 1861-1865* 4/6 (Hapeville GA: Longino & Porter, 1958), 606; Lucian Lamar Knight, *History of Fulton County Georgia* (Atlanta: A. H. Cawston, 1930), 252-253; and Franklin Garrett, *Atlanta and Environs* 3 vols. (New York: Lewis Historical Publishing Company, 1954) 3:122.

[8]Built by John Loyd in 1846, Washington Hall faced the Georgia Railroad and Loyd Street (now Central Avenue). S. M. Jones of Nashville, Tennessee, and Thomas E. Whitaker of Atlanta renovated the hotel in the spring of 1864. It burned later that year. Garrett, *Atlanta and Environs*, 1:237; and *Atlanta* (GA) *Daily Register*, 19 March 1864, 2, c. 8. A drawing of this building appears in Norman Shavin and Bruce Galphin, *Atlanta: Triumph of a People* 2nd ed. (Atlanta: Capricorn Corporation, 1985), 22.

[9]The City Hall/Court House building stood on the site of the present state capitol building and was erected in 1854-1855. In 1859, it was described as "70 by 100 feet in size, two stories high of fine architectural proportion and design." C. S. Williams, *Williams' Atlanta Directory for 1859-60* (Atlanta: M. Lynch, 1859), 13. Several photographs of this building survive.

[10]Sallie's version of these events is largely confirmed by an article in the *Southern Confederacy* (Atlanta), 7 June 1861, 3, c. 1 and 4, wherein a resident of nearby Decatur complained that these seven hundred Zouaves from Pensacola were shipped by train from Atlanta, unguarded, to Decatur for breakfast. Despite the earlier problems in Atlanta, the Decatur residents found the Zouaves to be perfect gentlemen.

done.[11] About the same time, or a little later, there was a hospital association, with Mrs. Isaac Winship president,[12] that rendered equally or more valuable service. The former held their meetings in the City Hall where work would be prepared. A good deal of sewing would be done there, though if the emergency were not very great many bundles were taken to the different homes. If an entire company was to be provided for immediately, we usually worked there at the Hall until it was finished. A room for hospital work was rented on the north side of Decatur Street, near Ivy, where numbers would meet for sewing, rolling bandages and scraping lint. All worked for one as much as for the other. At the hospital room different surgeons would come to see how we were succeeding in following directions as to bandages and lint, and where all was going well, nice compliments were paid us on our work. One to me of which I was very proud on account of its coming from a senior surgeon, was from Dr. Willis Westmoreland,[13]

---

[11]This organization was officially formed as the Ladies' Soldiers' Relief Society on 7 January 1862, with Mrs. Mariah Jourdan Westmoreland as president, and Mrs. Chisolm and Mrs. Root as vice presidents. *Southern Confederacy* (Atlanta), 10 January 1862, 2, c. 3-4; and Garrett, *Atlanta and Environs*, 1:531. The bundles, as Sallie described them, were sent in boxes with whatever books, foods, and other commodities that the women could afford for the soldiers. [Francis W. Dawson, comp.], *"Our Women in the War." The Lives They Lived; The Deaths They Died. From the Weekly News and Courier, Charleston, S. C.* (Charleston: The News and Courier Book Presses, 1885), 63, 437-439.

[12]Officially this organization was the Atlanta Hospital Association. They accepted donations for Atlanta's military hospitals from throughout the South. Sallie's mother not only served as a member but also helped collect the donations. Other hospital organizations included A. F. Freeman's St. Philip's Hospital Aid Association. Garrett, *Atlanta and Environs*, 1:531; and *The Commonwealth* (Atlanta), 6 November 1862, 2, c. 1. A paper written about Martha (Mrs. Isaac) Winship, described the work of the Atlanta Hospital Association: "Long trains of cattle cars loaded with dead and dying, with naked and starving, with sick and wounded were arriving at all hours. Not a train but was met by these women . . . who hastened with first aid, with hot coffee and food." Lucian Lamar Knight Scrapbooks, vol. 23, 117, Georgia Department of Archives and History. Also see Lee Kennett, *Marching Through Georgia: The Story of Soldiers and Civilians During the Atlanta Campaign* (New York: HarperCollins, 1995), 115.

[13]Dr. Willis Foreman Westmoreland, b. Fayetteville, Georgia 1 June 1828 d. Atlanta 27 June 1890, founded, with his brother John G. Westmoreland, the Atlanta Medical College. He served as a Confederate surgeon in the hospitals of Atlanta. Glenna R. Schroeder-Lein, *Confederate Hospitals on the Move: Samuel H. Stout and the Army of Tennessee* (Columbia: University of South Carolina Press, 1994), 195; Southern Historical Association, *Memoirs of Georgia*, 1:240-242; Joseph Jones, "Roster of the Medical Officers of the Army of Tennessee," *Southern Historical Society Papers* 22 (1894), 274; and Walter G. Cooper, *Official History of Fulton County* (Atlanta: self-published, 1933), 871-872.

himself.

On one occasion we were summoned to the City Hall to make clothes for the Gate City Guards. This was after their terrible experiences at Laurel Hill in West Virginia[14] where all their belongings were lost and almost their lives. Among the bundles of work given to a group of us was one marked "Quill Orme"[15] which pleased us very much for he was a favorite with each member of our little party numbering five. We wouldn't allow any one person to take the bundle, nor would we let any one sew on it long at a time. It must be done by the five of us, and we carried out our determination to the letter.

The work was trousers, and after we had finished one of the young ladies wrote Mr. Orme a note telling him how much pleasure it had given us to make the garment for him and that thinking he might need a little money we had enclosed what change we had with us. Each of us signed her name; Mrs. James Butler, Mary Clayton, Gussie Hill, Alice Gordon and Sallie Clayton. Then we put in some five and ten cent pieces and one or two quarters and sewed the note up in the watch pocket. And we learned later that after all our enthusiasm over those clothes Mr. Orme never saw the bundle or heard of it until we told him long afterwards.[16]

The children formed a society for knitting socks and elected Gussie Clayton president. Indeed, everybody was knitting, from old ladies to tiny tots between three and four years of age. Some became exceedingly expert in a short while; for instance, one day someone said his wife was not very

---

[14]She refers here to the Confederate retreat from Laurel Hill, in what became West Virginia, in July 1861, following the federal victory at nearby Phillipi. Mark Boatner III, *The Civil War Dictionary* (New York: Vintage Books, 1987), 907; and John C. Waugh, *The Class of 1846: Stonewall Jackson, George McClellan, and Their Brothers* (New York: Warner Books, 1994), 255-265.

[15]This incident must have occurred early in the war for 1st Corporal Aquilla J. Orme of Company F, "the Gate City Guards," 1st (Ramsey's) Georgia Volunteer Infantry Regiment, was discharged for medical reasons on 31 December 1861. His discharge stated that he was age 23 and born in Lancaster, Pennsylvania. Compiled Service Records of Confederate Soldiers Who Served in Organizations From the State of Georgia, microcopy M266, reel 145, National Archives, Washington, DC.

[16]Here she refers to the work of the Ladies' Soldiers' Relief Society, what she previously identified as the Sewing Society. They made c othes for the soldiers but also sent food, medicine, jams, and wine to the soldiers and to the Confederate hospitals in Virginia. Sallie's mother served in this organization. Garrett, *Atlanta and Environs*, 1:531-532; and *Daily Intelligencer* (Atlanta), 27 September 1861, 3, c. 1.

well, that she had finished only one sock during the day and when asked in surprise how many she usually made in that time he said, "Always three."[17]

On the first day appointed for fasting[18] we wanted to see what our youngest sister[19] understood about it, and while she was busy with her knitting, she was a little over three years of age, one of us asked if she knew what the day meant. "Oh, yes! she said, "Don't eat anything and don't do any work but knit." She was very fond of her knitting, and she was afraid if it was not included as part [of the] observation of the day it would have to be put aside. At first socks only were knitted for the soldiers but in course of time when we had to think also of ourselves, came stockings, plain and clocked, gloves, comforters, caps, hoods, shawls, capes, jackets, undervests, etc. Besides being knitted, many of these things were also crocheted, together with nets for the hair, long open-work summer gloves and broad-brimmed hats both of white cotton for the little children. Before putting a little ribbon trimming on them the hats were starched very stiff and lined with silk of a delicate color.

To the slow knitter came great rejoicing when someone introduced for stockings what was called railroad knitting. All one had to do was to begin as with the intention of making the accustomed foot covering, and after knitting one and a half to two fingers in length drop every third or fourth stitch, reduce the end sufficiently to close, stretch the work out to the beginning and there was a good open work stocking, or rather, a straight, narrow bag that some foot would shape.[20]

---

[17]An article on knitting socks for the army appears in the *Southern Confederacy* (Atlanta), 30 January 1864, 1, c. 3. The children's group was the Atlanta Juvenile Knitting Society. No member was over age fourteen. Gibbons, "Life at the Crossroads of the Confederacy: Atlanta, 1861-1865," *Atlanta Historical Journal* 23/2 (1979): 27, and *The Commonwealth* (Atlanta), 2 November 1861, 2, c. 4. Augusta "Gussie" King Clayton, b. 13 April 1849 d. 22 July 1864, is one of the major characters in A. A. Hoehling, *Last Train From Atlanta* (New York: Bonanza Books, 1958). Torrence, *Rootes of Rosewall*, 78. Her death in Atlanta from typhoid fever is discussed in chapter 5.

[18]Presumably she meant 13 June 1861, the day of fasting and prayer called for by Confederate President Jefferson Davis. Gibbons, "Life at the Crossroads of the Confederacy," 21.

[19]Almyra Cobb Clayton, b. near Kingston, Georgia 18 November 1857 d. Atlanta 16 December 1904, married Westwood Campbell Sayre. Torrence, *Rootes of Rosewall*, 79.

[20]For other accounts of knitting and providing for the soldiers see the memoirs of Mrs. Hubbard W. Cozart and Mrs. R. M. Massey, Atlanta Pioneer Women's Society Papers Collection, Atlanta Historical Society.

In later years northern people in hearing of things we did, have expressed surprise at our being able to be so helpful in so many lines, when they had always understood that everything in the way of work was done for us by slaves and they would ask why we kept so many in our houses. They didn't know that a great many southern parents were sensible enough not to wish their children to be entirely dependent upon slaves; they were aware that money often takes wings, that we might not have servants always; consequently they were wise enough to train their children in many useful ways and especially in needle work. It was true it was not necessary for us to do very much work, yet if there were no knowledge in the mistress of the different things to be done about a house, how was she to be able to direct her servants, provided she had them? As a general thing where young people could not sew and knew little or nothing about the housekeeping and especially such as cake, preserves, pickle and candy-making, it was a almost sure indication that they did not come of the best people, that their slaves were not inherited; indeed, that they had none until their fathers made money enough to buy them and then were ashamed to let their children do anything in the way of work.

Likewise the keeping of so many servants about a house was not because people were lazy and inert that it was necessary, but younger servants had to be trained and it was but another evidence of wisdom in the housewife to keep a number of them working in all lines with the older experienced ones, those who wore turbans and were privileged to call you "Chile" and "Honey." No younger used pet names to any but the little children nor did they wear the turbans. The latter was regarded as a badge of maturity and experience and the very high ones, without bright colors, and on state occasions, pure white or with a tiny leaf or flowers on a white ground were marks of aristocracy of which they were exceedingly proud.[21]

---

[21]This fragment of the manuscript ends here. I have been able to find few other references to the use of turbans (tied head scarfs) as a symbol of social status among slave women. The brightly colored turbans were a tradition brought from Africa, although white turbans were more popular with slave women. Confederate diarist Mary Chesnut saw elderly slaves taking communion wearing white turbans. After emancipation, ex-slave women celebrated their new freedom by abandoning their turbans for hats. Randall M. Miller and John David Smith, *Dictionary of Afro-American Slavery* (New York: Greenwood Press, 1987), 118; Elizabeth Fox-Genovese, *Within the Plantation Household: Black and White Women of the Old South* (Chapel Hill: University of North Carolina Press, 1988), 440, fn. 45; Roderick A. McDonald, *The Economy and Material Culture of Slaves: Goods and Chattels on the Sugar*

Several months before our school building [the Atlanta Female Institute] was taken for a hospital, my father had to give up the house on Mitchell Street in which we had been living on account of it being sold. Atlanta was then so very much crowded that it was difficult to get a house of any size.[22] We were anxious to get one somewhat larger than [we had before] for our personal accommodation, for owing to the exceedingly poor conveniences for laundry work to be found anywhere and the lack of open, or butler's pantries, the latter being unknown even in the most recently built large dwellings, we were obliged to reserve a room for ironing, and a small one where we could use for keeping china, and also to prevent crowding the dining room with cup-boards and presses.

The house of suitable size to be had, a very nice one, having more conveniences, than any house in town up to that time was Judge Cowart's[23] on Decatur Street between Courtland and Loyd streets. But in those days though while Decatur Street was nothing to compare to what it became afterwards and has been since, it was just beginning to be undesirable for residence and my father was not willing to rent that house.

Consequently we had been obliged to take a house in Courtland Street

---

Plantations of Jamaica and Louisiana (Baton Rouge: Louisiana State University Press, 1993) 127, 151; Mary Chesnut, *The Private Mary Chesnut*, ed. C. Van Woodward and Elisabeth Muhlenfield (Oxford: Oxford University Press, 1984), 52; and Eric Foner, *Reconstruction: America's Unfinished Revolution, 1863-1877* (New York: Harper & Row, 1988), 79. Lucy Hull, wrote of her "Mammy" walking with "her turban held high" in contempt of some poor whites she encountered. Autobiography of Lucy Hull Baldwin, MS 849, Southern Historical Collection, University of North Carolina at Chapel Hill.

[22]Annie Schor of Atlanta wrote as early as May of 1862 that rental houses in Atlanta were almost impossible to find but that even the best boarding houses were "miserable." Atlanta began to fill with refuges, especially from Tennessee, during the first year of the war. By 1862-1863, Atlantans lived in tents, old box cars, or whatever they could find. Annie M. Schor to John Kimberly, 27 May 1862, John Kimberly Papers, MS 398, Southern Historical Collection, University of North Carolina at Chapel Hill; and Mary Elizabeth Massey, *Refugee Life in the Confederacy* (Baton Rouge: Louisiana State University Press, 1964), 83-84, 105.

[23]Robert J. Cowart, b. 25 May 1811 d. Cherokee County, Georgia 27 January 1876, was not yet a judge although he had been an Atlanta attorney since 1860. In 1872, he became the first judge of the Atlanta City Court. In 1860, the census taker listed him as an Indian agent. Garrett, *Atlanta and Environs*, 1:861; Garrett Necrology, microfilm reel 2, frame 721, and reel 11, frame 110, Atlanta Historical Society; and Eighth Census of the United States (1860), Fulton County, microcopy M653, reel 122, 799, National Archives, Washington, DC.

that was about half the size we wanted.[24] However, the few months we held it we were not greatly inconvenienced as several members of our family were absent, and the rest of us had to leave Atlanta very soon on account of the prevalence of small-pox.[25] By the time we could return, or very soon after, one of our former neighbors, Mr. Gibbon, who lived then in Mr. Charlie Martin's house, in Capitol Square,[26] bought the Morell place, where St. Joseph's Infirmary [now St. Joseph's Hospital] stands,[27] and offered it immediately to my father for rent.

The house was quite a nice one of twelve rooms and a basement room for stores, though no attic; but, the unusual feature, except in a few cases where they were in basements, of a kitchen attached to the house. This was at the extreme end of a long hall and was not objectionable on account of cooking fumes, for the doors leading to it through a pantry were never opened except in very bad weather. There were servants rooms, carriage house, stables and other out houses, a large garden, fruit trees, etc. on the lot which was two acres in size. So, not withstanding what we thought [of]

---

[24]The 1864 tax digest of Fulton County listed for W. W. Clayton, fifty acres of land worth $300, six children between the ages of six and eighteen, three hands between the ages of twelve to fifteen, five hands between the ages of fifteen and fifty-five, town property worth $35,000, ten slaves worth $24,000, $960 in annual profits, $1,000 in debts, $2,000 worth of stock, $5,100 worth of furniture, and $1,000 worth of other property. Fulton County Tax Digest, 1864, 1026th District Atlanta, microfilm reel 70/29, Georgia Department of Archives and History.

[25]Sallie likely refers to the smallpox scare of the winter of 1862-1863 although it also returned in the winter of 1864. Red flags, posted to warn Atlantans of quarantined houses, dotted the streets. Annie M. Schor to Betty Kimberly, 3 January 1863, John Kimberly Papers, MS 398, Southern Historical Collection, University of North Carolina at Chapel Hill; and *Southern Confederacy* (Atlanta), 24 March 1863, 2, c. 3-4, 16 February 1864, 1, c. 4. Smallpox, passed from the Confederate soldiers to the civilian population, was the most feared disease in Atlanta. Rebel authorities created a contagious disease hospital outside of the city at the 155 acre William Markham farm and placed guards to keep the recovering (but still contagious) soldiers out of the city. Ralph Benjamin Singer, "Confederate Atlanta," (Ph.D. diss., University of Georgia, 1973), 152-153; and Garrett, *Atlanta and Environs*, 1:548.

[26]Clayton Torrence made a note here: "This location was at that time the streets surrounding the old City Hall, which occupied the site of the present State Capitol Building."

[27]This location is now 216 North Collins Street. Garrett, *Atlanta and Environs*, 2/:8-9; and Wilbur Kurtz Collection, MS 130, box 37, folder 12, Atlanta Historical Society. The deed from Bryan M. Morrel to George Gibbon is recorded in Fulton County Deed Book G (1863), microfilm reel 100/60, 91, Georgia Department of Archives and History.

the great distance from the heart of town, it was gladly taken.[28]

This house put us near the Female Institute.[29] The school closed early in the summer with pretty and appropriate exercises, which took place in the morning, instead of the evening. The graduating class was the third and the largest in the history of the school.

As we were now very near [to the hospitals], as soon as the hospital days began, we went every morning, accompanied by a servant, with a large tray of different things prepared for the sick and wounded. None of us, however, went into the wards, except our younger sister, Gussie.[30] We older ones simply assisted in arranging what was to be sent in by the servants and nurses.

That there might be proper system, certain ladies prepared for certain wards. Ours was the sick ward in the third story; though sometimes we took fruits enough to divide with the other wards.[31]

A pathetic incident took place when the wounded were first brought in. When taking the names and commands, of the different men, they came to one who could not talk, on account of having been shot in the mouth, and, it was difficult to find out where he came from, or to whose command he belonged.

To get the former he was asked every point south, to which he could give only a shake of the head. Then someone suggested that they cross the ocean to find his home. Germany proved to be his country, and he was a member of one of the numerous Federal commands. He had been brought

---

[28]Gussie Clayton, Sallie's younger sister, also approved of the new house and wrote high praise of its size, gardens, and orchards. Gussie Clayton to Mary Lou Yancey, 12 May 1863, Benjamin Cudsworth Yancey Papers, MS 2594, Southern Historical Collections, University of North Carolina at Chapel Hill. Ironically, Gussie would die of typhoid while the Battle of Atlanta raged over Oakland Cemetery, forcing her family to bury her in that garden, where she remained for some years before being removed to the cemetery.

[29]For the history of the Atlanta Female Institute see chapter 2.

[30]Although Sallie never explains this passage or the related references in this chapter, she implies that while children, like her sister Gussie, were allowed to visit the wounded soldiers, unmarried women were kept out of the hospital wards. Gussie later died of typhoid, likely contracted visiting the hospitals.

[31]A writer for the *Mississippian* (Jackson) wrote of Atlanta's women, "The Ladies of Atlanta are doing their whole duty to the gallant sick and wounded defenders of the country. Committees are appointed for a particular daily work in the hospitals. . . . There is a committee of daily visitors to each hospital, a committee appointed to stay at each hospital daily; a committee appointed to prepare food for the wounded daily arriving; and a committee to cook for the car shed." *Baptist Banner* (Atlanta), 5 December 1863, 1, c. 5.

in with our men through mistake, and was not moved, on account of his serious condition, though he managed to pull through, and the last time I saw him, he was arranging his cot.

The steward told me he thought some of the ladies were not acting right in not being willing for him to have a part of what they brought; that our men who were near enough, would reach over and divide with him what was given to them. After that, though the man was not in our ward, the steward was told to provide for him from our tray whenever there was need for so doing, and my sister was instructed in going around with fruit never to omit him.[32]

We were told to try not to let hatred of a cause extend to its advocates, and especially to anyone of them who was suffering.

Besides attending this hospital in the morning, we went to the receiving hospital in the afternoons, until early in 1864, when my Father bought Mr. Si Robson's home on Marietta Street.[33] It was then thought too much for us to do to attend both [hospitals], especially as most of our visits to the former had been before school, and we would not have time now to reach the latter by the opening hour, as the two places were far apart in opposite directions.

At the time we stopped our visits there were only a few tents in the yard, and they were used for attendants. Hospital tents were put up later in 1864, when so many more sick and wounded were sent into Atlanta.

The receiving hospital was called by several names: the Distributing

---

[32]A federal soldier in Atlanta, after it fell to Sherman, wrote that Atlanta's reported "hundreds" of Union sympathizers had tried to help the wounded federal soldiers captured by the Confederates, so much so that the Confederates finally banned civilians from the Atlanta hospitals. *Nashville* (TN) *Daily Times and True Union*, 17 September 1864, 1, c. 5-6. Also see Lee Kennett, *Marching Through Georgia: The Story of Soldiers and Civilians During the Atlanta Campaign* (New York: HarperCollins, 1995), 116.

[33]Clayton Torrence made the note that the Clayton House stood at the corner of Marietta and Spring streets. He was born there at 91 Marietta Street on 7 June 1884 and lived in this house until it was sold in 1891. For many years after the war, Marietta Street was considered the elite of Atlanta residential neighborhoods, home to Atlanta's most prominent doctors, lawyers, and judges. Even President Woodrow Wilson "entered the road to world-wide distinction through the gates of old Marietta Street." Sarah Huff, *My 80 Years in Atlanta* (Atlanta: n.p., 1937), 46; and Lucian Lamar Knight Scrapbooks, vol. 7, 53, Georgia Department of Archives and History. Merchant Sion R. Robson moved from Madison, Georgia to Atlanta in 1860. The Civil War memoirs of his wife, Kate Hester Robson, are in the Atlanta Historical Society. D. Louise Cook, ed., *Guide to the Manuscript Collections of the Atlanta Historical Society* (Atlanta: Atlanta Historical Society, 1976), 100.

Hospital and the Wayside Hospital (or Wayside Inn) were two of them. The hospital was at the southeastern corner of Alabama Street, now Waverley Place, and Loyd Street.[34] It was not a house but a large hollow square, with a covered platform about eight or ten feet in width, and raised one step, built around the inner wall, to each side of the broad and only entrance in the center of that part facing Alabama Street.[35]

On this platform, at short distances apart, were placed cots, wash stands or small tables, and chairs. The cots were arranged crosswise with heads to the outer wall. Sufficient room between them for the other pieces of furniture was allowed, and in this way we could not only have more of them, but plenty of room for waiting on those who occupied the cots.

When the trains came in with the wounded those of them who could walk the short distance from the railroad station were received here where they were furnished with refreshments, and could rest until sent to the different hospitals. Those who could not walk were kept in the station until it was determined where each would be sent.[36]

---

[34]This location is now Underground Atlanta. Loyd Street is now Central Avenue.

[35]Kate Robson would remember that the few men left in Atlanta would serve as stretcher bearers for the trains of wounded that arrived there. The hospital, as she described it, "was simply a shed, deep enough to hold the beds lengthwise, with rough plank floor, built around a hollow square–no doors or partitions–just one bunk after another, with room between for the doctor or nurse." Memoirs of Kate Hester Robson, MS 291F, Atlanta Historical Society.

[36]Atlanta's extensive railroad connections made it a prime location for Confederate hospitals and as a distribution center for wounded to other hospitals in Georgia and Alabama. It became known as "the hospital of the South" and the "Second Richmond." By the end of the war, an estimated eighty thousand Confederates and twenty-five thousand federal soldiers had been cared for in Atlanta's hospitals. V. T. Barnwell, *Barnwell's Atlanta City Director and Stranger's Guide* (Atlanta: Intelligencer Book and Job Office, 1867), 25; and "Liela" to Marylou Yancey, 21 October 1863, Benjamin Cudsworth Yancey Papers MS 2594, Southern Historical Collections, University of North Carolina at Chapel Hill. For an overview of the hospitals see Glenna R. Schroeder-Lein, "'To Be Better Supplied Than Any Hotel in the Confederacy:' The Establishment and Maintenance of the Army of Tennessee Hospitals in Georgia, 1863-1865," *Georgia Historical Quarterly* 76 (1992): 809-836. The Atlanta Female Institute became the Institute Hospital, the Gate City Hotel (also known as the American Hotel) became the Atlanta Receiving and Distributing Hospital, the Atlanta Medical College became the Medical Hospital, the Empire House became the Empire Hospital, and the Fair grounds became Fair Grounds Hospitals 1 and 2. The state of Georgia opened the Brown Hospital for Georgia troops at the Atlanta City Hall before turning the hospital over to the Confederate government. Other hospitals included Kile's Building, Hayden's Hall, and the Concert Hall. The Ponder home became a convalescent

The older ladies would go over and do what they could for the wounded men. One afternoon Mrs. Winship[37] started with some of the younger crowd, but before we reached there several surgeons stopped her, saying it was no place for us, and protested against our being taken in the midst of such sights as were to be seen unless it was absolutely necessary. So we were sent back.

I think it was about midsummer of 1863, I had been early one Sunday morning to Washington Street, as far as Peters Street, now Trinity Avenue, and on my return just before I reached the little frame church, that was St. Philip's,[38] I met two men carrying a litter on their shoulders, and seeing the arm of the wounded man hanging down as though he were too weak to replace it, I called attention to it. They stopped immediately, and lowering the litter, who should I see lying on it but Mr. Dan Pittman.[39] He had been

---

home during the federal siege of Atlanta. The Atlanta Hotel and its yard became a hospital so gory that citizens walked blocks to avoid it. Garrett, *Atlanta and Environs*, 1:530; Stephens Mitchell, "Atlanta: The Industrial Heart of the Confederacy," *Atlanta Historical Bulletin* 1/3 (May 1930): 24-25; Barnwell, *Barnwell's Atlanta*, 25; R. J. Massey, "Memories of Brown Hospital," *The Sunny South* (Atlanta), 26 October 1901, 5, c. 1-3; and Singer, "Confederate Atlanta," 150-151, 258. However, as Sallie points out, wounded continued to come even after no room remained in Atlanta's makeshift hospitals. In September 1863, following the Confederate victory at the Battle of Chickamauga, for example, Atlanta's hospitals had an estimated capacity of eighteen hundred but had to accept more than ten thousand wounded. Cunningham, *Doctors in Gray*, 125.

[37]Sallie previously identified her as Martha (Mrs. Isaac) Winship, president of the Atlanta Hospital Association. Martha Cook (Mrs. Isaac Winship), b. Fort Hawkins, Georgia 1813 d. Macon 20 June 1882, was the daughter of Philip and Martha Pearson Cook. Mrs. Winship turned the second floor of her home into a hospital, following the Battle of Shiloh in 1862. She made her slave coachman Booker her "surgeon in chief." Lucian Lamar Knight Scrapbooks, vol. 23, p. 117, Georgia Department of Archives and History; "Georgia's Twenty-Five Greatest Women," *Atlanta Journal*, 2 October 1923, n. p.; and Winship Flournoy Family Papers, 1822-1951, MS 209, Atlanta Historical Society.

[38]St. Philip's Episcopal Church was a small frame building on the corner of Washington and Hunter streets. Garrett, *Atlanta and Environs*, 1:587. An Atlantan wrote that it was the poorest church and had the smallest congregation in Atlanta, "its only attraction here is the sublime ritual, which, [even] when poorly read never fails in binding the heart and soul. . . ." *Southern Confederacy* (Atlanta), 24 March 1863, 2, c. 5.

[39]Captain Daniel N. Pittman of 2d Company C, 1st Confederate Infantry Regiment, had moved to Atlanta from Gwinnett County in 1855. His disability from a wound to his left leg at the Battle of Chickamauga, Georgia, 19 September 1863, was permanent but he did not resign until 29 August 1864, after being elected Judge of Probate of Fulton County. Memoirs of Abi Elder and Lucy A. P. Ivy, Atlanta Pioneer Women's Society Papers Collection, Atlanta Historical Society; and Compiled Service Records of Confederate Units Not Raised

brought into Atlanta that morning having been badly wounded, without his parents having any knowledge of the fact that he was in danger, and they were taking him to his wife at her father's, Mr. John Neal, who lived at the corner of Washington and Mitchell streets.[40]

Though so badly wounded, and very pale from suffering, he spoke to me with the accustomed cheerfulness which his friends all remember.

I asked the litter bearers to walk slowly and give me time to hurry back to Mr. Neal's and let them know they were bringing Mr. Pittman home in a seriously wounded condition. I found Mrs. Neal in the lower hall and Mrs. Pittman heard me telling her, so they were in time to meet him just as the men entered the gate.[41]

In the estimation of many persons about the greatest day ever seen in Atlanta was that on which General John H. Morgan[42] "came to town" after his escape from imprisonment in the Ohio Penitentiary.

The day of his arrival [6 February 1864] he was entertained at Colonel

---

by State, microcopy M258, reel 57, National Archives, Washington, DC.

[40]John Neal, b. 1796 d. 1886, of Zebulon, Georgia built his $25,000, two and one half story house in 1858. Neal and his family sold the house and returned to Zebulon early in 1864. Several photographs of the house survive because it was used by General Sherman as his headquarters during the federal occupation of Atlanta. The house was demolished in 1928 when the adjoining Atlanta City Hall was expanded. Garrett, *Atlanta and Environs*, 1:638-639. Portraits of John Neal and his wife hang in the Atlanta History Center.

[41]This fragment of the manuscript ends with this sentence.

[42]John Hunt Morgan, b. 1825 d. 1864, won fame as a Confederate general for his partisan raids in Tennessee, Kentucky, and Ohio. On 26 July 1863, he and most of his command were captured near New Lisbon, Ohio, although he subsequently escaped. Stewart Sifakis, *Who Was Who in the Confederacy* (New York: Facts on File, 1988), 203-204; and Jack D. Welsh, *Medical Histories of the Confederate Generals*, (Kent OH: Kent State University Press, 1995), 159. Guerrilla warfare as a subject fascinated many Civil War Atlantans. Annie Schor wrote to her brother that if she were a man, she would want to be one of Morgan's partisans. As early as 1861, H. B. Holiday of Griffin sought recruits for a proposed local guerrilla group, if needed. John M. Richardson offered a book for sale to Atlantans on partisan warfare. Just before Atlanta fell to the federal army, the *Atlanta Argus* newspaper urged the Confederate defenders to disperse into guerrilla bands. *The Commonwealth* (Atlanta), 30 May 1861, 2, c. 2; Schor to John Kimberly, 27 May 1862, John Kimberly Papers, MS 398, Southern Historical Collection, University of North Carolina at Chapel Hill; *Atlanta Intelligencer* (GA), 18 September 1863, 3, c. 2; and *Nashville* (TN) *Daily Times & True Union*, 5 August 1864, 1, c. 6. For theories on why the southerners did not engage in a general guerrilla war see Raimondo Luraghi, *The Rise and Fall of the Plantation South* (New York: New Viewpoints, 1978), 105-106.

Calhoun's,[43] at the corner of Washington and Alabama streets, and later in the morning he was to hold a reception at the Trout House,[44] on Decatur Street, after speaking from the balcony of the hotel.

Several of us went early to the head of Alabama Street, where the engine house stood, in order to see them start, and then we intended to leave the line of march, to shorten the distance, as well as to avoid the crowd, cross the ground in the rear of the Georgia Railroad Depot (between Alabama Street and the Tracks), which was not enclosed at that time, go through the freight depot to Loyd Street, by the Hotel, Washington Hall, and before the carriages reached there, secure a place on the narrow balcony of the Trout House.

We succeeded in carrying out our design, but we decided not to hold the position, after we had seen that the crowd on Alabama Street, not only from the head of possession way up to the turning point, was dense enough for an active boy to walk on the heads and shoulders of men for all that distance, but was not any less dense in Marietta Street, and the upper block of Decatur Street.

There was no telling how many of this number might, like ourselves, want to stand on the balcony of the Trout House, and, as we did not have entire confidence in the strength of the balcony's supports, we came down and stood opposite to the hotel against the fence to the City Park, so we could get into the park if the crowd around became too thick.

---

[43]Sallie presumably means Atlanta mayor and attorney James M. Calhoun, although she may have meant his law partner and son William Lowndes Calhoun, a later mayor of Atlanta. Williams, *Williams' Atlanta Directory*, 57; and Knight, *History of Fulton County*, 62. Photographs of both Calhouns are in Cooper, *Official History of Fulton County*. Antebellum attorneys were afforded the honorary title of colonel.

[44]The Trout House was Atlanta's largest hotel at that time and from its windows a visitor could see Stone Mountain and most of Atlanta. Jeremiah F. Trout built this four story structure on the northeast corner of Decatur and Pryor streets in 1854 although it changed ownership at least twice before being destroyed by the federal army in 1864. J. Cutler Andrews, *The South Reports the Civil War*, 1970 reprint. ed. (Pittsburgh: University of Pittsburgh Press, 1985), 429-430; *The Commonwealth* (Atlanta), 18 November 1861, 2, c. 4; *Daily Intelligencer* (Atlanta), 3 December 1862, 3, c. 1; and Garrett, *Atlanta and Environs*, 1:374. Insurance agent C. C. Hine wrote of the Trout House in 1859 "*name* suggests good living–illusory!" Robert S. Davis, Jr., ed., "Georgia Cities on the Eve of the Civil War: The Insurance Reports of C. C. Hine," *Atlanta History* 31 (1987): 52. For a picture of the Trout House see Garrett, *Atlanta and Environs*, 1:587. For an account of the social life there see the memoirs of Mrs. Alfred Austell, Atlanta Pioneer Women's Society Papers Collection, Atlanta Historical Society.

So dense was the body of human beings coming down the Street, that it was a puzzle to understand how the carriages could be brought to the stopping point. We knew the horses had been removed from the General's carriage early in the start of the procession and that it was being drawn by men; but, no one could possibly have seen it done; that is from the level of the Street, except those engaged in the work and all who stood directly around them.

After the hotel was finally reached, speeches were made by General Morgan, and General W. C. P. Breckenridge, and Colonel Robert Alston,[45] to all of which the people gave the closest attention.

Then the reception was held that so far was the largest ever seen, or heard of, in Atlanta. We were not directly in it, for we deemed it wise not to get caught in such a jam, but to be lookers on merely.[46]

Those of us who were fortunate enough to look upon the gallant General that day, could little dream that in one short year his brilliant career would be brought to a sudden close, through the treachery of a woman, that he would be not only killed, but afterwards his body before it was taken away, would be dragged through the streets of the town in which

---

[45]Colonel William Campbell Preston Breckinridge of the 9th Kentucky Confederate Cavalry Regiment was a former brigade commander under Morgan. He later served in Congress. Clement Evans, ed., *Confederate Military History*, 17 vols. (Atlanta: Confederate Publishing Company, 1899; reprint, Wilmington NC: Broadfoot Publishing Company, 1988) 11:287-288; and *Sunny South* (Atlanta), 12 October 1901, 5, c. 1-5. Robert A. Alston, b. Macon, Georgia 31 December 1831, although a lieutenant colonel and chief of staff under Morgan, was a Charleston, South Carolina merchant and lawyer at that time living in Atlanta. Morgan had promoted him from private to his personal adjutant. Alston died in a duel in Atlanta on 11 March 1879. Garrett, *Atlanta and Environs*, 1:958-959; Basil W. Duke, *A History of Morgan's Cavalry* (Bloomington: Indiana University Press, 1960), 203; Derrell Roberts, "Duel in the Georgia State Capitol," *Georgia Historical Quarterly* 47 (1963): 420-424; and *Southern Confederacy* (Atlanta), 24 March 1863, 2, c. 4.

[46]General Morgan and his wife Martha arrived in Atlanta on 6 February 1864. They were greeted by a cheering crowd of thousands at the railroad car shed and treated to a parade to their hotel. Men from the crowd unhitched the horses from the carriage and pulled it through the streets of Atlanta. James A. Ramage, *Rebel Raider: The Life of General John Hunt Morgan* (Lexington: University of Kentucky Press, 1986), 205. Atlanta and nearby Decatur became a base for veterans of Morgan's raiders and other Kentucky exiles. *Southern Confederacy* (Atlanta), 12 November 1862, 1, c. 6, 29 January 1864, 1, c. 5, and 30 January 1864, 2, c. 5-6.

he lost his life.[47]

The above was told to me by Tennesseans who knew what they were telling was true. Some years afterwards I was making my home temporarily in that State, and not far away from the scene of General Morgan's death.[48]

In June 1864 my brother, William H. Clayton[49] of the Seventh Georgia Regiment, returned home from Virginia where he had been wounded in the second battle of Cold Harbor. Now just a few words about the battle which is said to have been one of the greatest, if not the greatest ever fought. The Federal forces under General Grant far outnumbered the men under General Lee, according to their own accounts. Yet during an engagement within thirty minutes fifteen thousand of the enemy were slain and after a cessation of hostilities, when the Federal forces were ordered to renew the attack they silently ignored the order. You will not learn this from their reports for they acknowledge to the killing of seven thousand only, and of the latter they say that "For some reason" the attack was not renewed.[50]

I have already told of what was considered about the greatest day Atlanta had ever seen. We come now to one of the saddest, the bringing

---

[47]This version of Morgan's death on 4 September 1864 was a popular myth. He was actually shot and killed by a Union soldier for refusing to surrender during the federal attack on Greeneville, Tennessee. No woman had betrayed him and the federal troops were unaware of his presence until after his death. Morgan's corpse was thrown on a horse for an unceremonious removal because, in the midst of the fighting, a more respectful treatment was not possible. Ramage, *Rebel Raider*, 233-241; and *The Sunny South* (Atlanta), 7 September 1901, 5, c. 1-6.

[48]This fragment of the manuscript ends with this sentence.

[49]William Harris Clayton, b. Athens 7 November 1843 d. Atlanta 11 January 1891, served as captain of Company K, 7th Georgia Volunteer Infantry Regiment and was slightly wounded in the hip near Cold Harbor, Virginia on 1 June 1864. He never returned to his command and was officially dropped from the unit's rolls on 4 January 1865 as a deserter. He had previously written to his company from Augusta, Georgia that he had no intention of returning. Torrence, *Rootes of Rosewall*, 77; and Compiled Service Records of Confederate Soldiers Who Served in Organizations from the State of Georgia, microcopy M266, reel 216, National Archives, Washington, DC.

[50]Her brother did not participate in the events she describes as he was wounded on 1 June 1864 (see previous footnote) and the Battle of Cold Harbor that she describes occurred on 3 June 1864. It did result in seven thousand federal casualties within only one half hour but the last order to charge the Confederate lines was ignored by the federal troops. Although federal losses were not as great that day as Confederate sources would claim, the Union army had also lost five thousand other men in the fighting around Cold Harbor on the previous two days and would lose fifty thousand men in Virginia in just that month. John S. Bowman, ed., *The Civil War Almanac* (New York: Bison Books, 1983), 206-207.

into the city the remains of General Polk soon after he was killed on Pine Mountain, the middle of June 1864,[51] and their lying in state in St. Luke's Church in Walton Street.[52] The train came in quite early, and the body was taken to the "Little Refugee Church" as it was called. This was the original St. Luke's that was built through the efforts of Dr. Quintard,[53] the rector, for the accommodation of the refugees; as St. Philip's Church[54] was not then large enough to seat so many Episcopalians as were in Atlanta in addition to her own people. The building was a neat, commodious frame structure on the corner of Walton and Forsyth streets. After its almost destruction by Sherman it was never rebuilt and the parish never renewed though another at St. Stephen's afterwards took the members in. St. Philip's Church remained where they were through another church, [also] called St. Stevens [sic], gotten up by an almost entirely different set of people in a not altogether commendable spirit afterwards took the name of St. Luke's because it was found by so doing they could get possession, or the value, of the lot on which the former church stood.[55]

---

[51]Episcopal bishop and Confederate General Leonidas Polk, b. 1806, was killed by a federal shell while observing the federal lines from atop Pine Mountain, Georgia on 14 June 1864. Joseph H. Parks, *General Leonidas Polk, C.S.A.: The Fighting Bishop* (Baton Rouge: Louisiana State University Press, 1962), 382; Welsh, *Medical Histories of the Confederate Generals*, 174-175; and *Louisville* (KY) *Daily Journal*, 9 July 1864, 3, c. 3.

[52]St. Luke's Episcopal Church was erected in the Spring of 1864 on Walton Street, between Broad and Forsyth streets, by the Confederate garrison from donated materials. Gibbons, "Life at the Crossroads of the Confederacy," 30; Garrett, *Atlanta and Environs*, 1:587-589; Susan Elisabeth Leas, *Alive in Atlanta: A History of St. Luke's Church, 1864-1974* (Atlanta: self-published, 1976), 6; and *Southern Confederacy* (Atlanta), 23 April 1864, 2, c. 3. The congregation later petitioned the federal government for reparations for the destruction of their church during the Atlanta campaign. *The Miscellaneous Documents of the House of Representatives for the Second Session of the Fifty-third Congress 1893-1894* (Washington, DC: United States Government Printing Office, 1896), 274.

[53]Dr. Charles Todd Quintard of Tennessee served as both army chaplain and surgeon in Atlanta. Garrett, *Atlanta and Environs*, 1:586-588. Also see Arthur H. Noll, *Doctor Quintard, Chaplain C.S.A.* (Suwanee: University of the South, 1905) and Derrell C. Roberts, *The Gray Winter of 1864 in Dalton* (Dalton: self-published, 1991), 64-69. When General Polk was killed, he was carrying copies of Quintard's *Balm for the Weary and Wounded* as gifts for Generals Johnston, Hood, and Hardee. *Nashville* (TN) *Dispatch*, 9 July 1864, 4, c. 2.

[54]This small frame building stood at the corner of Hunter and Washington streets. Garrett, *Atlanta and Environs*, 1:587.

[55]Actually, the property upon which the second St. Luke Protestant Episcopal Church was built was purchased for $3,500 and is on the corner of Spring and Walton streets. Alex M. Hitz, "The Origin of and Distinction Between the Two Protestant Episcopal Churches

After reaching the church the casket was carried to the upper end of the nave and placed cross-wise in front of the chancels, or rather upon a broad & only step leading to the choir proper. Through the latter was not furnished with stalls, for male choirs and choir boys were at that time unknown to the vast majority of us and the ladies who were usually leading the congregation in the singing, occupied in a place from back to the right of the chancels though a little farther front.

Known as St. Luke's, Atlanta," *Georgia Historical Quarterly* 34 (1950): 1-7.

The Trout House Hotel in Atlanta after General Morgan's visit and during the federal occupation of Atlanta. (Courtesy Library of Congress.)

Sallie Clayton's family lived in this house on Mitchell Street in the early months of the Civil War. The photograph was made in 1863 and apparently belonged to Sallie. The handwriting at the top of the photograph appears to be that of her daughter Caroline and indicates "mother's" bedroom. (Courtesy Atlanta Historical Society)

4

THE BATTLE OF CHATTANOOGA

IN NOVEMBER 1863 THE FAMILY OF ADMIRAL SEMMES[1] WAS SENT BY General Burnside[2] from their home in Ohio (where they had been quietly living) out of the Union lines.[3] Mobile, Alabama was to be their refuge home. But they came first to Atlanta and after remaining our guests for a few days, went with two of my sisters and the Admiral's oldest son, Captain Spencer Semmes,[4] who was also with us, to Washington, Georgia, to attend the marriage of the latter to his cousin, Pauline Semmes, a daughter of my mother's brother, General Paul J. Semmes,[5] who was mortally wounded at the Battle of Gettysburg [on 2 July 1863] and died a few days later at

---

[1]Raphael Semmes, b. Charles County, Maryland 27 September 1809 d. Mobile 30 August 1877, was a Confederate admiral and the second highest ranking officer in the Confederate navy. He won fame as the captain of the raider CSS *Alabama*. Admiral Semmes was also the second cousin of Sallie's mother, Carolina Maria Semmes Clayton. Harry Wright Newman, *The Maryland Semmes and Kindred Families* (Baltimore: Maryland Historical Society, 1956), 70-71, 76, 78-80.

[2]Ambrose Everett Burnside, b. 1824 d. 1881, was federal commander of the Department of the Ohio. Ezra J. Warner, *Generals in Blue: Lives of Union Commanders* (Baton Rouge: Louisiana State University Press, 1964), 57-58.

[3]When the war began Admiral Semmes's wife Anne Elizabeth Simpson Semmes and their children went to live with her family in Cincinnati, Ohio. They were constantly harassed because of her husband's activities as a Confederate officer, although initially the federal authorities in Ohio would not allow them to refuge to the Confederacy. In the spring of 1863, General H. G. Wright, the federal commander in Cincinnati, finally allowed them to leave but they were required, at great expense, to enter the Confederacy through Fortress Monroe, Virginia. W. Adolphe Roberts, *Semmes of the Alabama* (Indianapolis: Bobbs-Merrill, 1938), 117, 223-24.

[4]Samuel Spencer Semmes, b. 4 March 1838 d. Osceola, Arkansas 24 January 1912, was at that time a captain and quartermaster in Atlanta. Newman, *The Maryland Semmes*, 90-92.

[5]Paul Jones Semmes, b. Wilkes County, Georgia, 4 June 1815 d. Martinsburg, Virginia 9 July 1863, and Sallie's mother, Carolina Maria Semmes (Mrs. William W. Clayton), were the children of Andrew Green Simpson and Mary Robertson Semmes. Newman, *The Maryland Semmes*, 70-71; L. P. Thomas, "Paul Jones Semmes," in *History Confederate Veterans' Association of Fulton County, Georgia*, Robert L. Rodgers, comp. (Atlanta: V. P. Sisson, 1890), 41-43; and Jack D. Welsh, *Medical Histories of the Confederate Generals* (Kent OH: Kent State University Press, 1995), 194.

Martinsburg, Virginia.[6]

The party returned the day following the marriage accompanied by the bride and groom, and the sister of the bride. A number of our gentlemen friends came and serenaded us that night, and the following evening, the party was tendered a reception by my mother.

We had heard of the beautiful view from Missionary Ridge [Tennessee, near Chattanooga], which was then held by the Confederates under General Bragg,[7] and Mrs. Semmes, Senior,[8] suggested a day's visit. We had a merry laugh over this when they told us that while the General was holding a council of war the night before and expecting important messages, a telegram was handed him, which visibly affected him. Sitting with his hand to his face, as he shook with laughter, he showed to his lieutenants[9] gathered about him a telegram from Mrs. Semmes, informing him of the number of persons in her party, and that they were then leaving Atlanta.

In this party were Mrs. Semmes, her three daughters, Electra, Kate and Anna;[10] Captain and Mrs. Spencer Semmes, and her sister Mary; Mrs. William W. Clayton, and four daughters, Julia, Mary, Sallie, and Caro,[11] Mattie Clayton, of Greensboro,[12] and Lou Shackleford, of Atlanta, and

---

[6]Clayton Torrence made the note here that the body of General Semmes was taken to his home in Columbus, Georgia for burial.

[7]Braxton Bragg, b. Warren County, North Carolina, 22 March 1817 d. Galveston, Texas 27 September 1876, was the commander of the Army of Tennessee. In November 1863, his army was besieging the federal troops that occupied the city of Chattanooga, Tennessee, at the foot of Lookout Mountain and Missionary Ridge. Ezra J. Warner, *Generals in Gray: Lives of Confederate Commanders* (Baton Rouge: Louisiana State University Press, 1964), 30 and Welsh, *Medical Histories of the Confederate Generals*, 23-4.

[8]She refers to Ann Spencer (Mrs. Raphael Semmes), the mother of the groom, Samuel Spencer Semmes. Newman, *The Maryland Semmes*, 76.

[9]The term lieutenants here means his subordinate officers of all ranks at the meeting, not just literally the officers of the rank of lieutenant.

[10]These daughters were Electra Louisa, Catherine Middleton, and Ann Elizabeth Semmes. Newman, *The Maryland Semmes*, 76-77.

[11]These daughters were Julia Frances, Mary Semmes, Sarah "Sallie" Conley, and Caroline Maria Clayton. William Clayton Torrence, *Rootes of Rosewall* (n.p., 1906), 77-78.

[12]Clayton Torrence notes here that Mattie Clayton was the daughter of Philip Clayton, the assistant secretary of the Confederate States Treasury. She was therefore Martha Harper Clayton, daughter of Philip Augustin and Leonora Harper Clayton. Torrence, *Rootes of Rosewall*, 70.

three young boys, Raphael Semmes Jr., and Smith and Tom Clayton.[13] Several young officers returning from leave of absence to attend Captain Semmes' wedding were also with us, among them Lieutenants Oliver and Gladden, of New Orleans, and Captain Sparks.

We left Atlanta late Saturday afternoon, traveled all night, and reached the point where we were to leave the railroad, Scottsburg[14] was, I think, the name of the little place, early the next morning. There were two ways of driving to headquarters called the short and the long ways. The first was behind Missionary Ridge over the Chickamauga River and through a large portion of the camps. Four miles was the distance. The other was a most beautiful drive of seven miles and for a long distance on the brow of the Ridge, giving us a full view of the surrounding country, and for this reason it was chosen, though it took three hours to make the trip. Clear, Bright, beautiful, neither too warm nor too cool, the day was all that could be desired for the drive.

Several officers, among them Major Ellis and Lieutenants Parker and

---

[13]Raphael Semmes was the son of Admiral Raphael and Ann Spencer Semmes. In the last days of the war, although only age thirteen, he would serve under his father in protecting the fleeing Confederate government. Smith and Tom Clayton were his third cousins, Augustin Smith and Thomas Andrew Clayton, the youngest sons (and Sallie's brothers) of William Wirt and Carolina Maria Semmes Clayton. Newman, *The Maryland Semmes*, 77; Burke Davis, *The Long Surrender* (New York: Random House, 1985; reprint, New York: Vintage Books, 1989), 54, 169; and Torrence, *Rootes of Rosewall*, 78. Mrs. Lou Shackleford has not been identified. Stephen J. Shackleford, male auctioneer and charter member of the Christian Church of Atlanta, is in the 1858 city directory and the 1850 and 1860 censuses of Atlanta. However, his wife is identified in the censuses as Melissa. He had two grown males in his household in 1860, presumably his unmarried sons. Seventh Census of the United States (1870), DeKalb County, microcopy M432, reel 67, 213, , National Archives, Washington, DC; and Eighth Census of the United States (1860), Fulton County, microcopy M653, reel 122, 810, National Archives, Washington, DC.

[14]This community in Walker County, Georgia is called Scott. However, as the railroad did not run through Walker County, Sallie must have referred to the Chickamauga Station. Marion R. Hemperley, *Cities, Towns and Communities of Georgia* (Easley SC: Southern Historical Press, 1980), 131; and Keith Bohannon to author, n.d., in the author's possession. Francis Lawley took the train from Atlanta to Chattanooga at almost this same time but complained that his passage took two days. Other travelers required four days by train, one way, to make the trip, which he believed took more time than if they walked. Francis Lawley, *Francis Lawley Covers the Confederacy*, ed. William Stanley Hoole (Tuscaloosa: Confederate Publishing Company, 1964), 75.

Cabell Breckinridge, were waiting to meet us,[15] and the three ambulances they had brought with them were soon filled by ourselves and a large hamper of provisions which we had brought to present to General Bragg and his staff.

On our arrival we found headquarters, situated on the very crown of the Ridge opposite to Chattanooga, about three miles distant, with Lookout Mountain some distance to the left, though nearly in a line with the Tennessee town. There were several two-roomed, frame houses, such as are called in the country "upright houses," from being built with planks placed up and down instead of being weather-boarded. These houses were not very far apart, and I think all were in an enclosure where there were also tents, though many of the latter were outside.

Besides the encampment of forces behind the ridge, in the valley in front of it, were the main corps. The entire front extended seven miles. General Bragg occupied the little house in the center of the enclosure, that sat with the end facing the valley. The front room was furnished as a reception, or sitting room, and behind that was General Bragg's own room and office combined.[16]

Soon after our arrival dinner was announced, and we were escorted into a tent, which served as a dining room. The rest of the day was spent quietly; and insofar as I was concerned it had to be, for traveling all night, and the long drive of the morning, had given me a severe headache. Dr. Urquhart, of Columbia, Georgia,[17] very kindly gave me the use of his tent in order that I might have a good rest. There, after the excitement due to the novelty of being in the midst of a great army, and in a soldier's tent, lying on a soldier's cot, had somewhat subsided, I fell asleep. When night came it was thought

---

[15]The Claytons were met by Lieutenant Francis S. Parker, Jr., aide de camp to General Bragg, and Lieutenant Joseph Cabel Breckinridge, aide to his father Major General John Cabel Breckinridge. Major Ellis must have been General Bragg's aide, Lieutenant (later Major) Towson Ellis. Compiled Service Records of Confederate General and Staff Officers and Non-Regimental Enlisted Men, microcopy M331, reels 32, 193, 86, National Archives, Washington, DC; and Keith Bohannon to author, n.d., in the author's possession.

[16]Almost no information survives on General Bragg's headquarters. An artist's rendering of the headquarters and the view of the area roads from there appears on page 127 of Richard O'Shea and David Greenspan, *American Heritage Battle Maps of the Civil War* (New York: Smithmark, 1994).

[17]Lieutenant Colonel David Urquhart was General Bragg's assistant adjutant general. Compiled Service Records of Confederate General and Staff Officers and Non-Regimental Enlisted Men, microcopy M331, reel 253, National Archives, Washington, DC.

best for me to be in one of the houses, and my cousin, Mary Semmes, insisted upon my coming, with my Mother, into a room that had been assigned to her, with the privilege of inviting as many others as it would accommodate. We accepted her invitation and slept on pallets. Pallets were also arranged for several other members of our party in General Bragg's reception room, and wherever house room could be found. Those who were not under a roof were quartered around in tents.

The original intention of our party had been to spend a day only, though I think no one had realized how far we had to go from the railroad, and that to return to that point in time for the train's departure would have hurried us considerably. Also General Bragg, and his officers, called our attention to the fact that as one feature of our entertainment a serenade had been planned, and he insisted that we spend the night.

As a further inducement they also promised to take us the next day onto Lookout Mountain, and let those who wished to do so, fire cannon. With these delightful inducements, and as time had then become very short in which to reach the station early enough to catch the train, we accepted, with great pleasure, the invitation to spend the night.

All of us were up bright and early the next morning and soon after breakfast we began preparing for the trip to Lookout Mountain. We asked if we had not been quite prompt in making our appearance, but we were compelled to engage in a hearty laugh when told that General Bragg had just said that he could have moved his entire army in the time it had taken us to get ready. This, however, turned to our advantage.

The entire party, with his officers, had gathered in his room for a social visit to him before setting out on our morning jaunt. When we began asking for his autograph the General did not seem inclined to comply. Then someone ventured to say something about him giving it to friends, to which he replied rather sadly, that sometimes he thought he had not a friend in the world besides his wife[18] Then came a chorus: "We are your friends, General," and our request was granted. He took his seat at the desk in the middle of the room, and with us all gathered around him, in a plain, bold

---

[18]Braxton Bragg was at odds with his generals and the Confederate press. Shortly before the arrival of the Semmes-Clayton party, Bragg had been retained in his command after a personal visit by his friend, Confederate President Jefferson Davis. His generals had petitioned Davis for his removal. James Lee McDonough, *Chattanooga–A Death Grip on the Confederacy* (Knoxville: University of Tennessee Press, 1984), 20-40.

hand, wrote his name "Braxton Bragg" on cards enough for each one of us to have one. How we prized them, and how very glad afterwards we were that we made him this visit and obtained his autograph when we did, for there was no time for such a visit and request later in the day.

In going to Lookout Mountain we went down in the valley where there was a level, comfortable road, that carried us through the camps of our army. An amusing sight, was the certain haste among some soldiers in getting a comrade under cover of a tent, when they saw that there were ladies in the ambulances driving their way. It was Monday [23 November 1863], wash day, and the poor fellow was busily washing his clothes; a very commendable thing to do, but they were evidently all that he had. With no one to wash them for him he was himself busily engaged at the wash tub.

After we had passed the camps some of us began to show the white feather. Mrs. Semmes and I were more nervous than the others and wanted to be left by the wayside until the party returned from the trip to Lookout. The young officers tried to encourage us, but when we began entreaties they told us it was out of the question: that we were outside of the lines, and if we were left there the enemy's picket might dash in and capture us at any minute.[19] This information had the desired effect and we said no more about leaving the ambulance in which we were riding.

When we neared Lookout Mountain there was a long wagon train going up in the road before us, and a Federal battery was shelling it. Knowing that it would be sometime before we could begin our ascent our party left the ambulances and gathered together on a low hill. However, we had not been there very long when the Chattanooga battery turned a gun and sent a shell in our direction. It fell very near and one of our escort said immediately: "That settles it, we will not attempt to ascend the mountain." I, for one, was heartily glad something would prevent it, for the danger in that ascent was quite apparent to me and I did not want to be one of the dead women to roll out of one of the ambulances when it was struck by a yankee shell.

The return was made by a different route. We did not go far before we began to cross Missionary Ridge, and at a very steep part of it, so steep that the horses could pull but a little way without giving out. To prevent the ambulances sliding back, at each stop several soldiers would take hold of the

---

[19]That very morning of 23 November 1863, General George Thomas's federal troops did rush and capture this Confederate picket line. McDonough, *Chattanooga–A Death Grip on the Confederacy*, 110.

wheels of each conveyance and let the horses rest sufficiently to continue their upward journey. It was fearful, and all were silent. Indeed if anyone had spoken I think but one sentence, a short one of but five words would have been uttered, and that would be, "I want to go home!"

The strain was not altogether over even when we reached the top of Missionary Ridge, for then we had to drive on a narrow ledge behind the mountain that was almost as frightful as the coming up had been.

On nearing headquarters we saw General Bragg and several others out in front looking through field glasses in the direction of Chattanooga. We joined them as quickly as possible, anxious to know what this meant. We could see nothing except long black lines outside of the town. Then we were permitted to look through the glasses, and the black lines changed into long rows of soldiers. When we asked what they were doing General Bragg said he was not yet sure whether it was a matter of dress parade or preparations for an attack.[20]

Just then, I heard one of his staff, who had been intently watching the movements of the lines through his glass say "General, have you observed that the litter corps[21] is also out. That is not done for dress parade."

My mother, Mrs. Clayton, asked if it would not be better for us to get out of the way immediately, but General Bragg said he thought we would have time to eat dinner, which was then ready.

With that we hurried into the dining tent, and had just seated ourselves when a messenger came running in with directions from General Bragg that we must be off in ten minutes.

At the same time there came the sound of a volley of musketry from the valley below. The drivers, with their vehicles, had already crossed over to the road leading to the railroad station, and were waiting for us, and all that

---

[20]Confederate prisoners taken after the battle claimed that they mistook federal General George Thomas's preparations for the attack of 23 November 1863 as only a dress parade. Confederate Commander Braxton Bragg voiced the opinion that the federal formations were only a review in honor of General Grant, for which one of his generals replied, "in about fifteen minutes you are going to see the damndest review you ever saw." Ibid., 111; and Peter Cozzens, *The Shipwreck of Their Hopes: The Battles for Chattanooga* (Chicago: University of Illinois Press, 1994), 129-30. Thomas deliberately paraded the vast numbers of his troops before the Confederate lines. Richard O'Connor, *Thomas: Rock of Chickamauga* (New York: Prentice-Hall, 1948), 249; and Freeman Cleaves, *Rock of Chickamauga: The Life of General George H. Thomas* (Westport CT: Greenwood Press, 1948), 194.

[21]The litter corps were the stretcher bearers for removing soldiers wounded in battle. H. L. Scott, *Military Dictionary* (New York: D. Van Nostrand, 1864), 391-92.

we had to do was to get our baggage and jump into the ambulances.

After all was over it was quite amusing to recall how different members of our party acted under each excitement. Two ran to the brow of the ridge to see what was going on, and another tarried to powder her face.

But, what these and other foolish things done, were seen by me early in passing for I was one of the number who was suddenly seized with a most ardent desire to obtain a seat in the leading ambulance, and it was apparent that we were making it somewhat after the fashion of Cinderella, leaving for home, when she found that she had overstayed her time at the ball. Though I think none of us really ran; we only thought we did so. All the time the firing continued, and we were told, as we were being seated in the ambulances, that our picket had already been driven in.[22]

So, without further delay, we set out at a brisk pace for the railroad station. On this return journey we took the short way right through the camps. The three little boys, Raph[ael] Semmes, Junior, Smith, and Tom Clayton, seemed to prefer the first ambulance also, and came as rapidly as they could until they overtook us, Smith Clayton putting up entreaties that would have gotten him in anywhere. The other two boys were quiet.

There was no escort on the return trip. The scene through the camp was one of wild confusion: the men were seizing their arms, and were almost running over one another, in their hurry to reach the front. You could see boxes, benches, and camp stools, upset and hear the jingle of pots and pans, as the men pushed things out of their way.

Couriers were riding rapidly here and there, still we had heard no call to battle, or if we had, we did not understand it. Yet there were those men seemingly as anxious to get into the foray as we were to get as far from it as quickly as we could. All this as I saw it may have seemed quite different to others.

When we got down behind the Ridge to the Chickamauga River a wagon train was coming over the pontoon bridge and we had to wait a long time for it to cross. It seemed like an hour. Driving over the pontoons[23] was something none of us had ever done before and we were much interested in trying to see how it was put and kept together.

---

[22]A picket is a line of sentries whose duty was to alert the army of the enemy's approach. Scott, *Military Dictionary*, 462.

[23]Pontoons were flat bottom boats used to support a makeshift bridge. Mark M. Boatner III, *The Civil War Dictionary* (New York: Vintage Books, 1987), 658.

After we reached the station there was another long wait; but, by this time, and at this distance from hostilities we were a little less nervous, and as it was almost dark, and the battle was well under way, we had a splendid view of the beautiful light above the trees, caused by the cannonading which we employed ourselves by watching.

We found afterwards that General Grant had not acted toward us with due consideration. He might easily have sent us a courier to inform us that he would devote more attention to Lookout Mountain than to Missionary Ridge that afternoon and have given us an opportunity of leaving our host with more civility, to say nothing of courtesy, then we did.[24] For on such a hurried breaking up of General Bragg's home, or tent party, I have never been fully assured that any of us said good-bye, or thanked him for his hospitality.

I think it was just after we had taken our seats in the train that we had quite a start given us by someone rushing into the car and calling out excitedly "Is Mrs. Clayton on board?" at which my Mother rose and answered "Yes." At the same time a lady in the other end of the car also rose and she proved to be the person the messenger was looking for. She was the wife of General Henry D. Clayton,[25] and there was a message for her from her husband.

So far as I know only one person who was in our party on this memorable visit to General Bragg's headquarters at Missionary Ridge was ever to met General Bragg again, and that was my sister Caro,[26] who later became Mrs. William George Irwin, and whose home was afterwards in Galveston,

---

[24]Sallie is being sarcastic here. Federal commander General Ulysses S. Grant's attack on the Confederate lines at Lookout Mountain and then at Missionary Ridge, 23-25 November 1863, took the Confederates by surprise and ended the siege of Chattanooga. Grant's subordinates were then free to begin massing forces for the invasion of Georgia that resulted in the capture and destruction of Atlanta. Warren Wilkinson, "Chattanooga Campaign," in *Encyclopedia of the Confederacy*, ed. Richard N. Current (New York: Simon and Schuster, 1993), 292-95.

[25]Henry DeLamar Clayton, b. 7 March 1827 d. 13 October 1889, commanded a brigade in the Confederate Army of Tennessee. Warner, *Generals in Gray*, 53; and Welsh, *Medical Histories of the Confederate Generals*, 40. His maps of the Atlanta Campaign are in the Alabama Department of Archives and History. See Robert S. Davis, Jr., "Every Crossroads and Farm: General Henry DeLamar Clayton's Civil War Maps of Northwest Georgia," *Georgia Historical Quarterly* 82 (1998): 151-67.

[26]Caroline Maria Clayton, b. Athens, Georgia 14 January 1847 d. Atlanta, 25 July 1876, married William George Irwin on 21 February 1871. Torrence, *Rootes of Rosewall*, 78.

Texas. When General Bragg and his wife heard that Mrs. Irwin was in Galveston they went immediately to see her, though they were just about to leave the city[27] for a long journey.

About this time, or a little later, more wounded soldiers were being sent into Atlanta than the hospitals, though numerous, could accommodate, and citizens were requested to take one or two more of the wounded men into their homes.[28]

While looking through the hospitals first to see if there was a relative, friend, or acquaintance, among the wounded, my father and mother found Captain Tom Sharp,[29] whose brother General Jacob Sharp,[30] had married my mother's niece,[31] and invited him to be our soldier guest.

Captain Sharp had been taken to the Empire House[32] on Whitehall Street, where we had frequently visited friends in the hotel days, and where once or twice at night we kept tally on the watchman, across the Street, and

---

[27]Braxton Bragg spent the last years of his life as a resident of Galveston and died there 27 September 1876. Warner, *Generals in Gray*, 31.

[28]The Atlanta press reported that hundreds of Atlanta households took in from one to eight wounded soldiers. Gibbons, "Life at the Crossroads of the Confederacy: Atlanta, 1861-1865," *Atlanta Historical Journal* 23 (2) (1979): 27.

[29]Captain Thomas J. Sharp of Company H, 10th Mississippi Confederate Volunteer Infantry Regiment was wounded at the Battle of Chickamauga on 20 September 1863 and killed at the Battle of Ezra Church, Georgia 28 July 1864. Compiled Service Records of Confederate Soldiers who Served in Organizations From the State of Mississippi, microcopy M269, reel 189, National Archives, Washington, DC.

[30]Jacob Hunter Sharp, b. Pickensville, Alabama 6 February 1833 d. Columbus, Mississippi 15 September 1907, commanded a brigade in the Confederate Army of Tennessee. Warner, *Generals in Gray*, 273; and Welsh, *Medical Histories of the Confederate Generals*, 194.

[31]Clayton Torrence made the note here that Caroline Harris, daughter of Judge William L. Harris and Frances Semmes, married General Jacob Hunter Sharp. Frances Semmes Harris was the sister of Carolina Maria Semmes Clayton.

[32]The Empire House Hotel stood on Whitehall Street. Mills B. Lane, ed. *Times That Prove People's Principles: Civil War in Georgia* (Savannah: Beehive Press, 1993), 83. The Confederacy had converted it into the Empire Hospital for wounded soldiers from Georgia and the Carolinas. The hospital retained the name of the Empire Hospital, even after it evacuated to Macon and other cities. Cunningham, *Doctors in Gray*, 60; and Henry Putney Beers, *The Confederacy: A Guide to the Archives of the Government of the Confederate States of America* (Washington, DC: National Archives, 1986), 184.

would laugh so when he would suddenly jump up from a sound sleep and cry the wrong hour.

The wounds. . . .[33]

[33]This fragment of the manuscript ended with this unfinished sentence.

This photograph of the John Neal House on Washington Street was made from the yard of a house once lived in by the Claytons but during the federal occupation of Atlanta in the fall of 1864. The site of the Neal house is now the Atlanta City Hall. (Courtesy of the Atlanta Historical Society)

5

THE EVACUATION

WHEN THE ARMIES MOVED FURTHER DOWN IN THE STATE AND OURS HAD reached Kennesaw Mountain,[1] there was said to be a finer view of them there than at Missionary Ridge, and a party of us began to make preparations to go on another viewing expedition.[2] But just as we were about ready another civilian was added to the list of those who had been killed, and an order was issued forbidding the visits of any more civilians.

This was a disappointment to all and especially to those who had missed a sham battle earlier in the Spring at Dalton, to which a large number of the young people of Atlanta had gone.[3] My sister, Julia,[4] and I were among those who failed to see it, for we were absent on a visit to friends in Alabama, and, therefore, we could know only from hearsay about the sights and scenery.

We were told of the delightful time had by all who attended, of the beautiful military maneuvers and especially of the great excitement in the crowded railroad coach in which they were returning home when it was

---

[1]Kennesaw Mountain, located twenty miles north of Atlanta, was the site of a Confederate victory in the repulse of federal attacks on 27 June 1864. Samuel Carter III, *The Siege of Atlanta, 1864* (New York: Bonanza Books, 1973), 160-165.

[2]Also see Carter, *Siege of Atlanta*, 154, and Albert Castel, *Decision in the West: The Atlanta Campaign of 1864* (Lawrence: University of Kansas Press, 1992), 306. A federal account of the view from Kennesaw Mountain and how Confederate young women had come to admire that view, despite the destruction and death there, appears in the *Louisville* (KY) *Daily Journal*, 12 July 1864, 2, c. 1.

[3]Her sisters Mary and Carrie Clayton were among the visitors at the sham battle, 7 April 1864. Benedict J. Semmes to Jorantha Semmes, 6 April 1864, Benedict J. Semmes Papers, MS 2333, Southern Historical Collection, University of North Carolina at Chapel Hill. Also see the reminiscences of Augusta Hill (Mrs. Joseph) Thompson, Atlanta Pioneer Women's Society Papers Collection, Atlanta Historical Society, and *Southern Confederacy* (Atlanta), 19 March 1864, 1, c. 2; Darrell C. Roberts, *The Gray Winter of 1864 in Dalton* (Dalton: self published, 1991), 46-47; and Janet B. Hewett, Noah Andre Trudeau, and Bryce A. Suderow, *Supplement to the Official Records of the Union and Confederate Armies* 100 volumes to date. (Wilmington NC: Broadfoot Publishing Co., 1996), pt. i, vol. 6, Serial 6, 210.

[4]Julia Frances Clayton, b. Athens, Georgia 6 October 1839 d. 10 August 1885, married Edward Foster Hoge, founder of the *Atlanta Journal*, on 21 November 1866. William Clayton Torrence, *Rootes of Rosewall* (n.p., 1906), 77.

found to be on fire. While they told me about their fright we could not understand how such a thing could happen at that time of the year, when it was too mild for stoves, or other heat in the car, nor could they tell if the fire had been caused by sparks from the engine.

Another event which we missed was the great military inspection that was held in Marietta Street and was said to have been so fine.[5]

You have already been told of what I considered the greatest day in Atlanta and now we come to one of the saddest: the bringing into the city of the remains of General [Leonidas] Polk soon after he was killed on Pine Mountain [on 12 June 1864] and their lying in state in St. Luke's Church, at the corner of Walton and [Forsyth] streets.

The train came in quite early and his body was taken to "the little refugee church," as it was called, under Dr. Quintard.[6] The casket was placed in front of the chancels and was then opened showing the flag that draped the remains, and all was covered in flowers from the beautiful magnolia down to the smallest one then blooming. In the present time we think of the latter as nothing unusual but in that day and generation it was the first and only time for some years to come that flowers were used in Atlanta on a funeral occasion, and these flowers were not sent by different persons, it was the thought of one or two only who collected and arranged them.[7]

I do not remember at what hour, but quite early, that the church was opened, and thousands who thronged the streets waiting for this were permitted to pass in. There were two doors in front and to prevent any disorder or crowding all were required to enter the door at the left, continue up the left aisle, pass in front of the casket and down the right hand aisle to the door on that side. I could not begin to say how many, many thousands marched through the little church on that occasion or how sad their mien.

---

[5]This fragment of the manuscript ends here.

[6]Dr. Charles Todd Quintard was the Episcopal minister of St. Luke's Church on Walton Street and Confederate army surgeon. Carter, *Siege of Atlanta*, 92. A photograph of Dr. Quintard appears in A. A. Hoehling, *Last Train from Atlanta* (New York: Bonanza Books, 1958), after page 224.

[7]A cross of white roses was laid across his chest and hundreds of magnolia blossoms made a bower of the transepts. Carter, *Siege of Atlanta*, 156. For contemporary accounts of the services held for General Polk in Atlanta see *Southern Confederacy* (Atlanta) 16 June 1864, 2, c. 1; *The Chattanooga Daily Rebel* (Griffin), 17 June 1864, 2, c. 4; and *Nashville* (TN) *Dispatch*, 24 June 1864, 4, c. 2.

The good old Bishop's[8] death seemed a personal loss to everyone who looked upon his bloodless face that day. Tears were shed by hundreds of those present, but very silently, not a sound was heard in the entire church but that of footsteps as the crowd passed through. Many, very many of the throng paused long enough when the casket was reached to stoop, for it was quite low, and take a leaf, or flower or twig. There was no cessation of the stream of humanity; except for a short religious service, until the time came to remove the remains to the noon day train to start for Augusta where the remains were to be buried in St. Paul's church yard.[9]

The crowd made way in the Street for the passing of the hearse and the carriages of the pallbearers, then quietly fell in line, and with bowed heads followed in their wake, while all the time the beauty of the morning seemed a mockery to the gloom and sorrow of Atlanta that day.

The state of affairs around Atlanta was growing daily more and more serious. It was not long before the cannonading could be heard above all the noises of the Street, and if anyone who wanted to hear it would go into a quiet place the sound of musketry was quite plain.

Yet with all this going on there were still a few parties, picnics and entertainments of different kinds.[10] The last of those we attended was a party at Colonel Tom Howard's out at what is now called Sherman Town,[11]

---

[8]General Polk was the Episcopal Bishop of Louisiana. Stewart Sifakis, *Who Was Who in the Confederacy* (New York: Facts on File, 1988), 228.

[9]The actual funeral for General Polk was held at St. Paul's Episcopal Church in Augusta, Georgia. Joseph H. Parks, *General Leonidas Polk, C.S.A.: The Fighting Bishop* (Baton Rouge: Louisiana State University Press, 1962), 383-384.

[10]Sallie Clayton made a note here that visits to Stone Mountain, near Atlanta, were a popular entertainment. An Atlantan wrote that Atlanta society had many pleasant parties, especially at the Navy Department's bachelor home called the "Anchorage." *Southern Confederacy* (Atlanta), 24 March 1864, 2, c. 3.

[11]This mansion was actually the country home of Augustus F. Hurt. It stood on what is now the site of the Carter Presidential Center, on Cleburne Avenue. Thomas C. Howard was only temporarily occupying the house because of the proximity to his distillery on Clear Creek. According to legend, General Sherman observed the siege of Atlanta from here. The federal soldiers later tore the house down for fire wood and for lumber with which to build huts. Part of the Battle of Atlanta occurred on this site. Franklin Garrett, *Atlanta and Environs* 3 vols. (New York: Lewis Historical Publishing Company, 1954) 1:618; Don O'Briant, *Looking For Tara: The Gone With the Wind Guide to Margaret Mitchell's Atlanta* (Atlanta: Longstreet Press, 1994), 90; Albert Castel, *The Campaign for Atlanta* (Washington: Eastern National Park and Monument Association, 1996), 40; and Wilbur Kurtz Collection, MS 130, Box 36, folder 3, Atlanta Historical Society. Annie Schor wrote very favorably of

and two and three weeks afterward his home was Sherman's headquarters at the Battle of July 22d.[12]

People were now leaving town on every train. Those of the men who could not go were sending their families to what they thought safer places and so far as I know, everything in the way of schools, except our own, which was open in the summer, was closed. The pastor of the Second Baptist Church,[13] Dr. Wm. T. Brantley,[14] was our teacher. At our solicitation he had begun in 1862 to give private lessons to four of us. Ella and Gussie Neal, Sallie and Caro Clayton, together with his own bright, beautiful and lovely daughter Lou, and his little son Theo. Mr. Neal[15] gave him for recitation rooms two unfurnished parlors for as long a time as he chose to use them in his new house at the corner of Washington and Mitchell streets, the original building of the Girls' High School.[16] All lessons were prepared at home and we recited in the mornings from nine to eleven. Dr. Brantley's idea was for us to have few studies at a time and after mastering them to pass others. In addition to his wise plan he was exceed-

---

the Hurt property when her husband was trying to rent it in 1862. Schor to John Kimberly, 27 May 1862, John Kimberly Papers, MS 398, Southern Historical Collection, University of North Carolina at Chapel Hill. A drawing of the house appears on page 38 of Wilbur G. Kurtz, *Atlanta and the Old South* (Atlanta: American Lithograph Company, 1969). The nearby unfinished Troup Hurt House is the focus of the Cyclorama, the enormous painting of the Battle of Atlanta on display at Atlanta's Grant Park.

[12]The Battle of Atlanta, fought 22 July 1864, took place on what is today Memorial Drive, east of Oakland Cemetery. Garrett, *Atlanta and Environs*, 1:616-618.

[13]The Second Baptist Church of Atlanta was organized on 1 September 1854. It stood on the northwest corner of Washington and Mitchell streets. The congregation founded several churches before they merged with the Ponce De Leon Baptist Church to form the Second Ponce De Leon Baptist Church in 1933. Garrett, *Atlanta and Environs*, 1:374.

[14]The Reverend William T. Brantley served as pastor of the Second Baptist Church from 1861 to 1871. Garrett, *Atlanta and Environs*, 1:374. He was the son of the minister of the First Baptist Church of Charleston, South Carolina. *Southern Confederacy* (Atlanta), 24 March 1864, 2, c. 3. His photograph appears on page 9 of *A History of the Second-Ponce De Leon Baptist Church Atlanta, Georgia Centennial Year 1854-1954* (Atlanta: Darby Publishing, 1954).

[15]John Neal, b. 1796 d. 1886, of Zebulon, Georgia built his $25,000 mansion in 1858 on the corner of Washington and Mitchell streets. It was used by General Sherman as his headquarters during the federal occupation of Atlanta. Garrett, *Atlanta and Environs*, 1:638-639.

[16]The Atlanta Female Institute reopened in Neal's house on 27 September 1863 and 1 February 1864. *Baptist Banner* (Atlanta), 23 January 1864, 3, c. 5, and 30 January 1864, 3, c. 5. For the history of this house see Garrett, *Atlanta and Environs*, 1:638-639.

ingly humane in the appointment of lessons, so there was no trouble in our being able to obey the one only rule which was to close all books by two o'clock and not to open them again until the following morning. In this way we might have plenty of time for recitation and be both school girls and young ladies if we liked.

The only thing to mar our pleasure and delight in the arrangement we had succeeded in making was that very soon after we began our little circle was broken into by death. Gussie Neal was taken ill with typhoid fever and lived but a few weeks afterwards. It was very sad for us to give her up and we felt her death very much. After this when we resumed our studies, for an entire change, Dr. Brantley had us go for several weeks to his residence on Pryor Street, near Richardson, and recite in the afternoon. Then Mr. Neal asked him to come back to his house, and as the weather was getting cold to use their large sitting room instead of the unfurnished parlor. We continued in this way with our studies until the Christmas holidays and when after a reasonable rest we were not recalled we began to be very anxious on the subject. Finally, my sister, Caro,[17] asked Dr. Brantley how long before we might begin; he told her the times were getting so hard he would have to make teaching more of a business, and if she would get him a class of twelve he would begin immediately and he would use the basement of the Second Baptist Church for recitations. It took a few days only to get the required number, and at our first meeting there were present; Ella Neal, Lettie Floyd, Corinne Lawton, Nannie and Jennie Logan, Eddie Spiller, Mary Smith, Anna Goldsmith, Leila Larendon, Sallie, Caro, and Gussie Clayton, and, of course, Lou and Theo Brantley were with us. Two of this number, Anna Goldsmith and Corinne Lawton soon withdrew, though the sister of the latter, Loulu, came from her home in Savannah to take her place. Afterwards three more were added by special request, Rebecca Erskins, Ann Lana Colquitt and Freddie Tarver. The recitations were in the morning from nine to eleven as at first. Indeed, everything was as it was before, except that the younger girls were in a class not so

[17]Brantley wanted a school that provided him an income of $100 per month. Sallie and Caro Clayton, with Ella Neal, recruited the students. Gussie Clayton to Mary Lou Yancey, 12 May 1863, Benjamin Cudsworth Yancey Papers MS 2594, Southern Historical Collections, University of North Carolina at Chapel Hill.

advanced as those of us who were older.[18]

There were no holidays except at Christmas. Sometimes our teacher would have to be out of town for a while, but our lessons were prepared as usual. None of us wanted holidays, and nothing disturbed us more than the thought of not being able to be present every morning. Some of us had been to various schools and in all had many teachers, but we thought no teacher was ever better than our present one; and nothing before could compare with the happy influence he exercised over his entire class and for it we returned veneration in the highest degree and love bordering on adoration.

In the spring of 1864 one day Dr. Brantley laughed and said as he had taught about all the French he knew. He had secured the services of someone to take us further on; and the next morning he brought with him and introduced Miss Sterchi,[19] who took charge of us in that language. It was not until June had well set in that our little band began to dwindle, and from that time its members fell off one by one almost daily.

Every boom of cannon heard in the distance was but another death knell to its existence and finally came that last day, the eighth of July. My sister and I had been notified in the early morning that the cases of two of our sisters, Mary and Gussie, were not well, were typhoid fever,[20] and as it

---

[18]Carolina Maria Clayton, b. near Athens, Georgia 13 April 1849 d. Atlanta, 25 July 1876, married William George Irwin. Torrence, *Rootes of Rosewall*, 78.

[19]Elizabeth Sterchi, born in Lausanne, Switzerland in 1824, by being a school teacher and a member of St. Philip Episcopal Church, was described as one of the few church women of Atlanta with a job outside of the home. After her education at the Moravian school at Montmirail, Switzerland and having taught in several Moravian schools across Europe, she moved to America with her brother and father in 1857. They settled in East Tennessee before coming to Atlanta. Adelaide L. Fries, ed., "The Elizabeth Sterchi Letters," *Atlanta Historical Bulletin* 5/21 (1940): 107; Julia Collier Harris, "Miss Sterchi's School," *Atlanta Historical Bulletin* 5/21 (1940): 104-106; and Harvey K. Newman, "The Role of Women in Atlanta's Churches, 1865-1906," *Atlanta History* 23 (1979-1980): 18. Gussie Clayton described "Mademoiselle Sterchi" as giving long but varied lessons. Gussie Clayton to Marylou Yancey, 1 June 1864, Benjamin Cudsworth Yancey Papers MS 2594, Southern Historical Collections, University of North Carolina at Chapel Hill. Elizabeth Sterchi presumably was the sister of J. H. Sterchi, b. Lucerne, Switzerland 1828 d. 18 August 1909, who came to Atlanta in the early 1860s and joined the Confederate army. Garrett Necrology, microfilm reel 16, frame 585, Atlanta Historical Society.

[20]Captain Benedict J. Semmes wrote from Atlanta at this time that Gussie Clayton suffered from typhoid fever and pneumonia but that Mary had a "nervous fever" that brought on hallucinations that she was about to die. Her parents were described as "worn out" but determined to stay with their sick children in Atlanta "happen what may." B. J. Semmes to Jorantha Jordan Semmes, 13 July 1864, Benedict J. Semmes Papers, MS 2333, Southern

was important to send as many of us away as could go, we and two servants were to leave for Montgomery, Alabama, that night. We must go over to school, however, and if Dr. Brantley was there, tell him good-bye. We took an early start that I might have time before I left Atlanta, to see once more a friend, Mrs. Robinson, afterwards Mrs. Bell,[21] who lived at the corner of Washington and Peters' streets (the latter now Trinity Avenue). After saying goodbye to her, and taking a few flowers she gathered on her way to the gate, I hurried to the class room. Besides ourselves there was present only one scholar, Lettie Floyd, afterwards Mrs. Laird.[22]

Dr. Brantley's family had been sent to Augusta but he left town and came to the school as usual. This morning we had no lessons. We talked about the situation and Dr. Brantley questioned us as to our understanding of the position of our forces above the town and requested me to draw my idea of it upon the black board. He made a few changes, but in the main points it was correct and he complimented me on it. This commendation was more than a pleasure to me afterwards when I found those little lines proved the finishing touch of school days for me; however, little I expected to be graduated at the mouth of cannon.

Before separating we had a short reading of Scripture and knelt in prayer. Our parting was a sad one, for we, then, had little hope of ever meeting again. When we reached the train that night among others who had heard of our going and came to say good-bye were Dr. Way[23] of

---

Historical Collection, University of North Carolina at Chapel Hill; and Hoehling, *Last Train From Atlanta*, 75.

[21]The widow Mrs. H. Hathaway and her daughter the widow Mrs. M. A. Robinson are listed in Eighth Census of the United States (1860), Fulton County, microcopy M653, reel 122, 756, National Archives, Washington, DC.

[22]Lettie Floyd is likely the Lellie Floyd listed in the 1860 census of Atlanta as age eleven and born in Virginia. She and Charles Floyd, age fourteen and born in North Carolina, were living in the household of Scotsman James Craig. Eighth Census of the United States (1860), Fulton County, microcopy M653, reel 122, 758, National Archives, Washington, DC. Lettie C. Floyd married William Laird, who came to Atlanta from Cincinnati, Ohio in 1869 and later served as Atlanta's police commissioner. Fulton County Marriage Book H (1892-1895), microfilm reel 110/72, 511, Georgia Department of Archives and History; and Garrett Necrology, reel 12, frame 228, Atlanta Historical Society.

[23]Dr. Samuel Way, b. July 1810 d. 1866, was actually from Liberty County, Georgia. Eighth Census of the United States (1860), Liberty County, microcopy M653, reel 129, 734, National Archives, Washington, DC; Robert Manson Myers, *The Children of Pride: A True Story of Georgia and the Civil War* (New Haven: Yale University Press, 1972), 1717; and William Donald Harley, *Thomas Jane Sheppard of Liberty County* (St. Simons Island GA: self

Savannah, Captain Henry Watterson,[24] and his friend Captain Roberts, "John Happy" in the world of letters.[25] The former Captain [Watterson] introduced two of his editorial friends from Mobile, the Messrs. Clark, and very kindly commended us to their care. Besides this my father had already placed us under the care of General Clement Evans.[26] The town was under martial law and on this trip we traveled the first time with passports.[27]

The following day when my uncle [Benjamin Conley][28] met us at Montgomery there was a touching meeting between him and the Messrs. Clark, for it turned out they were old, old friends who had not met in many years. After reaching Alabama we were in an exceedingly anxious state. We would see in papers accounts of deaths of citizens in Atlanta from the

---

published, 1957), 2.

[24]Henry Watterson, a former aide to Confederate General Nathan Forest and a newspaper man, blatantly published Confederate troop dispositions in the *Chattanooga Daily Rebel* (Marietta GA) in his editorials against Confederate General Braxton Bragg. He later worked as a spy for Confederate General John Bell Hood and wrote articles after the war as Marse Henry in the *Louisville Courier Journal*. Judith Lee Hallock, *Braxton Bragg and Confederate Defeat* 2 vols. (Tuscaloosa: University of Alabama Press, 1991) 2:39; *Chattanooga Daily Rebel* (Marietta GA), 21 April 1864, 2, c. 2; Hoehling, *Last Train From Atlanta*, 13; and Carl R. Osthaus, *Partisans of the Southern Press: Editorial Spokesmen of the Nineteenth Century* (Lexington: University of Kentucky Press, 1994), 150-155.

[25]"John Happy" was the pseudonym used by J. P. Roberts. John Edward Haynes, *Pseudonyms of Authors Including Anonyms and Initialisms* (Detroit: Gale Research, 1969), 50. A satirical article by John Happy appears in the *Southern Confederacy* (Atlanta), 22 November 1862, 1, c. 4-5.

[26]Clement Anselm Evans, b. Stewart County, Georgia 25 February 1833 d. Atlanta 2 July 1911, was an often wounded Confederate general and later historian of the Confederate military. Stephen Davis, "Clement Anselm Evans," in *Dictionary of Georgia Biography*, eds. Kenneth Coleman and Stephen Gurr (Athens: University of Georgia Press, 1983), 295-296.

[27]Confederate General Braxton Bragg first declared Atlanta and vicinity under martial law on 12 August 1862. Ralph Benjamin Singer, "Confederate Atlanta," (Ph.D. diss., University of Georgia, 1973), 123-125; V. T. Barnwell, *Barnwell's Atlanta City Director* (Atlanta: Intelligencer Book and Job Office, 1867), 25; and William A. Richards, "'We Live Under a Constitution': Confederate Martial Law in Atlanta," *Atlanta History* 33 (1989): 25-33.

[28]Benjamin Conley, b. Newark, New Jersey 1 March 1814 d. Atlanta 10 January 1886, was Sallie's maternal uncle by marriage, having married her aunt Sarah H. Semmes. Conley became Georgia's last Republican governor in 1871 when, as president of the Georgia State Senate, he succeeded Reconstruction Republ can Governor Rufus Bulloch, following Bulloch's resignation. James F. Cook, "Benjamin Conley," in *Dictionary of Georgia Biography*, eds. Kenneth Coleman and Stephen Gurr (Athens: University of Georgia Press, 1983), 215-216.

bursting of shells, but never once a name except that of a Street where a death would occur.[29]

Then we could get no answers to letters nor did we know that any of ours were received. I wrote to Mr. Quil Orme,[30] knowing he had a position with the West Point railway since his term of military service had expired,[31] to ask if he would carry letters to Atlanta and send them to my parents for me. Nothing came of this and two months afterward when we had reached Augusta [Georgia] he was in that city and came to see us, at which time he told me he had received my letter that day.

I think it was through a letter of my father's that managed to reach its destination, to my uncle, Mr. Conley, to thank him for so kindly writing and telling him if he could get out of Atlanta to go to Augusta and take his house which he had been obliged to leave vacant,[32] that we learned two

---

[29]The federal army sometimes fired more than five thousand rounds per day into the besieged and starving Confederate city of Atlanta from 20 July to 25 August 1865. Some of the worst shelling came in the middle of August, after a quiet period of some days, in response to the Confederacy firing a large siege gun brought into Atlanta. The federal artillery retaliated on the city. Captain Benedict Semmes reported that by 25 August the post surgeon had performed 107 amputations on civilian men, women, and children, all victims of the shelling. However, Orlando Poe, the federal chief of engineers, felt that the bombardment did not speed the surrender of Atlanta by even one day. Carter, *Siege of Atlanta*, 285; Stephen Davis, "'A Very Barbarous Mode of Carrying on War': Sherman's Artillery Bombardment of Atlanta, July 20-August 24, 1864," *Georgia Historical Quarterly* 79 (1995): 57-90; Garrett, *Atlanta and Environs*, 1:626-31; Benedict J. Semmes to Jorantha Semmes, 25 August 1864, Benedict J. Semmes Papers, MS 2333, Southern Historical Collection, University of North Carolina at Chapel Hill.; and Lee Kennett, *Marching Through Georgia: The Story of Soldiers and Civilians During the Atlanta Campaign* (New York: HarperCollins, 1995), 128. A picture of the Confederacy's large siege gun, abandoned when the rebels evacuated Atlanta, appears in *Atlanta* (Alexandria VA: Time-Life Books, 1996), 145.

[30]Aquilla J. Orme was a railroad conductor. C. S. Williams, *Williams' Atlanta Directory For 1859-60* (Atlanta: M. Lynch, 1859), 124.

[31]Actually, he was discharged for medical reasons on 31 December 1861. Compiled Service Records of Confederate Soldiers Who Served in Organizations From the State of Georgia, microcopy M266, reel 145, National Archives, Washington, DC.

[32]Benjamin Conley had been a successful shoe merchant and the mayor of Augusta before moving to Montgomery. The house on Jackson Street in Augusta had been a gift from Sallie's grandmother to her daughter, and Conley's wife, Sarah Semmes. Morris Conly [sic] Claim, Approved Georgia Claims Before the Southern Claims Commission, microcopy M1658, fiche 122, National Archives, Washington, DC; and Richmond County Deed Book QQ (1860-1863), microfilm reel 138/28, 14, Georgia Department of Archives and History. The house is today the Seymour Whitney House at 15 Eighth Street in Augusta. Eric

more sisters, Julia and Kate,[33] had been added to the fever patients and that our aunt, Mrs. William King,[34] had come over from her home in Athens to help in nursing the sick. Captain and Mrs. Spencer Semmes[35] who had been with us for some time [in Atlanta] were there when we left, and the latter had promised to stay as long as it was advisable and to do all she could to relieve my mother.

A letter written in Athens by Mrs. King after her return home[36] reached us the second week in August, just two weeks after the death of our sister, Gussie,[37] of which it told us; then it was some time longer before we began

---

Montgomery to author, 18 November 1994.

[33]Julia Frances Clayton, b. Athens, Georgia 6 October 1839 d. 10 August 1885, married Edward Foster Hoge on 21 November 1866. Katherine Winter Clayton, b. Cass County, Georgia 3 October 1854 d. Atlanta 10 April 1903, married John Early Torrence. Torrence, *Rootes of Rosewall*, 77, 79. Katherine was the mother of William Clayton Torrence (1884-1953), director of the Virginia Historical Society who came to possess his Aunt Sallie's memoirs.

[34]Augusta Columbiana Clayton, b. Washington, DC, 20 February 1833, married Dr. William King of Savannah, Athens, and Atlanta, (nephew of the famous Roswell and Barrington King) in October 1851. Her daughter Julia married Henry W. Grady, the famous writer and editor of the *Atlanta Constitution*. Torrence, *Rootes of Rosewall*, 72. For more than twenty years Mrs. King headed the "Women's Page" of Atlanta's *Weekly Constitution* and wrote an advice column as "Aunt Susie." Her autobiography can be found in the Atlanta Pioneer Women's Society Papers Collection of the Atlanta Historical Society. An 1864 journal by her father-in-law, William King, Sr., is published in Mills B. Lane, ed., *Times That Prove People's Principles: Civil War in Georgia* (Savannah: Beehive Press, 1993), 163. He carried a letter to Governor Joseph E. Brown from his friend General Sherman requesting that Brown take Georgia out of the war. William T. Sherman, *Memoirs of General T. Sherman* (New York: D. Appleton, 1875; reprint, New York: De Capo Press, 1984), 138; and Myers, *Children of Pride*, 1585-1586.

[35]Samuel Spencer Semmes married Pauline Semmes, his third cousin and the niece of Sallie's mother, Carolina Maria Semmes (Mrs. William Wirt Clayton). Captain Semmes was the oldest son of Confederate Admiral Raphael Semmes, the second cousin of Sallie's mother. Harry Wright Newman, *The Maryland Semmes and Kindred Families* (Baltimore: Maryland Historical Society, 1956), 76, 88.

[36]This letter, dated Athens July 1, 1864, is today in the Nicolson Family Papers Collection of the Atlanta Historical Society, MS 518. Mrs. King wrote that Gussie had repeatedly called out the names of Sallie and their sister Caro.

[37]Augusta "Gussie" King Clayton had written to a friend a month earlier of how she and her sister Sallie helped prepare the family's household goods to evacuate Atlanta should the Union army come closer. She hoped, however, that they would not have to leave. Gussie Clayton to Marylou Yancey, 1 June 1864, Benjamin Cudsworth Yancey Papers MS 2594, Southern Historical Collections, University of North Carolina at Chapel Hill. Ironically, by her death, Gussie became the only member of the family not to evacuate Atlanta. The four

to learn through a long letter from my mother written in August, some of the sad things that had been taking place in our absence.[38] She wrote that two nights after we left the 10th of July, our army crossed the Chattahoochee River[39] and a long wagon train camped in Marietta Street extending from way out to the middle of the town, the men in charge of it filling the Street and sleeping wherever they could lie down on porches of the different houses or on the ground. These were the sleeping men that had to be stepped over when some of our neighbors, among them Miss Annie Robson and Mrs. Morgan[40] made a move for safety.

I think it was before this the wounded soldiers in Atlanta were ordered

---

sick Clayton sisters were kept in two rooms, two to a bed, with their parents moving back and forth between the sick.

On the night of Gussie's death, they heard the tramping of feet as General Hood's Confederate army began a moonlight march past the house to the Battle of Atlanta. The battle being fought around the city cemetery forced the Claytons to bury Gussie in the garden and even then the funeral was interrupted when a federal shell burst not one hundred feet away. Gussie Clayton's burial in the garden for several years became a symbol for many Atlanta families of how the federal siege had impacted upon their lives. After the funeral, the other girls recovered and Mrs. King returned to her home in Athens, although she had to leave Atlanta riding in an open railroad box car filled with muskets and travel by way of Macon and Augusta. Memoirs of Mrs. William King and Mrs. M. B. Torbett, Atlanta Pioneer Women's Society Papers Collection, Atlanta Historical Society; and Sarah Huff, *My 80 Years in Atlanta* (Atlanta: n.p., 1937) 45.

[38]Sallie's parents, William W. and Caroline Semmes Clayton, stayed in Atlanta to nurse their three sick daughters and be with their youngest children, despite the federal shelling of the city. Benedict J. Semmes to Jorantha Semmes, 22 July 1864, Benedict J. Semmes Papers, MS 2333, Southern Historical Collection, University of North Carolina at Chapel Hill.

[39]See Garrett, *Atlanta and Environs*, 1:599-600.

[40]In 1867, Annie Robson lived on the north side of Marietta Street near Spring Street. Twenty-three year old Anna C. Robson lived in the household of English merchant John Robson in the 1860 census of Atlanta. Gussie Clayton would write that she loved Anne Robson "dearly," in part because she did not mind having a little girl for a friend. Mrs. Morgan was Eugenia Goode (Mrs. Joseph H. Morgan), the daughter of Hamilton and Annie Goode and secretary for three years during the Civil War of the Atlanta Hospital Association. Franklin Garrett to author, 13 December 1993; Eighth Census of the United States (1860), Fulton County, microcopy M653, reel 122, 719, National Archives, Washington, DC; Gussie Clayton to Marylou Yancey, 1 June 1864, Benjamin Cudsworth Yancey Papers MS 2594, Southern Historical Collection, University of North Carolina at Chapel Hill; Lucian Lamar Knight Scrapbooks, vol. 23, 117, Georgia Department of Archives and History; and Garrett, *Atlanta and Environs*, 1:706.

to Macon. Our brother[41] was then able to get about on crutches and went with the others.

In our own home to make the nursing of the sick easier, they were moved down stairs and three of the lower rooms were taken for their use. Dr. Logan had been our family physician but was then in the service and was at that time Post Surgeon of Atlanta.[42] As an accommodation he had made a few visits in the beginning until he found the cases were typhoid fever that would require long and constant attention, and as he could not give his time in this way to private patients. Dr. Thomas Price, an old man of long experience, whom our mother had always known, was put in charge.[43] The sick ones all knew, liked and wanted him.

When our army moved into the immediate vicinity of Atlanta, Dr. Ford [sic, Foard],[44] the chief surgeon, was requested to come to the house and to

---

[41]Captain William Harris Clayton, b. Athens, Georgia 7 November 1843 d. Atlanta 11 January 1891, was slightly wounded during the Battle of Cold Harbor, Virginia on 1 June 1864. After recovering in Georgia, he deserted. Torrence, *Rootes of Rosewall*, 77; and Compiled Service Records of Confederate Soldiers Who Served in Organizations from the State of Georgia, microcopy M266, reel 216, National Archives, Washington, DC.

[42]Dr. James Payne Logan, born Botetourt County, Virginia 1820 d. 1891, earned his medical degree in Philadelphia before moving to Atlanta in 1854. Glenna R. Schroeder-Lein, *Confederate Hospitals on the Move: Samuel H. Stout and the Army of Tennessee* (Columbia: University of South Carolina Press, 1994), 191-192; Lucian Lamar Knight, *History of Fulton County Georgia* (Atlanta: A. H. Cawston, 1930), 64; and Walter G. Cooper, *Official History of Fulton County* (Atlanta: self published, 1933), 874. A description of Dr. Logan appears in *Atlanta* (GA) *Constitution*, 26 November 1873, 3, c. 3.

[43]Sallie is very likely mistaken about Price's first name, although her mother, in letters reproduced in the appendix, also refers to Dr. Price. No Dr. Thomas Price has been identified but a wealthy Dr. James Price of Clarke County, Georgia, born North Carolina c1815, graduated from the University of Pennsylvania and received a medical license in 1842. He moved from Clarke County to Atlanta between 1850 and 1860, becoming a neighbor of the Claytons. During the Civil War, he served as a physician for the Georgia state troops. Board of Physicians Registry of Applicants 1826-1881, RG 6-10-10, and Alphabetical Card File of the Confederate Pension Office, Georgia Department of Archives and History; Grace H. Jarvis, *1850 Census, Clarke County, Georgia (Seventh Census of the United States)* (Jacksonville: Jacksonville Genealogical Society, 1981), 120; Fulton County Tax Digest, 1864, 1026th District Atlanta, microfilm reel 70/29, Georgia Department of Archives and History; *The Commonwealth* (Atlanta), 31 October 1861, 1, c. 1; and Eighth Census of the United States (1860), Fulton County, microcopy M653, reel 122, 751, National Archives, Washington, DC.

[44]Surgeon Andrew Jackson Foard, b. Milledgeville, Georgia about 1826 d. Charleston, SC, 8 March 1868, served as surgeon and medical director of the Confederate Army of Tennessee. Schroeder-Lein, *Confederate Hospitals on the Move*, 189-190.

give an opinion as to the management and condition of the cases. His visit was more than ever appreciated on account of its being made on the day after the battle of Peachtree Creek[45] when there was so much in his line of work to be done. It was most encouraging to have him think and say he considered all was being done that could be. He thought two of the patients were doing well, one, though not in a dangerous condition, was in a distressing nervous state, and one was very ill.[46] The latter [Gussie] died the following morning, Friday, the twenty-second of July, about two o'clock, just as the battle below Oakland Cemetery was beginning.[47] This sister [Augusta "Gussie" Smith Clayton] was named for her aunt, Augusta King and was fifteen years of age in April preceding her death.

Not long before it had been thought best for Mrs. [Pauline] Semmes to leave Atlanta, and her husband [Samuel Spencer Semmes] had taken her to her mother[48] and sister in Washington, Georgia, consequently only Mrs. King and our neighbor, Mrs. Goode, were with the family at this time.

In addition to the sickness and grief that had fallen upon the household there were outside happenings, consequent upon the battle, of which the invalids could not be ignorant, or unmindful, and which were but so much more to be borne.

For before day some of the wounded were being brought to the adjoining lot, where Miss Annie Robson's house had been taken for a hospital, and the groans and cries of those poor sufferers had to be heard; while horrible even to think of, amputations were being made, without anesthetics, some from tables in the yard and upon the small front porch.[49]

As it was not at all certain to which side the victory of the battle would fall, friends and neighbors, who were all kindness itself, and did everything in their power to help in some way, advised that funeral arrangements should not be delayed [for Augusta "Gussie" Clayton]. But amid the terror and demoralization throughout the town, the difficulty was in getting

---

[45]She refers to the unsuccessful Confederate attack on the federal lines on the north side of Atlanta, 20 July 1864. Garrett, *Atlanta and Environs*, 1:612-614.

[46]See note 20 above.

[47]Here she refers to the Battle of Atlanta, fought east of Oakland Cemetery on what is now Memorial Drive.

[48]Clayton Torrence notes here that "mother" is Mrs. Paul Jones Semmes, sister-in-law to Sallie's mother, Caroline Maria Clayton.

[49]See the memoirs of Mrs. M. B. Torbett, Atlanta Pioneer Women's Society Papers Collection, Atlanta Historical Society.

something done. Mr. Purse[50] went up town to see about a casket, but could not succeed in getting it home, and Captain Lowry[51] and his father-in-law Mr. Markham,[52] took a light wagon belonging to the latter, drove to the undertaker's and brought it to the house themselves.

Mr. Purse got the Reverend Mr. Freeman[53] of St. Philip's Church to come in the afternoon and officiate at the burial at which a number of friends were also in attendance, although of her sisters, only Mallie,[54] the youngest, could be present. To think of getting to the cemetery was out of the question and there was nothing else to do but to make a place of burial of the garden[55] and even that was dangerous for all who were there, as shells from the battlefield fell not many feet from them before the services were ended.

This was her resting place for years before a removal to the cemetery could be determined upon, and then in order to have it done as privately as possible, and to avoid the gaze of the curious, the very early morning was selected for the time; all preparations were made at three o'clock and the different members of the family going singly, or in pairs, met at sunrise for the interment in Oakland Cemetery.

That night [22 July 1864] after all the noise, dust, heat, fatigue and carnage of the day, who should come to extend his sympathy but our friend Captain Henry Watterson,[56] and how it was appreciated words could never

---

[50]Isaiah Purse is in the 1864 tax digest of Fulton County. Fulton County Tax Digest, 1864, 1026th District Atlanta, microfilm reel 70/29, Georgia Department of Archives and History. In 1867, he was a clerk and bookkeeper with the firm of Clayton & Adair, Atlanta Grocers and Commission Merchants. Barnwell, *Barnwell's Atlanta*, 239.

[51]Clayton Torrence identified Captain Lowry as Robert J. Lowry. He was a prominent Atlanta banker and grocer who had moved to the city from Greenville, Tennessee in 1861. Garrett, *Atlanta and Environs*, 1:514.

[52]William Markham, partner in the Atlanta Rolling Mill, was Atlanta's mayor in 1853. He was remembered for his many building ventures in Atlanta, including the Markham House Hotel. Williams, *Williams' Atlanta Directory*, 119; and Garrett, *Atlanta and Environs*, 1:356, 921-922.

[53]Reverend Andrew F. Freeman was the Episcopal rector of St. Philip's Church. Garrett, *Atlanta and Environs*, 1:587.

[54]Almyra Cobb Clayton, b. near Kingston, Georgia 18 November 1857 d. Atlanta 16 December 1904, married Westwood Campbell Sayre. Torrence, *Rootes of Rosewall*, 79.

[55]Clayton Torrence made the note that the burial was near the corner of Walton and Spring streets.

[56]See note 24 above for Henry Watterson. By carnage, she refers here to the Battle of Atlanta, fought near Oakland Cemetery on 22 July 1864.

express.

The following Sunday, early in the morning a shell struck a servant's room in the yard, went through the roof and fell into a bed where two little negro children were sleeping, burst and set the bed on fire.[57] My mother had just risen, and hurried out to help in the rescue. By the time she reached the yard a number of soldiers had run in and the servants were all there, but the smoke was so dense that it seemed an impossibility to reach or to even find the bed. Finally someone succeeded, and instead of bringing out mangled dead bodies they brought two perfectly sound little girls; that is, with the exception of a few tiny powder blisters on the hands and arms of the baby that was about eight months old. They were taken into one of the front rooms of the house and put where a thick chimney would be between them and the direction from which the shells were coming, with the hope that the chimney would prove some protection. The shells came from the Marietta side of the town at that time.

Nobody had recovered from the fright when soon after breakfast an ambulance was driven to the door and Mr. Oliver Jones,[58] one of Atlanta's most faithful citizens, with Captain Bransford,[59] the latter a young officer whom my older sisters [Julia and Mary Clayton] had known while on a visit to the family of Admiral Semmes[60] in Mobile, came and announced they had come to move them all to a safer place.

My father asked where they would take them, and if one place was not as safe as another. They said No, that so far only one battery was shelling the town and his house was directly in the range. They proposed to take them to the building of the Georgia Railroad Banking Company down by the railroad on the northwestern corner of Whitehall Street, which Street then extended to Marietta and Decatur streets. The building was small,

---

[57]For a contemporary account of this incident see the Clayton letters in the appendix. It is also mentioned in Benedict Semmes to Jorantha Semmes, 25 July 1864, Benedict J. Semmes Papers, MS 2333, Southern Historical Collection, University of North Carolina at Chapel Hill.

[58]Oliver H. Jones was the city marshal. Garrett, *Atlanta and Environs*, 1:567, 589.

[59]John S. Bransford was a major and quartermaster for the Georgia state military. John S. Bransford Letters, Incoming Correspondence of Governor Joseph E. Brown, RG 1-1-5, Georgia Department of Archives and History.

[60]Raphael Semmes, the second highest ranking officer in the Confederate Navy, was the second cousin of Sallie's mother, Carolina Maria Semmes (Mrs. William Wirt Clayton). Admiral Semmes commanded the famous Confederate raider, the CSS *Alabama*. Newman, *The Maryland Semmes*, 71, 76-80; and Sifakis, *Who Was Who in the Confederacy*, 254-255.

two-storied, light gray in color and faced the railroad,[61] and was my father's place of business as agent for the above company, until the danger of Atlanta rendered it necessary to remove the assets of the bank to Augusta.[62] After the move was agreed upon, the Post Commander[63] very kindly sent wagons to take mattresses and bedding, and the sick followed in the ambulance.

Food was prepared at home and taken down, and my mother would go to and from the house; especially after she had learned that after one shell there would be a certain number of minutes, five, before another,[64] and she could walk to the house in that time. This discovery proved well in another way; it was a comfort to the man who carried the tray of food for he could know when to start and get to his journey's end in safety. His demoralization was such that when he heard a shell coming he fell flat on the ground, face down, until it had burst, and his fear was that one would catch him with the tray on his head and he said if it did, "good-bye dinner," for down he was bound to go.

There was another fright about shells and the servants, whom nobody had thought it necessary to caution about touching one of the death dealers. The morning after the move a shell entered a window of my mother's room just about the time she would have been standing by a bureau, almost touching it, passed through the room, struck in the wall opposite, but did not burst, and one of the women [servants] rushed in, pulled it out and carried it into the Street where fortunately she laid it down carefully instead of throwing it, which gentle treatment of it may have saved her.

One shell passed between the trunks of a twin poplar tree in the garden near enough to their junction to tear out a piece out of each without cutting either entirely down. There were some remarkable escapes. One of

---

[61]The Georgia Railroad & Banking Building was erected in 1856 and destroyed, after severe artillery damage, during the federal occupation of Atlanta. Garrett, *Atlanta and Environs*, 1:408. A photograph of the ruins of the building appears in ibid., 692.

[62]As early as February 1864, Sallie's father, William W. Clayton announced that all deposits in the Georgia Railroad Bank must be withdrawn by 22 March 1864, as the bank was closing. *Atlanta* (GA) *Intelligencer*, 18 March 1864, 4, c. 1.

[63]Major J. K. McCall. Garrett, *Atlanta and Environs*, 1:591.

[64]This safety period between shellings ended on 10 August, when General Sherman ordered federal guns to be fired at random as they became ready, rather than with five minute intervals. Garrett, *Atlanta and Environs*, 1:627.

our neighbors, Mrs. Sells,[65] had three, I think she was living in the Kontz[66] house at the time. One morning as she stepped out of bed a shell fell into the place she had just vacated, right by her husband and little boy. Another time she had just reached the top of the stairs when one fell at her feet; and once afterwards, as she was coming out of a bomb-proof[67] one met her at the entrance. Almost enough to make anyone believe she bore a charmed life.

During Monday, a cousin of my mother, the late Major [sic, Captain] B. J. Semmes,[68] of Memphis, who was in the Commissary Department came to tell her he expected a train of supplies to come in that afternoon, or in the early morning, and it would go out empty late in the day, Tuesday. He wanted her to take as many cars as she needed, put down mattresses and take her sick daughters out of Atlanta to some safer part of the state. He thought she would also have time to save her furniture. Of course, they were all only too glad to accept such a thoughtful, kind, offer and scarcely

---

[65]No Mrs. Sells has been identified. H. Sells was listed as serving in the Atlanta local defense forces. *Southern Confederacy* (Atlanta), 27 May 1863, 1, c. 1. Several people in Atlanta were named Seals and Mell.

[66]The Kontz house on 80 Marietta Street was the home of Christian Kontz (d. 1881), German born shoemaker, grocer, and railroad fireman living at Marietta Street. Immediately after the war, his home would be used as the federal Headquarters of the South. Williams, *Williams' Atlanta Directory*, 111; Huff, *My 80 Years in Atlanta*, 46; and Garrett, *Atlanta and Environs*, 1:312.

[67]For protection from the federal bombardment, many Atlantans dug and/or reinforced cellars as bomb shelters known as bomb proofs. Memoirs of Mrs. M. B. Torbett and Lucy Aseneth Pittman Ivy, Atlanta Pioneer Women's Society Papers Collection, Atlanta Historical Society; and Gibbons, "Life at the Crossroads of the Confederacy: Atlanta, 1861-1865," *Atlanta Historical Journal* 23/2 (1979): 46. A drawing of an Atlanta bomb proof appears in Castel, *Decision in the West*, 465.

[68]Benedict Joseph Semmes, b. Georgetown, DC 15 June 1823 d. Memphis, 29 January 1902, the son of Confederate Admiral Raphael Semmes, began the Civil War as a sergeant enlisted from Memphis in the 154th Senior Tennessee Regiment. After being wounded at the Battle of Shiloh, he served as a captain and Assistant Commissary of Subsistence for the Army of Tennessee. His Civil War letters from Atlanta, mentioning his cousins the Claytons, are in the Southern Historical Collection, Wilson Library, University of North Carolina at Chapel Hill. Compiled Service Records of Confederate General and Staff Officers, and Non-Regimental Enlisted Men, microcopy M331, reel 222, National Archives, Washington, DC; and Newman, *The Maryland Semmes*, 81-82. A photograph of Semmes appears after page 224 of Hoehling, *Last Train From Atlanta*.

knew how to express their thanks.[69]

Preparations for moving were begun immediately. Fortunately, there was no shelling on Tuesday, which gave a fine opportunity to pack and bring the different things to the cars for loading. One or two of our neighbors very kindly took some of the furniture for keeping.[70] Mrs. Austell,[71] for one, and I think Mrs. Goode[72] took some; if so, it was left temporarily in her home opposite ours for she and her little daughter, Callie, now Mrs. Torbett,[73] who was not well, went as far as Barnesville with the others.

As the last wagon was driven off and my mother was leaving the house she saw a small piece of furniture belonging to me still on the porch, but the time to reach the train before its start was getting too short and she did not call them to get it. There was one consolation only to me in its loss. It was a tiny bookcase, and among some of its keepsakes and a few highly prized books, in it was an old-fashioned leather-backed Bible that had been the stay of my maternal grandmother Semmes[74] in her last days; and my hope is that whoever got it was made a better person by reading it.

A number of things in a pantry were to be sent by Captain Semmes the

---

[69]Semmes, in writing of this matter, added that the Claytons left in what was almost the last train from Atlanta. The Union army cut the last railroad from Atlanta on the following day. Hoehling, *Last Train From Atlanta*, 179.

[70]Much of the furniture of Atlanta's wealthier citizens was saved by storage in the Trinity Methodist Church, under the protection of the federal army, which also protected many of the expensive homes around the City Hall and on Peachtree Street. Barnwell, *Barnwell's Atlanta*, 30-31.

[71]Francina Cameron, b. LaGrange, Georgia 11 November 1833 d. Atlanta, April 1917, was the wife, although almost twenty years younger than her husband, of General Alfred Austell. She helped to organize the women and old men of Atlanta into a burial detail for the interment of the Confederate dead left on the field following the Battle of Atlanta. Cooper, *Official History of Fulton County*, 841; Lucian Lamar Knight Scrapbooks, vol. 7, 53; and Eighth Census of the United States (1860), Fulton County, microcopy M653, reel 122, 835, National Archives, Washington, DC.

[72]Mrs. Hamilton (Anne E.) Goode is identified by Sallie in chapter 6 as one of the founding members of the Ladies Memorial Association.

[73]Lucy C. Goode married Mathew B. Torbett on 9 April 1877. Her memoirs are in the Atlanta Historical Society. Fulton County Marriage Book D (1873-1880), microfilm reel 110/68, 369, Georgia Department of Archives and History; and memoirs of Mrs. M. B. Torbett, Atlanta Pioneer Women's Society Papers Collection, Atlanta Historical Society.

[74]Mary Robertson (Mrs. Andrew Green Simpson Semmes), b. Orange County, Virginia 23 June 1788 d. Washington, Georgia 24 December 1838 was Sallie's maternal grandmother. Newman, *The Maryland Semmes*, 70-71.

next day, but when he went to see about getting them to the railroad the door had been opened and everything was gone.

My father didn't want to go so far as Augusta if he could help it, and succeeded in renting some cars in Macon for the purpose of living in them, but the government needed and took them immediately.[75]

The plantation near Montgomery, Alabama, where my sister Caro and I had gone[76] came very near having a visit from Federal Troops before we had been there long. I was awakened one night by hearing low voices at a window of my aunt's room just below ours and soon after I heard the door open and my uncle went out with someone. Then I spoke from the upper window and asked my aunt what was the matter. She said she didn't know; that my uncle had received a message from the overseer on the Pickett plantation adjoining theirs, to take care of himself and he had gone over to see about it. She supposed it meant that Yankees were in the neighborhood.

I asked if it would not be better for us to dress and join her downstairs, to which she said yes, to come down as quickly as we could. By this time my sister, and Miss Julia Richards of Augusta, who was also with us, were awake and up. Just before we were ready there was a loud sound of tramping feet outside that alarmed us very much, for we thought our guests had arrived before anyone could hasten out to meet them.

The sound, however, came from the rear of the house, whereas our visitors were expected to come up the front way. On looking through a back window we saw in the beautiful moonlight the plantation hands all marching in a double column directly to the house, and, perhaps, strange to say, the sight did not rouse in us much more courage and pleasure than if they had been blue coats. However, when we went downstairs we found they had gathered up there from sheer fright. With a common bond of sympathy we stood in moonlight, at the head of an avenue of [hole in manuscript] leading up to the front of the house, awaiting developments.

Suddenly we heard a call that sounded to us like a command to halt, and every one of us, white and black, started in a run as fast as our feet

---

[75]The names Sharpe and Bransford were written into the manuscript here by Sallie Clayton, for reasons not known. See note 61 above for Branford. She may have meant that officers of those names ordered the railroad cars seized.

[76]As she explains elsewhere in this part of the manuscript, she and her sister Caro were staying at Cedar Park, the plantation of her uncle and aunt, Benjamin and Sarah H. Semmes Conley.

could carry us for the woods that lay some distance behind these servants' quarters in the rear of the home. Somebody got us stopped by explaining that what we heard was the men on the next plantation calling to their mules.

On my uncle's return we found a raiding party was reported to be on the way to Montgomery. The next morning they had reached town in due time and it turned out they had changed their course to burn a factory and after that they took another direction.[77]

They were on Alabama territory long enough to cut the railroad between us and Opelika, and thereby destroyed temporarily our hope for reaching Georgia. This midnight fright was followed by a great deal of sickness in our household, which was particularly bad as we were three miles in the country and had only one neighbor, a widow with two little children, a mile from us, besides the overseer on the next plantation, a mile in another direction. If any of the sick had died there would have been very few to attend the funeral. All this time it was comforting to know that the work of rebuilding was going on and it was finished just about the time we thought the sick ones who were going to Georgia were well enough to undertake the journey.

Of course, we were delighted by the thought of going to our friends once more, though there was a feeling of regret at our not being able to be contented and to feel safe where we were, for few places could have been lovelier than "Cedar Park" as that was called. It was two and a half to three miles from Montgomery and a mile from the Alabama River,[78] and while the

---

[77]She refers here to the raid by twenty-five hundred federal cavalrymen under General Lovell Harrison Rousseau, 9-22 July 1864. *Louisville* (KY) *Daily Journal*, 30 July 1864, 1, c. 1-5, 2, c. 1-2; *Augusta* (GA) *Constitutionalist*, 26 July 1864, 1, c. 3; and Mark M. Boatner III, *The Civil War Dictionary* (New York: Vintage Books, 1987), 711. Also see David Evans, *Sherman's Horsemen: Union Cavalry Operations in the Atlanta Campaign* (Bloomington: Indiana University Press, 1966) and William David Evans, *Rousseau's Raid, July 10-July 22, 1864* (Ann Arbor MI: University Microfilms International, 1994).

[78]The Cedar Park Plantation actually belonged to the estate of the deceased Morris Jones Conley, for whom Sallie's uncle and Morris's brother, Benjamin Conley served as administrator. Morris Conly [sic] Claim, Fulton County, Approved Georgia Claims of the Southern Claims Commission, microcopy M1658, fiche 122, National Archives, Washington, DC; and Montgomery County (Alabama) Conveyances Volume T (1843-1844), 195, 489, and "Conley, Morris J.," Montgomery County Estate Case Files (1838-1946), Alabama Department of Archives and History. The property was on the north side of Montgomery, around Conley Circle in today's Sheridan Heights neighborhood of the

plantation was not very large it was more of a model in its appointments and management than any I had ever seen. So much attention was paid to order and appearances; the laying off the ground in graceful walks and avenues; the cultivation of trees, shrubs, and flowers, that it was like living in a beautiful park. Many bushes, flowering plants and trees were trained by clipping in odd shapes, as barrels, tables, chairs, balls, etc.

To give an idea of the profusion of flowers in their season, besides others of its kind in various shapes, there was in the middle of a flower garden to one side of the house a cape jasmine bush fully ten feet in diameter and trimmed to represent a mound, that in full bloom was a marvel of beauty. No fences could be seen anywhere in front, but a broad, semi-circular hedge was prettily arranged some distance from the house to conceal a small pit for greenhouse plants.

I had been on many plantations yet never before on one where any regard for appearances extended to the servants' quarters. Here, the cabins were built on a broad Street, no back yards, but on the opposite side were a garden, fruit trees and a chicken yard for each cabin, a large barn with stalls for the pleasure horses, and at the upper end was the house, for the "head man," facing differently and a little more pretentious in appearance than the others.

A row of beautiful forest cedars stood in front of the cabins far enough to leave a broad, shaded walk. Then way down beyond "the Street," as it was called (never "quarters" as in other places) was a large enclosure for cribs, gin house, packing screw, stables, wagon sheds, horse and cattle lots. On account of the water power the [grist] mill was a quarter of a mile from the house. Everything was kept in good repair and no rubbish of any sort was allowed to be thrown around, consequently there was nothing ragged-looking about the place. Immediately in front of the dwelling was a grass plot, oval in shape, to represent a large mat for carriages to stop on.

One charm of the place was the number and variety of the birds. No shooting was allowed on any part of it, which, I suppose, caused more than its share to flock there for safety from others on which the game was common. In going through an avenue fifteen or twenty nests might easily be counted, and a small covey of partridges used to come in and feed with

---

Boylston Community. The ground that was occupied, according to Sallie, with an idealistic arrangement of slave quarters, today is covered by a middle class African-American neighborhood.

the chickens.

The first cabin in the row was set apart for a chapel where religious services were held by different clergymen, and although the [former] master, [the deceased] Mr. Morris Conley,[79] was a bachelor, the teaching and spiritual instruction that on many plantations was given by the ladies of the family, he did himself every Sunday afternoon to the time of his death in 1861.

It was on this place in the early sixties I saw for the last time the plantation Christmas feast, heard the songs of the merry crowd, watched them in their games and plays, and especially as their dusky forms wound themselves in and out in the mystic mazes of the grapevine dance while with melodious voices they sang, ending with the sad refrain:

Oh, who can tell where we shall dwell
To be merry another year,
to be merry another year!

At the end of one avenue there was a beautiful grove of magnolias, bays and other trees that was sometimes used for picnics, and was a camping place for men of both armies during the war. General Turner Clanton's[80] brigade was the Confederate command to occupy it, and they behaved remarkably well, though the servants were afraid they would find the wild strawberries they liked so much that grew in great profusion in a meadow field near the house.

On our way back to Georgia, when we reached Opelika we had to change cars and go down in a part of the state none of us had ever seen

---

[79]Morris Jones Conley, b. 1829 d. September 1861, was the brother and partner of Sallie's Uncle Benjamin Conley. Conley Family Folder, Family Files Collection, Alabama Department of Archives and History and Morris Conly [sic] Claim, Approved Georgia Claims of the Southern Claims Commission, microcopy M1658, fiche 122, National Archives, Washington, DC.

[80]She presumably meant Lieutenant Colonel Turner Clanton, Jr. and his 7th Alabama Volunteer Confederate Cavalry Regiment. Robert N. Scott, comp., *The War of the Rebellion: A Compilation of the Official Records of the Union and Confederate Armies* 128 vols. (Washington, DC: United States Government Printing Office, 1888-1900) Series I, vol. 39, pt. ii, 752. However, she may have confused him with Confederate General James Holt Clanton. Jack D. Welsh, *Medical Histories of the Confederate Generals* (Kent OH: Kent State University Press, 1995), 38, and David Evans, *Sherman's Horsemen*, 110-111. The flag of Clanton's Brigade is today at the Alabama Department of Archives and History.

before. As we traveled father south the difference in vegetation began to be quite noticeable and the weather was so warm anyway that it reminded one of nearing the torrid zone, when Columbus, the end of the line, was reached. We didn't have much time between trains to see much of the town for it was already late, and just before night we were on our way to Macon in order to reach our objective point, Augusta.[81] We had a long, slow, tedious ride that took the entire night. No sleeping cars in those days, and that night, no light in the car. While we had started with a dim one, before long there was still less, if any, except the reflection.[82]

---

[81]Her description of the terrain from Montgomery to Columbus is confusing as she traveled east by northeast during this entire trip and was never south of where she had been living near Montgomery. George B. Davis, Leslie J. Perry, and Joseph W. Kirkley, *Atlas to Accompany the Official Records of the Union and Confederate Armies* (Washington, DC: United States Government Printing Office, 1891) plates CXLIV and CXLVIII.

[82]This fragment of the manuscript ends with this sentence.

Photographs of the Georgia Railroad Bank before the Federal army marched from Atlanta. It had been W. W. Clayton's place of business and, during the federal shelling, a place of refuge for his family. (Courtesy Library of Congress)

Photographs of the Georgia Railroad Bank after the Federal army marched from Atlanta. (Courtesy Library of Congress)

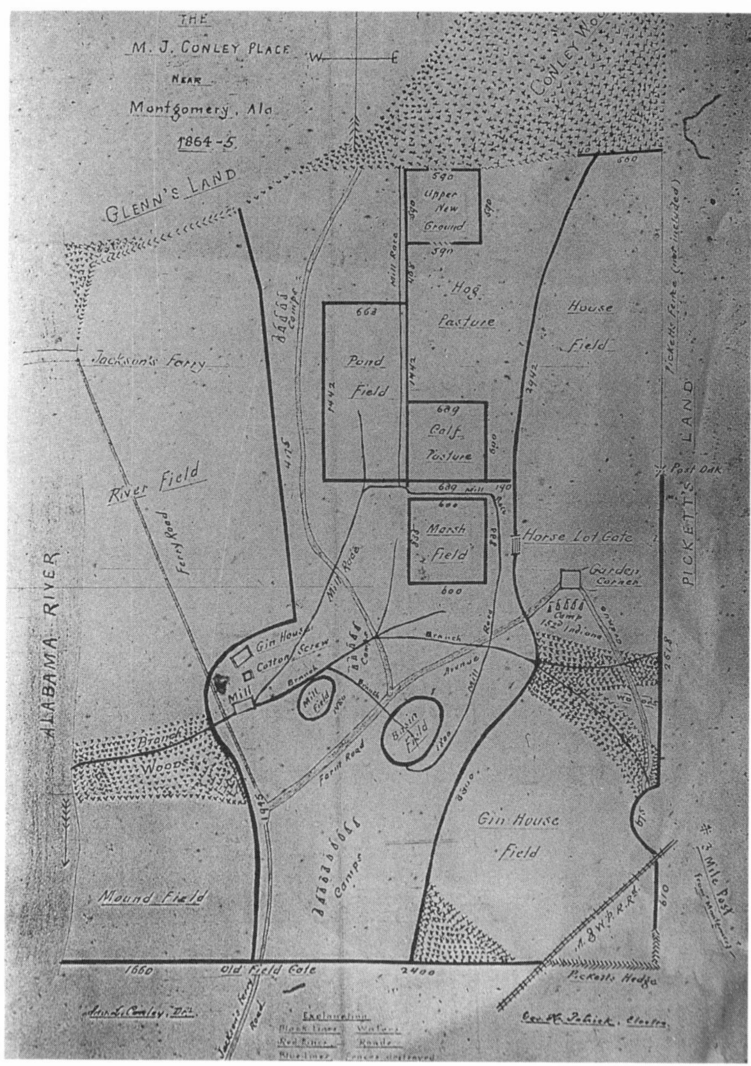

Benjamin Conley's plantation near Montgomery, Alabama, from the claim he filed on behalf of the estate of his brother Morris with the Southern Claims Commission. (Courtesy National Archives and Records Administration)

6

DEFEAT

OUR STAY IN AUGUSTA WAS SPENT WITH A QUIET AND SO MUCH GREATER sense of security than [had been our stay in] Alabama, I suppose from the mere fact of it being a city instead of a plantation. For some time there was excitement and the days passed and quickly. We found a number of our friends in the city and amongst them Captain Semmes,[1] who was stationed there and Dr. Brantley[2] who had rejoined his family and had opened a school. One of the first places we visited was General Polk's grave behind St. Paul's Church.[3] We went to it every walk, some times during the week, but, always on Sunday, usually before the service, and occasionally before Sunday school, as early as the large gate to St. Paul's church yard was opened.

In buying dry goods, and especially bread [sic? thread?], the prices were found to be very high, simple delaine was five hundred dollars for a dress pattern; alpaca, twenty-five and thirty dollars a yard; bombazine double that or more.[4] It was very much harder to get factory goods and knitting cotton as they had to be bought directly from the manufacturer and the purchaser was restricted in the amount or quality of his purchases. Probably there was

---

[1]She most likely means Samuel Spencer Semmes, b. 4 March 1838 d. Osceola, Arkansas 24 January 1912, a captain and quartermaster for the Confederate Army of Tennessee. Harry Wright Newman, *The Maryland Semmes and Kindred Families* (Baltimore: Maryland Historical Society, 1956), 90-92.

[2]Reverend William T. Brantley was pastor of the Second Baptist Church of Atlanta from 1861 to 1871. Franklin Garrett, *Atlanta and Environs* 3 vols. (New York: Lewis Historical Publishing Company, 1954) 1:374.

[3]Sallie discussed the death of Confederate General Leonidas Polk and the memorial service for him in Atlanta earlier in her memoirs. Polk was buried on 29 June 1864 at St. Paul Episcopal Church in Augusta, Georgia. William M. Polk, *Leonidas Polk: Bishop and General* 2 vols. (New York: Longmans, Green, and Co., 1915), 2:384-386; and *Funeral Services at the Burial of the Reverend Leonidas Polk* (Columbia SC: n.p., 1864), microfilm reel 81/8, Georgia Department of Archives and History.

[4]For definitions of these fabrics see Florence M. Montgomery, *Textiles in America 1650-1870* (New York: W. W. Norton & Company, 1983).

The ruins of the Atlanta Rolling Mill, where Sallie left the train the night that she returned to an Atlanta destroyed by war. (Courtesy Library of Congress)

fear of some one buyer's getting more than he needed and holding it for higher prices. Sometimes one or two friends would go with some of us to the factory to buy knitting cotton and we would have to sit in the waiting room several hours, like criminals waiting for the verdict of a jury before we could find out if we could get any and if we could pay twenty dollars a pound for it besides giving them many, many thanks. None of us wanted to go in bare feet so we were willing to go through with a great deal to prevent it. And, oh, soap! the fear that we couldn't buy, or the supply might give out was so great that every time I could spare money enough to pay for it, I would buy toilet soap in the cake, or Palm oil and English Castell in the bar. Fifteen dollars for a cake and twenty dollars for a bar though both were thoroughly good. Everything in the food cost was very high and what we managed was simple fare, expensive cakes and deserts had to be left off.[5]

[I know] how much better the appetite gets in proportion to a decrease in the quantity of food. Some insisted they had a sufficiency all this time, but in my own case doubt was raised not only by a constant desire to read all of the cooking books in the house, but also by thoughts of what we were then missing by being cut off from our plantation.

The few times that I was sure of being hungry, however, was during the winter while on a visit to Greensboro, Georgia. While the younger members of the family would be busy in the evenings with sewing or farm work my aunt Mrs. Philip Clayton,[6] would read some one of the Waverley[7] novels aloud, and when sometimes [the author Sir Walter Scott] stretched a description of one of them old time feasts such hunger would be awaked in

---

[5]By the time Sallie and her family had refugeed to Augusta, inflation had become so bad that the local textile factories no longer accepted Confederate money but sold only by barter. At the same time, $150 in Confederate currency might buy a single one hundred pound sack of flour, one bushel of salt, three hundred pounds of corn meal, or one cord of wood. Florence Fleming Corley, *Confederate City: Augusta, Georgia 1860-1865* (Columbia: University of South Carolina Press, 1960), 89.

[6]Sallie's uncle Philip Clayton married Leonora Harper, born October 1819 d. October 1895. They had only owned their home in Greensboro, Paradise Hill, since 1862. The house had been the home of United States Senators Thomas W. Cobb and William C. Dawson. Torrence, *Rootes of Rosewall* (n.p., 1906), 70; and T. B. Rice Collection, microfilm reel 91/78, Georgia Department of Archives and History.

[7]The Waverley was a series of forty-eight novels written by Sir Walter Scott (1771-1832), beginning in 1814. M. F. A. Husband, *A Dictionary of the Characters in the Waverley Novels of Sir Walter Scott* (London: George Rutledge and Sons, 1910), ix; and John O. Hayden, *Scott: The Critical Heritage* (New York: Barnes & Noble, 1970), 4-5.

the crowd that petitions would be put to the head of the house for permission to get the cook to prepare a feast for us. At first there would be a refusal, it was too late to disturb her, and, any way what would we have her to cook at such an hour, usually eleven o'clock. To the latter, we would always say, "something that could be [cooked] quickly." Of course, we would reward her for her trouble and, moreover, one of our number would go for her and quietly, and if she had retired, she would not be called. We knew Charlotte's lovely disposition and we had no fear of her ever failing us; she would then say, "we will make you some fatty bread" at which she was so adept, "and you some bacon, will that do?" "Oh yes! that will be splendid." And before very long here would come with her steaming dishes and we could enjoy what was brought, simple as it was, equally well with the partakers of Sir Walter's feasts. Indeed, I am inclined to think far more.

Immediately After the War[8]

The last winter we had very little tea or coffee. The usual substitutes for the former were sassafras, blackberry and raspberry leaves. The last was very good; better than many teas of these days. Before everything was over, the substitutes drank for coffee were rye, wheat, sweet potatoes, okra, parsnips, parched meal, chicory, etc. A substitute for chocolate was ground peas parched very broken and ground as fine as meal, then stirred in heated milk and water.

We had a good laugh on my uncle in Alabama[9] about a sack of coffee and other good things he had lain up in his store room. He wouldn't let us use them except when we were going some distance on the [railroad passenger] cars then we might have a nice cup of coffee, as it were a starter.

We tried to talk him into letting us have the benefit of what was there; that the Yankees might come along and use them for us. But he was firm in his determination to keep the supplies and a new buggy, the wheels standing in the carriage house, until the war was over and then he said he was going to "splurge." Just as we prophesied, when the Yankees really came

---

[8]This heading is the only heading by Sallie Clayton in the entire manuscript. All other headings used here are the editor's.

[9]She refers here to Benjamin Conley of Montgomery, Alabama, whose plantation she described in chapter 5. Sallie and her family stayed at Conley's Augusta house in late 1864 and early 1865.

they not only took the things but compelled him to hold bags while they filled them. Some of them also put a horse to his buggy and drove off with it.

Fortunately he and a faithful servant had taken what money he had out into the woods and buried it for after the buggy was gone and they had finished with the store room they turned upon him and said, "old man, you've got money, and we are going to have that." When he insisted that he had no money, they pointed eleven muskets at his breast (he said he counted them) and swore they would shoot him if he did not give it up; to which he said, "well, you will have to shoot for I have no money"; and strange to say they not only did not kill him, but afterwards, when they found he was opposed to secession, they paid him for the buggy and some of the other things that been taken.[10]

The citizens and refugees in Augusta were greatly excited when Sherman drew near on his most wonderful march to the sea, with nothing to oppose him, as there were only a few old men, invalids, women and children in his line, and [as if] they were actually going to make a show of resistance.[11] Even old men were called out for military duty and with others, my father and my uncle, Mr. Philip Clayton[12] had to go. We were sorry for

---

[10]Benjamin Conley, as administrator of the estate of Morris J. Conley, received $5,288 of a $6,868.35 claim that he made with the federal Southern Claims Commission after the Civil War. Claim of Morris Conly [sic], Approved Georgia Claims Before the Southern Claims Commission, microcopy M1658, fiche 122, National Archives, Washington, DC; and J. B. Holloway, *Consolidated Index of Claims Reported by the Commissioner of Claims* (Washington, DC: United States Government Printing Office, 1892), 54, reproduced in Records of the Commissioners of Claims (Southern Claims Commission) 1871-1880, microcopy M87, reel 14, National Archives, Washington, DC.

[11]By November 27, 1864, all local men were called to Augusta, the city was ringed with forts, the stores were closed, important Confederate generals had arrived to add prestige to the defense, some ten thousand to fifteen thousand troops had assembled, and movement into and out of the city required written passes. Edward J. Cashin, *The Story of Augusta* (Augusta: Richmond County Board of Education, 1980), 126.

[12]Philip Augustin Clayton, b. Athens, Georgia 19 March 1815 d. 22 March 1877, served as assistant secretary of treasury in the federal government before the war and later for the Confederacy. He had also been Secretary of State Howell Cobb's assistant secretary. Confederate Secretary of the Treasury Christopher G. Memminger fired him for such unbusiness-like practices as entertaining friends while at work. Jon L. Wakelyn, ed., *Biographical Dictionary of the Confederacy* (Westport CT: Greenwood Press, 1977), 138-139; Douglas B. Ball, "Treasury Department," in *Encyclopedia of the Confederacy*, ed. Richard N. Current (New York: Simon and Schuster, 1993), 1614; and Douglas B. Ball, *Financial Failure and Confederate Defeat* (Urbana: University of Chicago Press, 1991), 29. Confederate diarist

them but our amusement at their appearance as soldiers was very great. In the first place each weighed in the neighborhood of three hundred pounds and in the second they had to wear what they had in the way of clothing and put their soldiers accouterments outside of their citizens dress.[13]

My father didn't make quite the show that his brother did for his suit was dark whereas the other was still wearing a summer suit of white dress homespun with a little brown stripe in it that one of his daughters had made for him. He was jolly and cheerful as men are ever made, and he enjoyed the picture he presented as much as we. They were not kept in camp very long but had to report for duty during the day. In the late afternoon my father would usually get h me first and soon after somebody would call out, "Uncle Philip is coming!," and he was such a show there would be a rush for the Street, and a number of us, joined by the neighbors, would hurry to meet him so we might enjoy seeing im march sch long as we could. Sometimes that winter, for want of a more suitable garment, he had to wear a dark blue broad cloth dress coat that he had used on social occasions in Washington City, where he had been assistant United States Treasurer under three presidential administrations.[14]

He told us he was going to take a train car and at his home in Greensboro when he met a man on the platform who threw up his hands and exclaimed, "my God! mister where did you get that coat? my great grandfather had one just like it."

Instead of stopping with us in Augusta and without coming close

---

Mary Chesnut referred to Clayton several times in her writings. He should not be confused with Confederate Marshal Philip A. Clayton of Randolph and Calhoun counties in Georgia. Claim of Philip A. Clayton, reel 17, Pardon Petitions and Related Papers Submitted in Response to President Johnson's Amnesty Proclamation of May 29, 1865, National Archives, microcopy M1003, Washington, DC; and Bradley W. Steuart, *Georgia 1870 Census Index* (Bountiful UT: Precision Indexing, 1990), 574.

[13]For a very similar account of Georgia's very democratic, if oddly equipped militia, see Gary Livingston, *Fields of Gray: The Battle of Griswoldville* (Cooperstown NY: Caisson Press, 1966), 30. Gross obesity was not uncommon among the white male planters. Among the many "big" men of nearby Hancock County, a jury weighed in at approximately thirty-six hundred pounds, or an average of three hundred pounds per juror. Colin Campbell, "Sparta's Song," *Atlanta Journal/Atlanta Constitution*, 20 November 1994, C3, c. 2-4.

[14]Actually Philip Augustin Clayton only served as assistant secretary of the treasury under United States President Buchanan and Confederate President Davis, although he was also second auditor in the US Treasury from 1849 to 1857; acting treasurer of the United States in 1859; and, as a Republican, consul to Peru, beginning in 1874. Wakelyn, *Biographical Dictionary of the Confederacy*, 138-139.

enough even to throw us a shell, the valiant General [Sherman] passed on to Milledgeville[15] and thence through South Carolina to Columbia, the burning of which an attempt is now made to teach our children and grand children was accidental. If so, how did the originator of the accident story account for the flaming balls of rosin turpentine and cotton that were thrown through doors and windows into the midst of terrified women and children? Friends of mine were told in Atlanta by members of Sherman's army that they dreaded to go with him into Carolina because his men were to be allowed to burn and kill as they pleased. And a very short time after the burning, long, long before a question of accident was raised I was told of a gentleman who just as the day was closing, was talking on a Street in Columbia, with one of the enemy when he saw a rocket shoot up in the air, and, upon inquiring what it meant, his companion replied, "my friend that is the signal for firing your city."[16] My informant was the late Mr. Isaiah Purse,[17] a man of unquestioned probity and assiduity. I think he told me the person who saw the rocket and who told it to him himself was his brother in law, a resident of Columbia but whose name has escaped my memory.

---

[15]Despite various stories of personal attachments to Augusta as the reason for his not capturing that city, the reason General Sherman gave for avoiding Augusta was that he wanted to reach a sea port for resupplying his army, while avoiding a battle. Augusta had an ad hoc garrison of 10,000 to 15,000 men but would not have been serious opposition to Sherman's army of 60,000. Edward J. Cashin, *The Story of Augusta,* 126.

[16]For popular accounts of the burning of Columbia similar to what Sallie wrote, see John G. Barrett, *Sherman's March Through the Carolinas* (Chapel Hill: University of North Carolina, 1956), 81-90. Only some one third of Columbia, South Carolina was burned and the federal soldiers did not intentionally start the fire. The fire, more likely accidental, resulted from a number of causes although southerners from that time since have repeated stories that the defenseless, surrendered, city of Columbia had been destroyed for no reason but revenge against the South. Some drunken or vindictive northern soldiers reportedly helped spread the flames, without orders, although even more federal soldiers, including General Sherman, worked to stop the fire. James M. McPherson, *Battle Cry of Freedom: The Civil War Era* (New York: Ballantine Books, 1989), 829; John F. Marszalek, *Sherman: A Soldier's Passion for Order* (New York: The Free Press, 1993), 324-325; Burke Davis, *Sherman's March* (New York: Random House, 1985; reprint, New York: Vintage Books, 1988), 165-166; William Gilmore Simms, *Sack and Destruction of the City of Columbia* (Columbia, SC: Power Press, 1865; reprint, Atlanta: Oglethorpe University Press, 1937); and James G. Gibbes, *Who Burnt Columbia?* (Newberry SC: Elbert H. Aull, 1902).

[17]She refers here to Charleston, South Carolina railroad conductor Isaiah Purse, b. c. 1832 d. Atlanta 9 October 1881. Eighth Census of the United States (1860), Charleston County, South Carolina, microcopy M653, reel 1215, 467, National Archives, Washington, DC; and Garrett Necrology, reel 7, frame 631, Atlanta Historical Society.

After Sherman had passed on everything settled down into the same quiet way in which we were living before he came. The people ceased to wonder why he changed his mind about spending the winter in Atlanta for which he seemed to have prepared so much, in some instances, tearing down new dwellings to put the material into winter quarters for his men,[18] or so long as he did leave at that point, why he didn't go by Andersonville[19] and release those starving prisoners[?][20] Occasionally something would happen to afford us a good deal of amusement and [without] our seeking it. For instance, one of our friends, a young man whom we knew very well and who was a frequent visitor whenever he was in the city was at one time superintending the shipment of some cattle for the use of the army and he was not very anxious for us to know why he was in Augusta. But sometimes ["]murder will [be found] out.["] Now it happened that without our knowing it a yard adjoining ours had been rented to put a number of cattle

---

[18]Federal General Sherman originally intended to leave a heavily fortified garrison in Atlanta. Many of the city's buildings, including Sallie's Atlanta Female Institute, were demolished for that chain of interconnected forts. *Macon* (GA) *Daily Telegraph and Confederate*, 10 December 1864, 2, c. 2; William T. Sherman, *Memoirs of General William T. Sherman* (New York: D. Appleton, 1875; reprint, New York: De Capo Press, 1984), 129; and Robert N. Scott, comp., *The War of the Rebellion: A Compilation of the Official Records of the Union and Confederate Armies*, 128 vols. (Washington, DC: United States Government Printing Office, 1888-1900) Series I, vol. 39, pt. i, 137 and 139. Photographs and a map of Sherman's forts appear in George B. Davis, Leslie J. Perry, and Joseph W. Kirkley, *Atlas to Accompany the Official Records of the Union and Confederate Armies* (Washington, DC: United States Government Printing Office, 1891) plate LXXXVIII, map 1, and plates CXXVI and CXXVII.

[19]"Andersonville" was the popular name for the Confederate prison Camp Sumter in Sumter County, Georgia. By August 1864, it held more than thirty-three thousand federal prisoners. Richard N. Current, ed., *Encyclopedia of the Confederacy* (New York: Simon and Schuster, 1993), 38-40; and *Nashville* (TN) *Daily Times & True Union*, 25 August 1864, 1, c. 4.

[20]General Sherman was somewhat concerned with the condition of the federal prisoners held at the Confederacy's prison Camp Sumter, popularly called Andersonville. He negotiated with Confederate General John Bell Hood about releasing the healthy prisoners. Sherman also sanctioned an impractical and disastrous federal cavalry raid to reach Camp Sumter. By the time Sherman began his march from Atlanta, the Confederacy had evacuated all but the most desperately ill of the federal prisoners to other camps to prevent their rescue by Sherman. In his hurry to reach the security of the federal navy, Sherman did not detour more troops to another Andersonville rescue attempt. Sherman, *Memoirs*, 112, 115, 143; and Albert Castel, *Decision in the West: The Atlanta Campaign of 1864* (Lawrence: University of Kansas Press, 1992), 442, 569.

in for the night, and, while my sister Mary[21] and I were in the parlor with our friend, who had come in for the evening, someone rang the door bell and calling for him, notified him that the cattle had broken the fences and were getting into our yard and into the Street. Of course he hurried off, and we prepared to leave the room. We knew the back of the house was only one step from the ground but we did not know the door was open, and we would not have thought anything of it if we had; to our astonishment and fright on opening the parlor to go up stairs, [which] were by no means slight, when we met a cow with a bell on her neck, running up the hall. We managed to reach the stairs just in time to escape her and stood in our place of safety, half way up, to watch [the] proceedings. She couldn't get through the front of the house. As the door was closed, and she didn't seem to know how to turn around, so some of the men, who were helping with them, had to come in and get her headed the other way so they could take her out. After that our friend was always, "General B. of the cow brigade."

Later in the winter we had another laugh at his expense for he called one cold evening when we had no heat, on account of the furnace being out of order. We couldn't have fires at all down stairs for furnaces were very rare in the south in those days and as they were put in after the houses were built the chimneys to the lower rooms were used to carry the heating pipes to the upper story. While we were sitting there in the cold trying to talk, there was a rap on the door and a little servant asked to speak to my sister. On returning to the room she seemed somewhat embarrassed, and, shortly after, when another rap came she asked me what the servant wanted. When I went into the hall the girl was standing there with a very broad smile on her face, and a package in her hands and she said it was a hot brick that my sister Caro,[22] had sent with a message to put it in the middle of the floor and sit around it so we could warm our feet. I sent her upstairs again, but the desire for fun wouldn't be quieted in that way for before long she came down and this time without tripping opened the door and delivered her message while she put the brick in the middle of the room. The occurrence gave as an excellent idea. The churches were very cold on Sundays but we

---

[21]Mary was Mary Semmes Clayton, b. Athens 16 January 1842 d. Atlanta 31 July 1899 (later Mrs. Cary Wood Henderson). Torrence, *Rootes of Rosewall*, 77.

[22]Sallie refers here to her sister Caroline Maria Clayton, b. Athens, Georgia 14 January 1847 d. Atlanta 25 July 1876, later Mrs. William George Irwin. Torrence, *Rootes of Rosewall*, 78.

didn't suffer much after this for we carried hot bricks under our cloaks and kept our feet comparatively comfortable.

There were a number of gunboats lying in the Savannah river in the Spring,[23] and, on the invitation of some of the officers, we made them one or two visits. The only one I had ever seen before was one just built that was launched in the Alabama river at Montgomery in the presence of an immense crowd, earlier in the sixties.[24] Besides visiting and going over a large boat, two of its officers, W. F. Clayton[25] and Lieutenant Floyd[26] invited us, with some young lady friends to go up the river one beautiful moonlight night in a rowing party. There was another party on the river and in their boat, one of the young ladies was singing to the accompaniment of a guitar. As we passed them, she was singing, "On the banks of the Blue Mosille." She had a sweet voice and heard upon the water that evening her song was very beautiful. We had another lovely moonlight view of the Savannah River through the kindness of Mr. Quill Orme,[27] who managed one evening to get to our house during a freshet that had put the city under water.[28] Soon after he came in he said he wanted us to go down the Street with him and see a beautiful sight. We laughed at the idea of going out in the water until he explained that although we were living so near the river we were

---

[23]What survived of the Confederate fleet at Savannah, the CSS *Sampson* and CSS *Macon*, moved to Augusta after Savannah fell to the Union army. Civilians were invited to make tours of the gun boats. Berry Fleming, *Autobiography of a City in Arms: Augusta, Georgia 1861-1865* (Augusta: Richmond County Historical Society, 1976), 140-143; Cashin, *The Story of Augusta*, 126; and Corley, *Confederate City*, 90.

[24]The Confederate gun boat *Nashville* was launched in Montgomery in 1864, but finished in Mobile. After heavy fighting in Mobile, it surrendered to the federal forces on 10 May 1865. Tony Gibbons, *Warships and Naval Battles of the Civil War* (New York: Gallery Books, 1989), 43. A model of the *Nashville* is in the Museum of the City of Mobile.

[25]William Force Clayton of Georgia served as a midshipman on several Confederate gunboats during the Civil War. Thomas Truxtun Moebs, *Confederate States Navy Research Guide* (Williamsburg: Moebs Publishing Company, 1991), 200.

[26]The only Lieutenant Floyd in the Confederate navy was Richard S. Floyd of Georgia but at the time Sallie was in Augusta, he was in federal custody, having been captured on the Confederate raider *Florida* off the coast of Brazil on 7 October 1864. Charles R. Floyd, however, served as a master's mate in the Savannah squadron in 1864. Moebs, *Confederate States Navy Research Guide*, 210.

[27]Aquilla J. Orme, Atlanta railroad conductor.

[28]This flood occurred on 12 January 1864 and, for the poor people of Augusta, proved a blessing, as the water deposited enough driftwood for them to have fires for the rest of the winter. However, the flood water increased unsanitary conditions and encouraged the spread of disease. Corley, *Confederate City*, 89; and Cashin, *The Story of Augusta*, 127.

on higher ground than most people, for we could walk to the corner, down the Street, which was Reynolds, a block, and then turn and walk a block to the river and that was where he wanted us to go.

We started with him and soon found he was right for we got to the river on dry land, where we stood on a long porch facing the water and saw the Savannah, under a full moon, spread out of her banks not only into the city but so far on the Carolina side that no land was left in sight.

Just after the surrender of General Lee's army my sister Julia and I were spending a few days on the Sand Hill with Mrs. L. H. Davis,[29] who had also with her Miss Tuny Glen of Atlanta. One morning about midday while we young ladies were sitting together Mrs. Davis came in and told us Lincoln had been killed. We asked how she had heard such a thing; she said one of the men on the place had been sent to town in a wagon for something and on his return as he neared the house she could see him dancing up and down in the wagon and hear him calling out something that before long she could understand and it was: "Lincoln is killed! Lincoln is killed!" Of course she couldn't understand a darkee's hilarity over the killing of Lincoln so when he drove near enough to hear her she called out: "you mean Jeff Davis don't you?", but he said no, he meant Lincoln that someone shot him the night before. This report was confirmed by Mr. Davis on his return from the city and I will say for the household that, while we were not overwhelmed with grief, there was no rejoicing; we were filled with wonder and amazement.[30]

We had been waiting a long while for the Georgia Railroad to be rebuilt, after having been torn up so badly by Sherman's army when he began his march through the state, so we might return to Atlanta. At one time we intended to go farther up in the state and be ready to go in on the first train, and having this intention in view rooms were rented for us in Madison, but

---

[29]Sallie must be referring to Elizabeth E. Morris, the second wife of commission merchant Larkin H. Davis. His first wife, Melinda Fowler, died 14 January 1864, and he married Elizabeth on 16 March 1865. Garrett Necrology, microfilm reel 5, frames 405 and 528, Atlanta Historical Society; *Atlanta* (GA) *Intelligencer*, 20 January 1864, 1, c. 6; Fulton County Marriage Book B, 326, microfilm reel 110/66, Georgia Department of Archives and History; and Garrett, *Atlanta and Environs*, 2:67.

[30]President Lincoln's assassination, however, was actually a full page and front page story in Augusta's *Daily Chronicle and Sentinel* of 25 April 1865. Also see Carolyn L. Harrell, *When the Bells Tolled for Lincoln: Southern Reaction to the Assassination* (Macon GA: Mercer University Press, 1997).

the government had a way of fancying just what we liked so a claim was made here and we had to give them up.[31] Then we concluded it would be better, anyway, to have cars and follow the road as it was being built but although we had already secured several [railroad cars] the government spoke again and they had to go as the rooms did. It was a great disappointment to some of us; for seeing others living in them, by the way side, and seeming so cozy, so long as we could not have our own home, made us anxious to give that mode of life a trial. By this time large numbers of our men were passing through Augusta on their way home; yet it had not occurred to us how full the cars would be in traveling, and we appointed a day for three of us to start for visits to Athens and Greensboro until we could get to Atlanta. Two evenings before we were to leave we were all sitting together in the parlor talking over the state of affairs when Captain Semmes[32] who was in the Quartermaster's department, said from what he could hear he was satisfied the soldiers intended to help themselves to all government stores the next day [1 May 1865] and if they did, of the few things left in his office the best was a bolt of uniform material known at that time as "Joe Brown blue,"[33] which he was going to try to save, and, if he succeeded, he would give it to my mother to make cloaks for us the following winter. We were almost overcome with [laughter at the thought of being] dressed in black, and wearing cloaks of clear, bright, "Joe Brown blue." The Captain joined in the laugh but insisted it was thick enough to keep out the cold and if we didn't like the color we might resort to dyes.

True to report, the following day all places containing government stores were attacked by thousands of our own men, who claimed they were entitled to everything that was left. Two of our sisters and two young ladies of our neighborhood were walking up Broad Street at the time the trouble

---

[31]A letter from William Wirt Clayton to Sallie, 31 January 1865, about his obtaining a home in Madison and getting railroad cars in Augusta is in the unprocessed papers in the Nicolson Family Papers Collection at the Atlanta Historical Society, MS 518. For the condition of the Georgia railroads see John F. Stover, "The Ruined Railroads of the Confederacy," *Georgia Historical Quarterly* 42 (1958): 376-388.

[32]Samuel Spencer Semmes, b. 4 March 1838 d. Osceola, Arkansas, 24 January 1912, was a captain and quartermaster for the Confederate Army of Tennessee. Newman, *The Maryland Semmes*, 90-92.

[33]She refers to the material of the flannel sack coats worn as fatigue uniforms by the Georgia militia, named for Governor (and commander of the Georgia militia) Joseph E. Brown. Philip Katcher, *The Civil War Source Book* (New York: Facts on File, 1993), 248.

began. They had forgotten the rumors of the day before until they heard a roaring noise and a sound of many tramping feet and turning to see what caused it they found the Street thronged with soldiers coming at a rapid pace in their direction. There was not even an opportunity of getting into a building, and their only hope of escaping the crowd was to out run them. Success crowned their efforts and when they got way up Broad Street they found a side Street sufficiently clear for them to turn towards the river and come down a back way. When they reached home and told their experience they expressed a fear, as no other women were visible on the Street at the time, of being considered leaders of the mob. But we hadn't long to jest about it for just then there was a roar and sound of many voices and a glance toward Broad Street from the pavement where we were standing, showed an immense crowd rushing into Jackson Street. We thought this could mean nothing else than an attack on private property, and our neighborhood gathering was quickly scattered as we started into our homes to try to save some clothing if nothing more.

However, we very soon found Warren Block to be their destination and, we afterwards heard, that their object was the baggage of General Beamesard [sic, Blanchard],[34] which was said to be stored in that building. Why the General's baggage was so dangerous as to bring on the attack couldn't be learned, but the satisfaction of knowing it didn't fall into their hands was very great. As soon as it could be done, cannon were planted at four points in Broad Street, two at the upper end and two at the lower, and the commander, General Raines,[35] declared the Street would be swept by them if the rioting men could be quieted in no other way. There were no casualties in the city though one man was killed when the arsenal on the

---

[34]Albert Gallatin Blanchard, b. Charlestown, Massachusetts 10 September 1810, d. New Orleans, Louisiana 21 June 1891, was commanding several regiments of South Carolina reserves with the Army of Tennessee in North Carolina at that time. William C. Davis, *The Confederate General* (Washington, DC: National Historical Society, 1991), 104-105.

[35]Colonel George Washington Rains, b. Craven County, North Carolina 1817 d. Newburgh, New York 21 March 1898, was neither a general or commander at Augusta. He built and directed the Confederate States Powder Works at Augusta, one of the most successful munitions works of the Civil War. Wakelyn, *Biographical Dictionary of the Confederacy*, 360-361. The commander at Augusta was actually Confederate General Ambrose Ransom Wright, b. Louisville, Georg a 26 April 1826i d. Augusta, Georgia 21 December 1872. Cashin, *The Story of Augusta*, 125; Jack D. Welsh, *Medical Histories of the Confederate Generals* (Kent OH: Kent State University Press, 1995), 240; and Davis, *The Confederate General*, 161-162.

Sand Hill was attacked.[36]

Captain Semmes gave an amusing account of the raid on him. He said they ran completely over him, knocking him to the floor and preventing his saving anything not even a pair of new shoes he had for his wife. Afterwards he picked up a large spool of black flax someone had dropped and, on examining a little farther, he found the package of "Joe Brown blue" must have been overlooked for there it was, so we got it after all, and, later in the year, we made it into suits for an uncle and a brother who needed clothes more than we needed cloaks.

The following morning when the three of us, who expected to leave Augusta on that day went to the depot, we found a long train that seemed to be packed with soldiers to its utmost capacity. It was crowded on the roof as well as inside and there seemed not the remotest probability of our being able to get even standing room. My father thought it was useless for us to go into a car and we had turned to leave the depot when we met coming in, one of our friends, Captain Dennis Harris[37] of Nashville. The latter said it was too bad for us to be disappointed for the trains would probably be crowned in this way, daily, for sometime to come, and that if we were entrusted to his care he felt sure he could get us in among the soldiers and we would reach our destination in safety.

Sure enough, some of the "boys" made room for us, and, with only one other woman in the car besides ourselves, we started on our way. Although every particle of space seemed to be already occupied, at every station, more

---

[36]The Augusta riot of 1 May 1865 was the high point of lawlessness that had been taking place in the city for months, as the Confederacy collapsed. Similar riots by Confederate soldiers took place across the South. The Augusta riot was quelled by the resistance of hastily organized bands of citizens, a speech by Confederate General Ambrose R. Wright, and the fatal shooting of one of the riot leaders on Kollock Street. The crews of the Confederate gun boats were ordered to dump arms and ammunition that might have been captured by the rioters. As a result, one of the sailors was shot for insubordination. *Macon* (GA) *Daily Telegraph*, 8 February 1865, 2, c. 2; Lee Ann White, *The Civil War as a Crisis in Gender: Augusta, Georgia, 1860–1890* (Athens: University of Georgia Press, 1995), 127-128; Corley, *Confederate City*, 93-94; Cashin, *The Story of Augusta*, 127; Dan T. Carter, *When the War Was Over: The Failure of Self Reconstruction in the South, 1865-1867* (Baton Rouge: Louisiana State University Press, 1985), 12-13; and Salem Dutcher, *Memorial History of Augusta* (New York: D. Mason, 1890; reprint, Spartanburg SC: The Reprint Company, 1980), 186.

[37]Assistant Commissary of Sustenance Dennis B. Harris was from Davidson County, Tennessee. Compiled Service Records of Confederate Non-Regimental Staff Officers and Enlisted Men, microcopy M331, reel 119, National Archives, Washington, DC.

soldiers would crowd on. And to the remonstrances of the conductor that the engine could pull no more, and the tops of the cars would certainly give way under each strain, their only reply was: "We are walked enough, we'll be d--d if we are not going to ride home." The consequence was, before the train reached Union Point, where two of us were to change cars for Athens, every little while a stop was made and stout saplings were cut down and placed as supports under the weakened roofs of the cars. I do not know that it was true, as I did not see it, that two of the tops had broken through as we were told, but I believed it for that we were in was propped in three different places and we were heartily glad when our ride ended. It would be always well in giving an account so out of the ordinary to produce at the same time proof of its truthfulness but, at this late day, that would be somewhat troublesome as it would necessitate advertising for some participant of that memorable ride to come forward and testify. Then, too, the date has been forgotten, though that might be supplied by designating the time as: "Early in May 1865, the day after the sacking of Augusta, Georgia" [2 May 1865].

In order to reach Greensboro my sister, Caro, had to go seven miles farther. When we started, the crowd was so great that Captain Harris had been separated from us, but as we left the car to take the train for Athens he managed to get near my sister, which proved to be most fortunate for when a stop was made at Greensboro, owing to some mistake, there was no one to meet her and it was found our soldiers were sacking the town also. A great many of them were in the neighborhood of the depot and the fear of their attacking that for freight and baggage was such that, while the conductor held the train long enough for him to do so and get back, Captain Harris took my sister's trunk on his shoulders and carried it to a private house and put it in safe keeping until it could be sent for.

When we reached that point, Athens was also being sacked.[38] We thought all such behavior was very wrong at the time, but, later, there was general rejoicing that our men got as much as they did when the hordes of our enemies seemed so disposed to strip us of the little that was left. The boys seemed to be helping the soldiers in Athens, for during our ride through town we could see them from the windows of the omnibus with

---

[38]The Athens riot occurred on 3-4 May 1865. Kenneth Coleman, *Confederate Athens* (Athens: University of Georgia Press, 1967), 176; and *Southern Watchman* (Athens), 17 May 1865, 1, c. 2.

their arms filled with tins of various shapes and many other things.

My uncle, Mr. E. P. Clayton,[39] paid a boy a good price for four tin pans and thought he had made a good bargain until he got back and found his young son had brought in four dozen. We had been in Athens about two weeks and the pleasant stay we were having with our friend, Miss Caro Yancey,[40] was drawing to a close when we unexpectedly found the town filled with Yankees.[41] The first we knew of it was one morning Mr. Hamilton Yancey ~~now of Rome, GA,~~[42] who was then a young boy, came to us and said he had taken a prisoner. Of course we laughed, thinking he was jesting, but he insisted not and said we might go on the back porch and see him for ourselves. He saw a man prowling around the stable and thinking he was a Texas Ranger,[43] he ran into the house for his gun, made him surrender and marched him on the back porch to his father. Major Yancey[44]

---

[39]Edward Patrick Clayton, b. Athens, Georgia 14 July 1820 d. Augusta, Georgia 1888, was an Augusta merchant and cotton factor. Torrence, *Rootes of Rosewall*, 71.

[40]Caroline Yancey, later Mrs. Hugh Nesbitt Harris of Athens, was the only child of Benjamin Cudsworth Yancey (1817-1891) by his first wife Laura Hines (d. 1844). Patton and Pitts, *The Benjamin Cudsworth Yancey Papers*, 7, 9; and Charlotte Thomas Marshall, *Oconee Hill Cemetery* (Athens: Athens Historical Society, 1971), 2.

[41]The first federal troops actually arrived in Athens at almost the same moment as Sallie, on 4 May 1865. However, after doing some looting, these men of the Thirteenth Tennessee Regiment were replaced by a federal garrison under General Palmer. Coleman, *Confederate Athens*, 177; and *Southern Watchman* (Athens), 17 May 1865, 1, c. 2-3.

[42]Hamilton Yancey, b. 27 September 1848 d. Rome, Georgia 15 November 1931, was the son of Benjamin Cudsworth Yancey and his second wife Sarah Hamilton. Patton and Pitts, *The Benjamin Cudsworth Yancey Papers*, 7, 9; Shirley Kinney, Madge Tate, and Sandra Jenkins, *Floyd County, Georgia Cemeteries* (Rome: Northwest Georgia Historical and Genealogical Society, 1985), 578; and Hamilton Yancey to Ruth Blair, 27 June 1927, File II Names, Georgia Department of Archives and History. The reference to Rome does nothing to help date the manuscript as a search of the city directories in the Sara Hightower Regional Library in Rome shows that Yancey lived there at least as early as the 1880, long before Sallie's manuscript was written, and still lived there in 1927, after Sallie's death.

[43]Reference is made here to a band of deserters from the 8th and 11th Texas Confederate cavalry regiments under a Captain Jack Colquitt. They had been raiding civilians in North Georgia. *Augusta* (GA) *Constitutionalist*, 11 February 1865, 1, c. 2; *Macon* (GA) *Daily Telegraph*, 18 November 1864, 1, c. 3; and George Magruder Battey, Jr., *A History of Rome and Floyd County* (Atlanta: Webb and Vary Company, 1922), 206-207.

[44]Benjamin Cudsworth Yancey, b. 27 April 1817 d. Rome, Georgia 24 October 1891, was the younger son of Benjamin Cudsworth and Caroline Bird of Charleston, South Carolina. A businessman, he also served in the state legislatures of South Carolina, Georgia, and Alabama. His older brother was Confederate politician William L. Yancey. Coleman, *Confederate Athens*, 61; Patton, *The Benjamin Cudsworth Yancey Papers*; and Kinney, et al.,

asked his name and command that he might report the matter and have him punished, to which the man, though wearing a gray overcoat, replied he was a Federal soldier. His statement seemed so improbable that it brought forth a severe reprimand from the Major, but the stranger, who was trembling visibly, insisted and said he would unbutton his overcoat and show his uniform. This he did, and the view of his blue suit caused him to be asked when he came into town; to which he said, "This morning." "With how many?" "A command of two thousand." In some way or other this determined the Major not to detain the man any longer, so he told him that, as, under the circumstances he had no right to hold him, he was at liberty to go. The man not only seemed to be but was frightened and asked that young Hamilton Yancey might be allowed to go down town with him. To this Major Yancey consented and afterwards went down himself to see if he could secure a guard for his premises, for although hostilities had ceased, no one knew how these men would behave. It didn't take anybody long to find out when they were seen to take watches, jewelry and silver, horses from carriages and riders, and, indeed, anything they seemed to fancy just as in days of yore.

Although a guard was sent, the next morning while a number of us were sitting on the front veranda, an officer with a party of men appeared. He first stepped over to where the guard was sitting a little apart from us, and after a few minutes conversation with him, turned and demanded all keys that he might search the premises. Miss Yancey informed him the master of the house was not present but [she] should like to know by what authority he demanded keys. Brother yank must have forgotten the war ended nearly two months prior to that time for he got angry, jerked a paper from his pocket and thrusting it at her said: "By that authority," she didn't examine his paper but told him she was well aware we were living in a day when might made right, and started in to send for her father, who had gone with his wife across the Street to see her mother. As she passed me I managed to give her a little warning to try to keep cool if she could. The officer wouldn't wait but calling to his men to follow him, he walked rapidly into the hall. I thought of my trunk upstairs and thinking what the contents would mean to me, prompted a feeble effort on my part for its salvation. I followed the leader into the hall and offered him the key at the same time explaining that I did not know whether trunk keys were also meant and

---

Floyd County, Georgia Cemeteries, 577.

how I should dislike to have my trunk broken open, especially as I was away from home. The young man was very polite to me; he told me to keep the key and assured me the trunk should not be disturbed. Emboldened by my success a plea for the house was then offered by my asking if he would not wait until the master could reach home. He said he would have done so but the young lady had been so rude to him he did not feel that he could. Just then Major Yancey, with a number of others entered the back door and I feared for his welfare when I found he was not any more cordial to the newcomers than his daughter had been.

The view he took of the matter was that having a guard in the house protected him from such intrusion. However, after a stormy parley of a few minutes, comparative quiet was restored and the order to search was carried out. When the smoke house was opened there was no meat for that had all been carried to the attic either the day before or early that morning; but with the hope of saving them, a pretty pair of carriage horses had been put in [the smoke house?]. The officer stated they were not after horses and they would not be disturbed. In going through the dwelling the door to the attic was overlooked but Major Yancey called attention to it and showed them the meat. Of this, he was allowed to keep a certain number of pounds; I think it was two hundred. It was thought after this nothing else would be taken, but when the officer made his report down town, one higher authority sent an order back for the horses. At this Major Yancey went himself to headquarters, and, for a wonder succeeded in getting them again. Then there was some fear that a party might be sent to burn the house, so we contrived to set out as much of the silver and wearing apparel as we could and took them some distance where they were left with friends, by making several trips and in different directions, in the hope of not arousing the suspicions of the guard.

It was whispered this band was hunting for Mr. Davis, but some of us thought bread and meat were more important objects to them just then,[45] though they didn't hesitate to take anything else that suited them. The general belief was that many of them came into our states for nothing more than they could steal, and, occasionally, some of them would let the cat out

---

[45]The first federal troops to reach Athens were searching for Confederate President Jefferson Davis. They did engage in looting. However, the systematic search for food that Sallie describes was an attempt to locate the Confederate stores seized by Athens citizens during the riot of 3-4 May. Coleman, *Confederate Athens*, 176-177.

of the bag. As for instance, one of our friends said to a man, who was taking her silver from a wardrobe in her bedroom where she had put it, "you wouldn't take an old lady's silver would you?" to which he replied: "Well, I'd like to know what I came here for if I wouldn't.["] and, oh, the damns they did use even to and about babies and children. Here are a few sample sentences. A charming little girl not more than three years, old, and so small that she looked like a large doll, called out one morning in a most friendly way to a passing blue coat, "Howdy Yankee," and his reply was ["]shut your mouth, you d--d little rebel." Another told a nurse who was walking with her little charge three months old to throw the d–d little rebel down and break its neck. The same nurse asked one of them if Confederate money would ever be good again and he told her no, he had been lighting his pipe with the d–d trash for two months. While all this excitement of this Yankee visit was going on we were thankful the sun shown by day and the moon by night[46] and we enjoyed everything funny that came our way. One our first laughs was at the blank expression of Ham Yancey when a day or two after the Federal command reached town some of their little darkies, who had taken advantage of their newly acquired freedom to go hunting came running in exclaiming "Marse Ham, ain't dese your powder horns?" and gave him some hunting pouches; which he told us afterwards he had taken more than a mile from home and hidden in a hollow tree, and their dogs had taken them directly to the spot. But when some one was heard one night prowling around the garden, which required investigation by the guard and the master of the house was found while he was trying to hide something we had to laugh, on the sly, for fear of offending for he was very indignant at the thought of his not being able to go about his own premises

---

[46]Much more lurid tales of robberies and atrocities committed by federal troops were spread by southerners. Reasons for animosity towards southerners, including long absence from home, deaths of friends in the war, and the treatment of federal soldiers as prisoners of war, are discussed in Joseph T. Glatthaar, *The March to the Sea and Beyond: Sherman's Troops in the Savannah and Carolinas Campaigns* (New York: New York University Press, 1985), 76-77. Federal General Sherman defended his army against the charges of needless cruelty. He argued that the Confederate army's needs had caused far more suffering and refugeeing than anything done by the federal forces. He also pointed out that while the federal government was feeding thousands of southern civilians, the Confederate military starved far more. Sherman, *Memoirs*, 127. However, historian Albert Castel called Sherman's evacuation of the civilians in Atlanta the harshest measure taken by federal authorities against civilians in the Civil War with the exception of the expulsion of civilians from guerrilla infested Missouri. Castel, *Decision in the West*, 549.

without being brought in by a Yankee guard. My sister Julia and Caro Yancey came in from the garden one morning where they had been eating strawberries from the plants and the under lip of the latter was so badly swollen that we asked immediately what had caused it. She said it was a case of "curses, like chickens, coming home to roost" that my sister had been telling her of our aunt Mrs. King's[47] wish when she had to let one of the soldiers have strawberries from her garden that while he was eating them he would bite a pumpkin bug and have the taste of it forever after.[48] As she was enjoying the joke and saying what a good wish that was, without looking at it, a berry was carried to her lips with one of the very bugs on it and she got a severe sting. The wishes of Mrs. King, who was always all of fun, were many and varied and always amusing. But on one occasion after a pleasant evening our party had spent with her and her husband had to see us home she got a little nervous at his having to be out so late while the town was full of our enemies, and began to take back all she had said with two exceptions, that about the pumpkin bug, and that every Yankee might have a darkey strapped over his shoulders and be compelled to carry him through all eternity. What soon followed, the soldiers, had they heard it, might have considered swift punishment even just retribution. For a cool morning came along and while she was bathing her baby near a stove in which a fire had been made, she noticed smoke and the draught didn't seem to be right; so a little servant in the room was told to run into the yard and look up at the chimney to see if it was on fire. Before the girl got back it was remembered that some boxes of jewelry, and a set of case knives one of the servants had committed to her care had been concealed as high up the flue as they could be put and their burning was the cause of the trouble. The loss, though regretted, was cheerfully borne, and great comfort was deprived from the knowledge of the fact that no blue coat could carry them away with him.

After leaving Athens we spent a few days at the home of my uncle Mr. Philip Clayton, in Greensboro where we found several of our returning

---

[47]Augusta Columbiana Clayton, b. Washington, DC 20 February 1833, married Dr. William King of Savannah, Athens, and Atlanta, Georgia in October 1851. Torrence, *Rootes of Rosewall*, 72.

[48]Mrs. King also tells this story in her memoirs in the Atlanta Pioneer Women's Society Papers Collection at the Atlanta Historical Society.

soldier friends and with them a gallant young Englishman Dr. Chaffers,[49] who had been helping to fight our battles for the past few years and who showed us his last pay from the Confederate government of one dollar and fifty cents in silver. He seemed to appreciate very much the kindness of my uncle in inviting him to share his home until he could sail for England. He also expressed a regret for having when a young boy, chucked with stones the statue of one of his hosts ancestors in London[50] declaring could he have known then of meeting descendants of the man whose representation it was and receiving such kindness and consideration from them he never would have been guilty of such mischief.

On our way to Atlanta[51] we were accompanied by Major Baylor[52] and Lieutenant Floyd[53] who were to be our guests for a few days. After going slowly for several hours in good daylight, when that gave out, we traveled

---

[49]Edward Chaffers of Manchester, England studied surgery at St. Thomas Hospital, London and became a member of the Royal Society of Surgeons in 1863, before serving as a captain and assistant surgeon in the 2nd Tennessee Confederate Cavalry Regiment. He was paroled by the federal army at Charlotte, NC on 3 May 1865. Compiled Service Records of Tennessee Confederate Soldiers, microcopy M268, reel 5, National Archives, Washington, DC; and Jones, "Roster of the Medical Officers of the Army of Tennessee," 183, 190. By 13 April 1866, he was working at the North Riding Lunatic Asylum in Clifton, Yorkshire, England. Chaffers died in Lancashire on 4 May 1909.

[50]Chaffers probably referred to Sir Robert Clayton (1629-1707), Lord Mayor of London, whose marble statute stands before St. Thomas Hospital in London. Ben Weinreb and Christopher Hibbert, *The London Encyclopedia* (London: Book Club Associates, 1983) and George Smith, *Dictionary of National Biography*, 22 vols. (Oxford: Oxford University Press, 1882-1952), 11:473-475. The Claytons had many distinguished English relations. See Claud Franklin Clayton, *Family Notes and Recollections* (Knoxville TN: self-published, 1959).

[51]The final destruction in Civil War Atlanta occurred on 15 November 1864. The rebuilding of the city began almost immediately. Citizens remaining after the fire appointed a provisional mayor and vigilante police force. Confederate troops reoccupied the city on 2 December. Later that month city elections were officially held in Atlanta, a salt factory began operations, the post office reopened, the trains again ran, and the *Atlanta Intelligencer* newspaper resumed operations. Gibbons, "Life at the Crossroads of the Confederacy: Atlanta, 1861-1865," *Atlanta Historical Journal* 23/2 (1979): 57; *Macon* (GA) *Daily Telegraph*, 11 April 1865, 2, c. 2; Davis, *Sherman's March*, 13; and Wooten, "New City of the South," 115.

[52]Major Eugene W. Baylor was an assistant quarter master. Compiled Service Records of Confederate General and Staff Officers and Non-Regimental Enlisted Men, microcopy M331, reel 18, National Archives, Washington, DC.

[53]As this lieutenant traveled with Assistant Quarter Master Baylor, he is most likely acting Assistant Quarter Master J. M. Floyd of Spututa, Clark County, Alabama. Ibid., reel 95.

in the dark as was customary in those days. The train reached Atlanta about eleven o'clock p. m. or rather the nearest point to which the tracks had been rebuilt.

In the midst of doleful and dangerous surroundings all the passengers left the cars at this stopping place, which was way down near Oakland cemetery,[54] about where the old rolling mill[55] used to stand. By this time the moon was giving a hazy light through clouds which had concealed it until then. In this kindness and thoughtfulness on the part of the moon we were truly thankful for without its faint shimmer it would have been impossible to have found our way through the burnt buildings, piles of bricks, rubbish of all sorts, heaps of ashes and clay and odds and ends of almost everything.[56] As none of us fell into one, it was fortunate we knew nothing of the danger of wells whose covers had been destroyed for it was one thing less on our minds. We understood better about such as this later or especially when some of us were stopped one day not more than inches from the brink of one. When we got further in town the walking was better as space enough to drive and walk had already been cleared.

The enemy claimed to have burned the business part of Atlanta only

---

[54]Atlanta's City Cemetery began in 1850. In 1876 it was officially named Oakland Cemetery and, on Memorial Drive, it still exists today. Garrett, *Atlanta and Environs*, 1:315. Sallie Clayton and her family are buried at Oakland Cemetery, near the main administrative building and the grave of novelist Margaret Mitchell.

[55]The Atlanta Rolling Mill, erected in 1858, had been Atlanta's most significant manufactory before the war. There tracks were refurbished for the railroads. During the war, the plant made iron plate for Confederate gun boats. The original owners, Lewis Schofield, James Blake, and William Markham sold the company to Trenholm, Frazer & Company in 1863. It was destroyed when eighty-one ammunition cars were detonated by the retreating Confederate army on the night of 2 September 1864. *Albany* (GA) *Patriot*, 15 December 1859, 2, c. 1; *Nashville* (TN) *Daily Times & True Union*, 3 August 1864, 2, c. 2; and Garrett, *Atlanta and Environs*, 1:427, 633-634.

[56]V. T. Barnwell wrote of the ruins of Civil War Atlanta, including the hordes of howling stray dogs, crows, vultures, and thieves, amid the "ruin, death, and devastation." Sydney Andrews still saw piles of burned and broken debris everywhere a year after Sherman left. V. T. Barnwell, *Barnwell's Atlanta City Directory* (Atlanta: Atlanta Intelligencer Book and Job Office, 1867), 31-32; and Sidney Andrews, *The South Since the War: As Shown by Four-teen Weeks of Travel and Observation in Georgia and the Carolinas* (Boston: Ticknor and Fields, 1866), 339. Also see John Richard Dennett, *The South As It Is: 1865-1866*, ed. Henry M. Christman (New York: The Viking Press, 1965), 267-269.

but many dwellings were burned also and others were torn down.[57] Miss Mecca Joyner,[58] who was with us for a few days in Augusta, said one of the last things she saw as the train in which she was riding rolled out of town was a lot of soldiers taking down a new house that her father had just built. And Mr. Ormond's[59] pretty home at the end of Washington Street was so needlessly burned for from its isolated location it could not have hurt or helped either side.[60]

The greatest destruction was in streets where so many people of small means had left comfortable homes to find nothing on their return but chimneys, loose bricks and ashes. We considered ourselves so very fortunate in that our house was not only not burned, but was damaged [only] very slightly, and that in one room only. The one shell that struck it had been very considerate in entering through a window and sticking in the wall opposite without bursting. The officer who used the house for his quarters

---

[57]Sidney Andrews wrote that only half of Atlanta had been destroyed in the war and the loss appeared less severe than that suffered by Columbia and Charleston. He wrote that most of the housing of all types had been spared. Andrews, *The South Since the War*, 339.

[58]A Mrs. Joyner and one servant were among the Atlanta civilians ordered evacuated by General Sherman. Robert S. Davis, Jr., "The General Sherman Census of Atlanta," *Georgia Genealogical Magazine* 31 (1991): 138. Mecca Joyner, b. 1842 d. 1885, became the second wife of Clinton Independence Brown. George W. Clower, "Thomas Winn (c. 1741-1797)," *Atlanta Historical Journal* 12/4 (1967): 43. Very likely, she was Pamelia Joyner, daughter of Richard W. Joyner. Seventh Census of the United States (1870), Cobb County, microcopy M432, reel 66, 175, National Archives, Washington, DC; and Ninth Census of the United States (1870), Fulton County, microcopy M593, reel 151, 277, National Archives, Washington, DC.

[59]James Ormond and his home are referred to in chapter 1.

[60]Federal General Sherman did not order Atlanta burned but the overall damage sustained by the city during the Atlanta Campaign achieved the same end. The federal shelling of the besieged city; the destruction caused by the Confederates building defenses and their withdrawal; the pulling down of houses and buildings to build a chain of federal forts; and the destruction of manufactories by the federal army upon abandoning the city before the march to the sea, resulted in the destruction of all but a fraction of Civil War Atlanta. During the destruction of the Confederate factories and other major buildings of military value, Sherman and his engineers actually worked to protect many Atlanta homes. Report of Captain John C. Van Duzer, 15 November 1864, John C. Van Duzer Collection, Special Collections, Perkins Library, Duke University; *Macon Daily Telegraph and Confederate* (GA), 10 December 1864, 2, c. 2; Marszalek, *Sherman*, 299; Davis, *Sherman's March*, 6-7; and Thomas Conn Bryan, *Confederate Georgia* (Athens: University of Georgia Press, 1953), 165. V. T. Barnwell wrote in 1867 that Atlanta's spectacular growth in manufacturing immediately after the war would not have happened if the city had not been destroyed in the war. Barnwell, *Barnwell's Atlanta*, 24.

must have taken this room for his kitchen for there was a hole cut in the chimney for a stove pipe.

The man who was sent from Augusta in advance of the family's return to give everything a thorough cleaning said he thought bacon had been intentionally used to grease the floors, especially the stairs, and the drippings from candles on the steps were so thick that there was not sufficient space between any two spots for a pin to rest. We excused the occupant for that since he proved himself such a good housekeeper in other respects. The paint was not injured or badly soiled, and the door bell, all that houses in Atlanta had them at that day, the keys and knobs were all there when from so many houses these things were taken and used for no other purpose than to add on the harnesses of horses. Even our gardens were not disturbed, not a tree, hedge, rosebush or flower of any sort was missing; though a small collection of geraniums had been taken from a porch. While the house was not particularly pretty, being true colonial in style, the materials of which it was built, the workmanship and, especially the enamel paint throughout were all that could be desired, moreover, it was home, and we were so thankful to have it not only still standing but in such good condition as well. In getting everything moved in there had been one little accident that inconvenienced the household somewhat for the time being. The dray man let the last boot box, and it proved to be one packed with china, fall and many pieces in it were broken especially cups and saucers. Five of one and six of the other were left for the use of fourteen or fifteen people, yet, we were thankful it was nothing more serious. Besides finding our house safe we were also most fortunate in having a car load of provisions. For while some of the neighboring planters around Kingston near which we had lived before and coming to Atlanta, rented their plantations or got some one to live on them while they refugee, my father sold his,[61] and hoping to get entirely out of the way of the Federal army, sought one twenty miles from the railroad in southwestern Georgia to which

---

[61]W. W. Clayton sold his Bartow County property to Nevil Rogers of Virginia on 24 October 1863. Bartow County Deed Book P (1861-1867), microfilm reel 153/13, 446, Georgia Department of Archives and History; and Martha H. Mullinax, *We Remember Kingston* (Marietta GA: Woman's History Club and Others, 1992), 49. Sallie likely refers to General O. O. Howard's occupation of the neighboring Goulding house. Ronald Casey, interview with the author, 25 January 1997

he moved his Negroes in the latter part of 1864.[62] So, in a few months, when the former home was headquarters for a Federal general, and the Federal folk twenty to thirty thousand strong were camped around on both sides of the little creek commonly called "Two Run," though in Indian parlance, "Tala-Tana-rah," from which last the place took its name[63] our Negroes were busy making a crop which was to be not only such a godsend to us, but saved the United States the expense of feeding so many of us for even a short time.

For awhile we thought our treasure had run into the hands of the enemy on its way and was lost, but my father went down the Macon railroad to hunt for it, and was delighted to find the agent, recognizing the danger, had kindly stopped the car just in time to save it. As there were no mills on the new plantation and we needed a man servant to take the place of the butler, Ned Rucker, whose health was too poor for him to continue work, our miller, Willis, had remained with us when the other plantation lands had been moved and had been for some time installed as the man of general work, and to his faithfulness we owed it that we got along in many ways as well as we did. For in leaving Augusta the under butler and the principal woman had chosen to remain in that city and very soon after reaching Atlanta our other women left and another one, whose husband did not belong to us, and who had gone to Alabama in refugeeing was so anxious to find him that she could not take my father's advice to wait and let him come to her.

As the force decreased, Willis became more and more helpful; he cooked or did anything he could in the house or yard. I believe he would

---

[62]As early as 1862, planters began moving slaves, for safety from federal forces, to southwest Georgia, driving up the land prices. *Nashville* (TN) *Daily Press & Times*, 28 June 1864, 1, c. 4; MS 291F, memoirs of Kate Hester Robson, Atlanta Historical Society; and Clarence L. Mohr, *On the Threshold of Freedom: Masters and Slaves in Civil War Georgia* (Athens: University of Georgia Press, 1986), 103. Ironically, the Bartow County planters fleeing to Atlanta were replaced by wealthy Virginia planters, fleeing the war in their own state. Frances Thomas Howard, *In and Out of the Lines* (New York: Neale Publishing, 1905), 53.

[63]William W. Clayton's plantation in Bartow County was on Two Runs Creek, immediately east of the present town of Kingston, which he also owned. Bartow County Deed Book P (1861-1867),. 369, 370, 446, microfilm reel 153/13, Georgia Department of Archives and History, Bartow County Courthouse, Cartersville, GA; and Martha H. Mullinax, *We Remember Kingston*, 49. Two Run Creek became an important position for the Confederate army during the Atlanta campaign and almost became the site of a major battle.

have undertaken the washing had it been allowed, but for a while we put that out and paid for it in the novel way of getting our young brothers to sell to the Federal soldiers a lot of ground peas [i.e. peanuts] that had been sent with the car load of provisions. We soon hired three women but they were so demoralized they could not be depended upon for steady work, but when any one of them failed Willis was there to see that everything went right. He tried to get us to apply to the Federal authorities for rations and when we told him it was not necessary he amused us very much by saying the way he looked at it was the Yankees had stolen what we had and it was nothing but fair for us to get anything from them we could whether we needed it or not. While we were living on the plantation I had been giving him and the blacksmith lessons in spelling and reading that they might be on the same plane with the butler, Ned Rucker, who knew already. So after freedom, I advised Willis to be diligent and persevere in getting an education; that in slavery he could get along without it as he then had a master to supply all his wants, but, now, that he had to take care of himself, he would need all the education he could get and he ought to go to school. His amusing reply was: "Well, you see I would but it makes my head ache so bad to study so hard." However, since he thought himself thus incapacitated for gaining knowledge from books, and he did not wish to go back into the country to run mills, he did, probably the next best thing by going under the tutorship of a Federal carpenter, who kindly befriended him, until he knew the trade.

On Marietta Street, where the post office stands, there were at that time two residences: Dr. Willis Westmoreland's[64] and a house that was formerly the home of Mr. Merring.[65] The latter was taken as headquarters for General Winslows, the cavalry commander.[66] We were near neighbors

---

[64]Dr. Willis Foreman Westmoreland, b. Fayetteville, Georgia 1 June 1828 d. Atlanta 27 June 1890, of the Atlanta Medical College. Walter G. Cooper, *Official History of Fulton County* (Atlanta: self-published, 1933), 871-872.

[65]No one named Merring has been found in the Civil War Atlanta records. She likely refers to Jethro W. Manning, b. 1815 d. 11 October 1883, judge of the Fulton County Inferior Court and Fulton County's first school commissioner. He lived on Marietta Street, at the corner of Simpson Street. C. S. Williams, *Williams' Atlanta Directory For 1859-60* (Atlanta: M. Lynch, 1859), 119; Garrett Necrology, roll 8, frame 135, Atlanta Historical Society; and Fulton County Tax Digest, 1864, 1026th District, microfilm reel 70/29, Georgia Department of Archives and History.

[66]Colonel Edward F. Winslow, breveted brigadier general on December 12, 1864, had commanded the Second Division of Brigadier General Benjamin H. Grierson's Cavalry Corps and had been chief of cavalry on the staff of General William T. Sherman. At the end of the

and our young brothers Smith and Tom[67] soon made friends of the officers and after that I think they were their daily visitors. Sometimes they were invited to dine and the younger one day horrified us by saying he told a certain captain of whom he was very fond that he would like to invite him home to dine with him some time but he didn't know how his sisters would take it.

Our first meeting with any of the soldiers on the opposite side was one evening soon after we had returned home. I was in an upper room about ten o'clock and was startled by hearing someone in the lower hall playing a violin very vigorously, and soon after my brother hurried into the room and said to let him get his pistol for two drunken soldiers had gotten in and he didn't know but they might give some trouble. When we joined the part of home folks and our visitors, they were all in the parlor and the fiddlers had by repeated requests prevailed on my sister Julia to accompany them on the piano. The men were having a joyous time while the others looked on with much amusement depicted on each countenance. As soon as one piece would be finished another would be begged for until several had been played and the pianist wanted to stop but she was entreated to go on, and to overcome her reluctance one stepped closer and offered her a quarter which she was indignantly refusing while the other one was saying to our mother that her daughter was a lovely young lady. But by this time the fun ended for someone had notified headquarters and several men were sent up to take them out.

---

war, however, he was serving as the federal quartermaster in Atlanta. Scott, *The War of the Rebellion*, Series I, vol. 38, pt. ii, 559; *Official Army Register of the Volunteer Force of the United States Army For the Years 1861, '62, '63, '64, '65* (Washington, DC: United States Government Printing Office, 1865), pt. vii, 233; Pioneer Citizens' Society of Atlanta, *Pioneer Citizens' History of Atlanta 1833-1902* (Atlanta: Byrd Publishing, 1902), 92; and Roger D. Hunt and Jack R. Brown, *Brevet Brigadier Generals in Blue* (Gaithersburg MD: Olde Soldier Books, 1990), 683.

[67]Augustin Smith and Thomas Andrew Clayton.

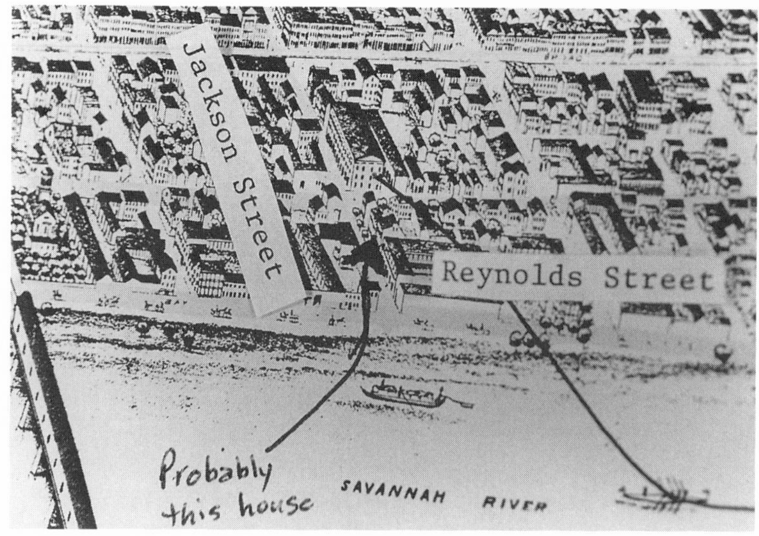

The Semmes-Conley (today the Seymour Whitney) House, appears on this 1872 aerial view of Augusta, just below the corner of Jackson and Reynolds streets, as indicated by the arrow. (Courtesy Eric Montgomery)

7

POSTWAR NOTES[1]

PEOPLE WERE DREADFULLY EXCITED BY HIS [ABRAHAM LINCOLN'S] ELECTION to the Presidency. I mean of course those of the South, and he was generally hated, and nobody stopped to inquire whether or not he was a good man;[2] but by the time he was killed there were many in the Southern States who thought he was in favor of paying for the slaves and that all together we would have gotten much better terms in dealing with him; and when reconstruction days, with their horrors set in, they were sure the South would have escaped that. He probably was a good man, but like all men North he knew nothing about negro character and evidently believed all that was told of bad treatment to them.[3]

There is no denying the bad treatment nor is there in any other state of life, marriage, parentage, etc., etc., but they cannot understand that the negro as a race was not as anxious for freedom as they thought. In the main he was a contented creature caring only for his physical needs and pleasures with no higher idea of freedom than the license he thought it would give

---

[1]Sarah "Sallie" Conley Clayton (Mrs. Benjamin Elliot Crane), in the following fragment, discusses her views of slavery, emancipation, and the aftermath of emancipation. It is reproduced here to include all that she wrote. It reflects the views held by her class, including many ideas that are not factually correct. For more on this subject see the sources cited in the footnotes and John David Smith, *An Old Creed for the New South: Proslavery Ideology and Historiography, 1865-1918* (Westport, Connecticut: Greenwood Press, 1985).

[2]For a discussion of the fears in Georgia that Lincoln's election posed a threat to slavery, see Clarence L. Mohr, *On the Threshold of Freedom: Masters and Slaves in Civil War Georgia* (Athens: University of Georgia Press, 1986), 40.

[3]Abraham Lincoln's personal contact with African-Americans was limited. However, he had seen slavery in slave states. He came from an abolitionist background and his wife, a Kentuckian whose family owned slaves, boasted of being the Lincoln family's real abolitionist. Lincoln, throughout his political career, condemned slavery, even at political risk, and made a thorough study of slavery as a member of Congress. Benjamin Quarles, *Lincoln and the Negro* (New York: Oxford University Press, 1963) 15-39. Many persons who knew Lincoln, however, believed that he had southern political credentials and could be considered a southerner by the South. Robert Walter Johannsen, *Lincoln, The South, and Slavery: The Political Dimension* (Baton Rouge: Louisiana State University Press, 1991) 2-3.

Shown in this Civil War drawing of Atlanta's Five Points is the Athenaeum Theater and the Trout House. (Courtesy Atlanta Historical Society)

him to do as he liked, whether good or evil, and do no work. All of that cry about cruel overseers being put over them to watch and drive them every moment to get as much work out of them as possible is nonsense; they [the overseers] were put with them to prevent their spending all the time sleeping in the fence corners. The Yankee idea was we were holding gentlemen and ladies in slavery instead of a poor depraved race that can under no circumstances take care of itself in the way of carrying on a government, and if they don't believe it all they have to do is remove him from the white man's influence and example and see that back to barbarism with few exceptions he would go. It would not have been many years before the south would have freed them herself, for there were many opposed to the institution[4] and occasionally a man freed his [slaves] but the majority did not feel able to give up their property for nothing. With all of the talk of ill treatment, including starving them, it has been shown they were better fed and cared for than the lower classes in any country.[5] They were as a whole fat, cheerful, jolly, all of which could only be from a life free from care; they didn't have to trouble about food, clothing, house rent, fire, old age or medical attention. Their health was almost perfect; little or no consumption; no cases of derangement, idiocy or insanity (this last can be positive about for no one was required to pay tax on such cases)[6] there was no feeble person among them; no suicide. I never heard of but one and I did not hear of that until after freed.

---

[4]Historian Carl Degler researched southern opposition to slavery and found it "always minuscule." Carl N. Degler, *The Other South: Southern Dissenters in the Nineteenth Century* (New York: Harper & Row, 1974) 13-96. Despite the North's victory in the Civil War, even the slave-holding states that remained in the Union refused to consider gradual, compensated, emancipation. Eric Foner, *Reconstruction: America's Unfinished Revolution, 1863-1877* (New York: Harper & Row, 1988), 6.

[5]Modern studies of slave diet in the South concur with this statement although the reason given is the ready availability of food in the United States rather than the paternalistic kindness of the masters. Peter Kolchin, *American Slavery 1619-1877* (New York: Hill and Wang, 1993), 113-114.

[6]Sallie Clayton makes the note here "(40 in Georgia)." Slave owners took at least an economic interest in maintaining the good health of their property. Health care of slaves was generally better for slaves than for most white southerners. Kolchin, *American Slavery*, 114-16. Slave owners in Civil War Atlanta reportedly would not allow their slaves to work in the military hospitals, even though he sick and wounded in those hospitals were often literally dying for the slave owners' cause, from fear of the slaves contracting diseases. Ralph Benjamin Singer, "Confederate Atlanta," (Ph.D. diss., University of Georgia, 1973), 205. However, the slave owners did send their wives and daughters to work in the hospitals.

The Yankee held slaves also, but in his climate he could not make them profitable so they were freed; and although they were paid for them,[7] what did they do; slipped them down South to Cuba, and sold them again.

It wasn't so much the bad time the negro was having that through good management of political speakers fired the northern heart in his behalf, but the good time they [the Abolitionists] feared the upper class [of the South] was having with his [the slaves's] services, and for this there is no blaming them when one takes into consideration the feeling of their wives and children who are nothing more than slaves, and that under the name of freedom; nobody south ever got as much work out of a negro as most Yankees do out of their wives and children. All the talk of fighting for the Union was folly; the number was comparatively small; but few are honest or truthful enough to acknowledge it. The great cry with L [Abraham Lincoln] was the Union, yet a reading of his second inaugural address will show what he was for.[8] He may have been a great and good man, but to the Southern people there is one blot not easily forgotten, and that was the signing of the Emancipation proclamation at the time he did. Its emancipation of slaves was not general, but for the belligerent [Southern] States, and the belief was, it was done then under the impression that the slaves in their great eagerness for freedom, as was the supposition of the North, would rise in insurrection and wipe us off the face of the earth, and that while they were thus busily engaged our men would of course rush to the rescue and leave them [the federal armies] to have things their way.[9] And, lo and behold! the negroes still took the utmost care of us.[10]

---

[7]The northern states that did not completely abolish slavery during or just after the American Revolution actually used a system of emancipating slave children upon the children reaching adulthood. Kolchin, *American Slavery*, 78.

[8]Lincoln's Second Inaugural Address maintained his claim that the Civil War was fought to preserve the union of the states. However, he did blame secession upon the slave-owning interests of the South. Mark E. Neely, Jr., *The Abraham Lincoln Encyclopedia* (New York: McGraw Hill, 1982), 271-272.

[9]This belief that the motive behind the Emancipation Proclamation was to encourage slave revolts was widely held in the Confederacy. However, the proclamation calls for slaves to abstain from all violence except when necessary for self-defense. John Hope Franklin, *The Emancipation Proclamation* (New York: Doubleday & Company, 1963), 137.

[10]Contrast this statement with the 1864 letters of her mother reproduced in the appendix, wherein Sallie's mother writes of her fear of the family being murdered and her daughters being raped by slaves. Fear of slave revolts became an obsessive fear of Southerners throughout the Civil War. Mohr, *On the Threshold of Freedom*, 40-46.

Now whether he [Abraham Lincoln] was urged into this [signing of the Emancipation Proclamation] or did it voluntarily is not yet clear to me. (It was far worse than the robbery of us.)

In speaking of the negro there was one fortunate quality given him that made the unkind treatment many had to bear very much easier for him than it would have been possible for the white man, that was his childlike disposition, very soon forgetting his sorrows or inquires, this was the black man; a mixture of blood brought desire for freedom, the more the greater and harder for him to bear his troubles [illegible words] while the greatest number were, by far, better off, the children, the old, the sick, it is far better to have them free; there was great responsibility attached to owning them. But if the Northerner thinks he has ended their suffering instead of changing it, all he has to do is to come down and investigate for himself; let him see something of the treatment of the old and the poor children, the way husbands and wives beat each other, and the way the sick have to suffer; the chain gang, the penitentiary. And as to morality, they say we fail to teach them. If there has been any improvement nobody has found it out, their own preachers fail on that and other crimes. And I should like to know what is thought of his [the negro's] criminal tendency these days. He was saved temptation to that in slavery, for in rare cases did it amount to more than lying and stealing, with his inborn immorality.[11]

Mrs. M[organ][12] was the prime mover in Atlanta in keeping Memorial Day.[13] Mrs. Williams[14] of Columbus [was] the originator. She came over to

---

[11]This fragment of the manuscript ends with this sentence. Clayton Torrence noted at the beginning of the next fragment reproduced here: "The following item begins on page immediately following the item in regards to Lincoln and the Negro problem."

[12]Torrence identified her as Mrs. Morgan here and as Mrs. Joseph Morgan in a footnote. She was Eugenia Goode (Mrs. Joseph H. Morgan), the daughter of Hamilton and Annie Goode and served as secretary of the Atlanta Hospital Association for three years during the Civil War. Lucian Lamar Knight Scrapbooks, vol. 23, 117, Georgia Department of Archives and History; and Franklin Garrett, *Atlanta and Environs*, 3 vols. (New York: Lewis Historical Publishing Company, 1954) 1:706. She was also the first president of the Atlanta Pioneer Women's Society. Memoirs of Mrs. Josephine Thompson, Atlanta Pioneer Women's Society Papers Collection, Atlanta Historical Society.

[13]She refers here to Confederate Memorial Day or 26 April, the anniversary of the surrender of the Confederate Army of Tennessee, the largest surrender of the Civil War. Garrett, *Atlanta and Environs*, 1:706.

[14]She was Mary A. (Mrs. C. J.) Williams. The idea for a Confederate Memorial Day came to Mrs. Williams in 1866 when she and her young daughter were putting flowers on the grave of her husband, a colonel of the First Georgia Regulars, at Atlanta's Oakland

Father's[15] one night in 1866 not long before April 26, and said she had been thinking of it, but was waiting for some older lady to take the initiative, and as no one had moved in the matter she proposed that our families united and begin preparations, to which we agreed, and all of hers, with most of ours, spent the week before the twenty sixth in working at the cemetery, to try to make it somewhat presentable, by gathering up fallen limbs of trees and sweeping leaves in piles for burning. We carried our dinner and stayed from early morning until quite late.[16]

Faithful Mrs. Goode[17] helped in every way and especially in keeping us with a fire for the weather was quite cool.

Sister Mary[18] and the boys were particularly helpful in getting the cemetery ready.

Soon after the first decoration we called a meeting of citizens, ladies in particular, at the First Methodist Church, the Old Wesley Chapel, that

---

Cemetery. Her daughter wanted to place flowers on the graves of the other Confederate dead. Ibid., 1:706; and A. C. Whitehead, *Makers of Georgia's Name and Fame* (Boston: Educational Publishing Company, 1913), 227-228. However, Sallie Clayton's former neighbors in Kingston, Georgia also claimed the first Confederate Memorial Day, their commemoration being in April 1864. Carroll Proctor Scruggs, *Georgia Historical Markers* (Helen GA: Bay Tree Grove, 1973), 22.

[15]Torrence added that Mrs. Morgan lived with her parents, the Goodes, across Marietta Street from where Sallie and her family were living. "Father" is William Wirt Clayton, b. Athens, Georgia 29 December 1812, d. Atlanta 20 July 1885. William Clayton Torrence, *Rootes of Rosewall* (n.p., 1906), 74.

[16]Garrett credits Mrs. W. W. Clayton and her daughters Sallie and Julia, with Mrs. Morgan, for this first commemoration of Confederate Memorial Day in Atlanta. He adds that the wife of Dr. J. N. Simmons raised $350 for the clearing of the cemetery and obtained cedar from Stone Mountain for making wreathes and crosses. Garrett, *Atlanta and Environs*, 1:706. Mrs. Morgan, Sallie Clayton, and other women worked for days to clean up the cemetery and then sent slips of paper to hundreds of Atlanta's merchants asking that they close their shops for the first Confederate Memorial Day. *History of the Confederate Memorial Associations of the South* (n. p.: Confederate Southern Memorial Association, n. p., 1904), 88-91; Richard Barksdale Harwell, "Our Confederate Dead," *Atlanta Historical Bulletin* 20 (1976): 100; and memoirs of Mrs. Joseph Thompson, Atlanta Pioneer Women"s Society Papers Collection, Atlanta Historical Society.

[17]She refers to Eugenia (Mrs. Hamilton) Goode, Mrs. Morgan"s mother. Garrett, *Atlanta and Environs*, 1:706.

[18]Torrence makes the note here that she is Mary Semmes Clayton, who married Cary Wood Henderson, the son of Confederate General Robert J. Henderson, in 1871. The younger Henderson saw service in the war as a Georgia Military Institute cadet.

stood at the junction of Peachtree and Pryor,[19] to organize an association. The women who had worked together so beautifully all during the war now began to show their little jealousies, and rather than give the first presidency to Mrs. Morgan, voted to have a male president, and Dr. J. P. Logan was elected for the office.[20] Mrs. Morgan was made vice president. There may have been more than one vice president,[21] I do not remember; the book of the Association shows it all. Miss Lizzie Hoge[22] was recording secretary. I do not remember who was treasurer.[23] I was corresponding secretary.

Just as those of us who did not want a man for president knew, Dr. Logan would not give his time for attending to what we expected, which was to collect the dead of our army from the different battlefields and inter them in the cemetery to which the city had made an addition just at this. . . .[24]

---

[19]This church was organized in 1847 and its building was dedicated in 1848. A photograph of the old Wesley Chapel appears in Garrett, *Atlanta and Environs*, 1:269. Also see the memoirs of Mrs. Anthony Murphy, Atlanta Pioneer Women"s Society Papers Collection, Atlanta Historical Society.

[20]Logan declined to serve, making Mrs. Morgan the first president. Garrett, *Atlanta and Environs*, 1:707; and Alberta Malone, *History of the Atlanta Ladies Memorial Association 1866-1946 Markers and Monuments* (Atlanta: n.p., 1946), 12.

[21]Mrs. E. B. Walker was elected second vice president and Mrs. J. N. Simmons was elected the third vice president. Garrett, *Atlanta and Environs*, 1:706.

[22]Torrence identifies her as the daughter of James and Catherine Mayson Hoge. Her brother, Edward Foster Hoge, formerly colonel of the 9th Georgia Confederate Volunteer Infantry Regiment, married Sallie Clayton"s sister Julia Frances on 21 November 1866. Also see Torrence, *Rootes of Rosewall*, 77.

[23]The treasurer was her mother, Mrs. William Wirt Clayton. Walter G. Cooper, *Official History of Fulton County* (Atlanta: self published, 1933), 821.

[24]This fragment ends with this incomplete sentence. The Confederate dead from battlefields within ten miles of Atlanta were eventually reinterred at Atlanta's Oakland Cemetery, largely through the efforts of Mrs. John M. Johnson, sister of Confederate generals Howell and Thomas R. R. Cobb, and president of the Ladies Memorial Association from 1868 to 1881. Mrs. Morgan remained active in the Ladies Memorial Association for fifty-eight years, until her death in 1924. Garrett, *Atlanta and Environs*, 1:707. Also see notes 11 and 19 above.

This eyewitness Civil War sketch illustrated the last civilian families from Atlanta being ordered from the city by Federal General Sherman. (Courtesy Library of Congress)

Appendix: The Clayton Letters

[Editor's note: The following letters from Sallie's parents, William Wirt and Caroline Maria Semmes Clayton, were written during Sallie's stay in Montgomery, Alabama and in Augusta, Georgia. The letters are preserved in William Clayton Torrence's papers in the Virginia Historical Society, along with Torrence's annotated typescripts of these letters and Sallie's memoirs. The letters are included here because they provide a contemporary account of some of the events Sallie describes in her memoirs.]

Atlanta July 25th 1864

My Dear Sallie & Caro[1]

The raid upon the Montgomery and Westpoint [sic, West Point, Georgia] Railroad[2] has prevented us from imparting to you the heart rending intelligence that our dear darling Gussie[3] sleeps her last sleep. The vital spark ceased about 3 o'clock Friday morning the 22nd inst. and she now reposes in our garden where we had to lay her for the present on account of the incessant shelling of the City by our cruel, barbarous and relentless enemy. Oh! my dear children this sad bereavement is terrible, almost insupportable. Did we not have the Strong arm of the Almighty to lean on our condition would be hopeless, but he is able and willing to sustain us in all our trouble; then let us look to him and he will give us strength. We hope Julia, Mary & Kate[4] are improving Slowly, they now sit up most of the time particularly the former but are very weak with occasional slight fever. I pray that God will spare them to us.

We moved down in the Ga RR Bank [Georgia Railroad Bank] yesterday & are now camping here believing it to be a safer place than our home, our

---

[1]Sarah "Sallie" Conley Clayton and her sister Caroline "Caro" Maria Clayton, are William Wirt Clayton's daughters. Sallie is the author of the memoirs reproduced here.

[2]He refers here to the raid by twenty-five hundred federal cavalrymen under General Lovell Harrison Rousseau, 9-22 July 1864. Mark M. Boatner III, *The Civil War Dictionary* (New York: Vintage Books, 1987), 711.

[3]She means Augusta "Gussie" King Clayton, their sister.

[4]Julia Frances Clayton, Mary Semmes Clayton, and Katherine Winter Clayton were his other daughters.

house being in the range of the batteries of the enemy where their shells fall thickest. Our servants room was struck by a shell on yesterday morning & [the slave children] Mollie & Clara escaped unhurt almost miraculously. On this morning while we were here in [the] bank a shell struck our house & passed through your Mother's room. We were fortunate in being away. Atlanta will not be given up. this is gen'l belief. It will be defended at all hazards. What will be the result time alone can tell.

All unite in love to you both & Aunt Sallie's family.[5] Yours in deep distress.

Wm. W. Clayton

Augusta Sept 18th '64

Dearest Husband [William Wirt Clayton]

Yours of the 11th was rec'd last night & I write immediately to beg you will bring the Boys back right away if they are able to travel.[6] Caro is better & I hope will be up in a few days.

Lucinda has been sick ever since her return, indeed came home sick. Sallie had a severe chill last night & is quite sick to-day. Mally has been a little sick but is better today. Betsy has been ill with Typhoid fever. Catherine has had chills & fever, so you see we have a hospital of our own.[7] Now that Mr. Robinson[8] is at home there is no necessity in your staying on

---

[5]He refers here to his wife's sister, Sarah H. Semmes (Mrs. Benjamin Conley), with whom Sallie and Caro were staying, near Montgomery, Alabama.

[6]She refers here to their youngest sons, Augustin Smith Clayton and Thomas Andrew Clayton. William Clayton Torrence, *Rootes of Rosewall* (n.p., 1906), 78.

[7]Caro, Mally, and Sallie are her daughters. Clayton Torrence identifies this Catherine and Betsy as household servants. Apparently Sallie and Caro, after leaving their uncle's plantation near Montgomery, Alabama in August 1864, traveled by train to Augusta, Georgia, where they were reunited with their mother and sisters at a house owned by Benjamin Conley. Ironically, Sallie and Caro had gone to Montgomery in part to escape the sickness in Atlanta that took the life of their sister Gussie. This letter explains that upon arriving in Augusta they too became sick, likely contracting fevers from their sick sisters from Atlanta. Their father (William Wirt Clayton) and their two sick, youngest, brothers, were at the family plantation in southwest Georgia.

[8]Clayton Torrence notes here that Robinson was the plantation overseer.

the plantation, so please come right back. I am so uneasy about you all—there is no use in making arrangements about our going down there to stay (if we can afford to live here) without you, to be murdered by the negroes or meet a worse fate—no—we must stay together as long as we can—if our Army is not reinforced Sherman will separate us ere long. I believe it will kill me, the way things are going on, our people driven out of Atlanta,[9] the soldiers told to tear down our dwellings & our men looking on, apparently unconcerned & indifferent. We are looking for the downfall of Richmond & then there will be really the "tug of war." This could all be prevented if there were any manhood & patriotism in the South. I presume you have seen from the papers Hood's & Sherman's correspondence relative to the removal of the citizens from Atlanta & the exchange of prisoners;[10] and seen also what buildings are occupied by Sherman & his staff &c. &c. It will almost shake my faith in God if Sherman is allowed to be farther successful. How humiliated we have been as a people!

I sent the articles you wrote for some days since. Will not send the slippers & cream of Tartar, for you must come home. Gus[11] came down yesterday. Mother[12] had written to you to go up & advise them what to do about the negroes, &c. as the enemy can go to Athens at any time & it is supposed will do so as soon as the armistice expires. Willie King[13] has rec'd an appointment of Asst. Surgeon in some command. I greatly fear Mother will suffer if left in the Yankee lines. She & Gus have determined to remain.

When you come bring the knitting cotton, 3 or 4 balls of sewing thread. I have one middling[14] of bacon, no hams, the meat was so much injured that

---

[9]General William T. Sherman ordered the evacuation from Atlanta of all civilians in mid-September 1864. Franklin Garrett, *Atlanta and Environs*, 3 vols. (New York: Lewis Historical Publishing Company, 1954), 1:642; and Robert S. Davis, Jr., "The General Sherman Census of Atlanta, September 1864," *Georgia Genealogical Magazine* 31 (1991): 132-141.

[10]This correspondence is reproduced in Garrett, *Atlanta and Environs*, 1:640-642.

[11]Clayton Torrence identifies her as Augusta "Gus" Columbiana Clayton, sister of Sallie's father William Wirt Clayton.

[12]Clayton Torrence identified "mother" as the mother of William Wirt Clayton, Julia Carnes (Mrs. Augustin Smith Clayton). She was born 2 July 1787 and died in Athens, Georgia 3 June 1873. Torrence, *Rootes of Rosewall*, 69.

[13]Clayton Torrence identifies him as Dr. William King of Athens, Georgia, b. 6 October 1830, d. 10 July 1917, the husband of William W. Clayton's sister Augusta.

[14]A medium but undetermined amount. Lewis Mulford Adams, ed., *Webster's Unified Dictionary and Encyclopedia* (New York: H. S. Stuttman Co., 1961), 2781.

a number of hams were lost. Of those brought here 10 or 12 were unfit for use. The hogs Mr. Robinson had in the horse lot I suppose will be ready for killing the first cold spell.[15] I wish you would [bring] all the young chickens the negroes have to sell. We should have 100 laying hens another year. As to the cows it is very bad our having to buy butter. I am sorry our cattle [here] were not sold & more bought in S[outh] W[est] Ga.

We feel so sorry the Boys anticipation of a pleasant time were not realized.

Our Doctor's bills this year will be ruinous. All join in love & kisses to you all.

Your devoted wife,
C. M. Clayton

Augusta Sept. 25th 64

Dearest Husband

Your last two letters were rec'd last night the latest dated the 19th & I am surprised at none of my letters having reached you. I have written some three or four times. We were much relieved to hear the Boys were better—have had quite a hospital here. Caro came home sick on the 10th & did not get up until the 21st. She is now able to come down stairs. Lucinda also came home with fever & came down stairs yesterday. Sallie was quite sick for several days but is well enough this morning to go to Church. The Doctor only saw Sallie once—she took Quinine & pepper tea with salt in it until a profuse perspiration was produced & the fever broken up. This is the best treatment I think in all cases of intermittent fever take Quinine for three days, when clear of fever warm pepper tea with salt in it & keep covered closely to produce perspiration—the trouble is when one feels better they wish to get up but this should not be allowed until the fever is broken.

---

[15]Hogs were traditionally slaughtered in the first cold weather of the season so that the lower temperature would make the blood congeal faster and to keep the bacteria low. Waiting later than the first cold to kill the hogs would have left the animals with little to eat.

Dr. Bebhart[16] says Caro has had Typhoid fever. If Smith[17] had been here I expect his would have become Typhoid. All fever here has a tendency that way.

You speak of building. What do you think after viewing the matter in every light will be the best for us to do. It will cost us not less than $1,000.00 to remove to the plantation to remain part of the year as nothing could induce me to stay during August & September. This money will a great deal more than keep us in wood this Winter. I wish we could decide what to do, as it will be best to remove our furniture from the ware room [warehouse?]. The bedding will be ruined by the rats & moreover if this place is occupied by the Yankees, nothing in the ware houses will escape. My only objection in going to the plantation (if you think it will save money) is fear of the negroes. I cannot believe it will be well to risk the girls there. It is much safer in a City <u>now</u> than anywhere else. I will not stay there without you.

The articles you wrote for were sent immediately, before your letter asking for Cream of tarter & slippers & as we thought you would return as soon as the Boys were well enough to travel, I concluded not to send. In letters rec'd yesterday you said nothing of coming home. If you think after considering the matter it will still be best for us to go to the plantation, go ahead & get ready as soon as possible. There is some fear here of Yellow Fever. Of the Yankees or fever I prefer the former. Of the exiles from Atlanta we have only seen Mrs. Joiner[18] who had a great deal to tell us. She was very kindly treated by the officers, but annoyed by the men's pilfering; indeed they would come before her face & take what they wanted. Instead of the people being humiliated she says they were exasperated & said what they chose. A soldier told her such a damned rebel as she was ought to be shot. She dared him to shoot.

---

[16]She refers here to Dr. Frederick William Gebhardt, Augusta physician, born in Baden, Germany c. 1817. Richmond County Tax Digests, 1861-1865, microfilm reel 186/6, Georgia Department of Archives and History; and Ninth Census of the United States (1870), Richmond County, microcopy M593, reel 72, 57, National Archives, Washington, DC.

[17]She refers here to their son Augustin Smith Clayton, b. Athens, Georgia 9 December 1850, who after the war was a prominent columnist for the *Atlanta Journal* and the *Atlanta Constitution*. Torrence, *Rootes of Rosewall*, 78.

[18]A Mrs. Joyner and one servant were among the Atlanta civilians ordered evacuated by General Sherman. Davis, "The General Sherman Census of Atlanta," 138.

Mr. Markham & Lowry[19] were acting as Secretaries for the Yankees. She could not tell whether they would remain in Atlanta or go North. Schofield, Solomon, Rawson all hail fellows well met with the Yankees.[20] Genl. Austell,[21] she thought, would come South. I hope he will & bring our plunder with him. Our house, we hear, is occupied by officers. You saw Sherman's order allowing his men to use all building material for constructing their huts or tents. A negro fellow demanded the key of our house from Austell saying he wished to take his family in!

Mrs. Joiner's house was being torn down when she left! Persons were allowed to bring all their clothing & such furniture as could be transported in wagons. about half, she thinks, of the poorer class came this way. Mr. Root[22] did not reach Atlanta before his family left for the South. Mrs.

---

[19]William Markham, partner in the Atlanta Rolling Mill, was a native of Connecticut nearly killed in a knife attack because of his suspected support for the Union. Mary A. De Credico, "Georgia's Entrepreneurs and Confederate Mobilization, 1847-1873" (Ph., d. diss., Vanderbilt University, 1986), 95; and Garrett, *Atlanta and Environs*, 1:629. Robert J. Lowry was an Atlanta banker and grocer from Greeneville, Tennessee. He married the daughter of one the wealthiest men in Atlanta, the northern born Thomas G. Healey (Markham's brother-in-law). Ibid., 514; and Lucian Lamar Knight, *History of Fulton County Georgia* (Atlanta: A. H. Cawston, 1930), 62. Markham filed a claim after the Civil War as a southern unionist in which Robert J. Lowery, among others, testified. William Markham vs. the United States, case 11137, Records of the US Court of Claims, RG 123, National Archives, Washington, DC.

[20]Lewis Schofield, partner in the Atlanta Rolling Mill and suspected unionist, was from Connecticut; and Edward Everett Rawson was from Vermont. De Credico, "Georgia's Entrepreneurs and Confederate Mobilization, 1847-1873," 95; Garrett, *Atlanta and Environs*, 1:431, 629. Solomon Solomon was a German. Eighth Census of the United States (1860), Fulton County, microcopy M653, reel 122, 835, National Archives, Washington, DC. However, the reference here may have been to Sallie's elderly neighbor William Solomon of North Carolina. Ninth Census of the United States (1870), Fulton County, microcopy M653, reel 122, 209, National Archives, Washington, DC; and Garrett, *Atlanta and Environs*, 1:908.

[21]General Alfred Austell, b. 1814, d. 1881, raised in Jefferson County, Tennessee and resident of Campbell County, Georgia, was a wealthy planter and brigadier general of the Georgia militia. Walter G. Cooper, *Official History of Fulton County* (Atlanta: self published, 1933), 841. A photograph of Austell appears in ibid., 308.

[22]Sidney Root, despite being born in Montague, Massachusetts in 1824, actively supported the Confederacy by captaining a ship that ran the federal naval blockade. He represented the Confederate government in London and Paris. His autobiography is in the Atlanta Historical Society., D. Louise Cook, ed., *Guide to Manuscript Collections of the Atlanta Historical Society* (Atlanta: Atlanta Historical Society, 1976), 100; Frank J. Byrne, "Rebellion and Retail: A Tale of Two Merchants in Confederate Atlanta," *Georgia Historical*

J[oiner] says it was clearly prove[d] if he had been there they would have gone the other way. At any rate his furniture is deposited at Trinity Church[23] with that to be sent North. Markley[24] of the firm of Hamilton & Joiner also goes the other way. From all we hear, however, there is but a small proportion of tories.[25]

Quarterly 79 (1995): 30-56; Walter McElreath, "Sidney Root: Merchant Prince and Great Citizen," *Atlanta Historical Bulletin* 7/29 (1944): 171-183; and Knight, *History of Fulton County*, 67.

[23]Clayton Torrence identifies this building as the Old Trinity Methodist Church on Whitehall Street.

[24]She refers to the Thomas C. Markley of Markley & Joyner, wholesale druggists, formerly Hamilton, Markley, & Joyner, Atlanta grocers. Markley, of neighboring Cobb County, was a wealthy book seller in the 1860 federal census. He enlisted in the first Confederate company raised in Cobb County but resigned and saw no service. Although he was born in South Carolina, his much older wife Louisa Turpin was born in New York. In late 1862, he called for the creation of a free market in Atlanta for distributing donated goods to the poor. Eighth Census of the United States (1860), Cobb County, microcopy M653, reel 117, 230, National Archives, Washington, DC; Sarah Blackwell Gober Temple, *The First Hundred Years: A Short History of Cobb County, In Georgia* (Atlanta: Walter Brown, 1935), 236; *South Carolina Magazine of Ancestral Research* 15 (1987): 68; *Southern Confederacy* (Atlanta), 29 November 1862, 3, c. 1, 8 January 1863, 4, c. 4; Hamilton, Markley & Joyner file, Confederate Papers Relating to Citizens or Business Firms, National Archives microcopy M346; and *Atlanta* (GA) *Daily Reveille*, 16 April 1864, 2, c. 5.

[25]Tories were Americans supporting the British during the American Revolution (1775-1783). She uses the term here to refer to Southerners opposed to secession. Northerners in Atlanta were suspected of being spies and secret abolitionists by their Confederate neighbors. Persecutions of suspected northern sympathizers did take place. Dr. John Thompson Darby of South Carolina confided in Mary Chesnut that he had nearly been hanged in Philadelphia as a southerner, only to later nearly be lynched in Atlanta as a northerner. Atlanta did have a significant community of persons opposed to the Confederacy. They were organized and provided some aid to the federal soldiers held prisoner in Atlanta by the Confederates. A Union soldier, after Sherman's capture of the city, wrote reports of hundreds of Atlanta Unionists and that wounded Union soldiers had been found in Atlanta, protected from the Rebels in stolen Confederate uniforms provided by the pro-Union civilians. The Western & Atlantic Railroad, the Confederacy's critical link between Tennessee and Atlanta, reportedly had several suspected Unionists and potential saboteurs among its employees. Gibbons, "Life at the Crossroads of the Confederacy: Atlanta, 1861-1865," *Atlanta Historical Journal* 23/2 (1979): 23, 31-33; James Michael Russell, *Atlanta 1847-1890: City Building in the Old South and the New* (Baton Rouge: Louisiana State University Press, 1988), 94-95; Mary Chesnut, *The Private Mary Chesnut: The Unpublished Civil War Diaries*, eds. C. Vann Woodward and Elisabeth Muhlenfeld (New York: Oxford University Press, 1984), 72; De Credico, "Georgia's Entrepreneurs and Confederate Mobilization, 1847-1873," 95; *Report on the Treatment of Prisoners of War by the Rebel Authorities* (Washington, DC: United States Government Printing Office, 1869), 40th Congress, 3d Session, Report 45, 885-886; *Nashville* (TN) *Daily*

Mr. Davis [Confederate President Jefferson Davis] is now at the front in Ga. Said in a speech in Macon two thirds of our Army are absent; some sick, others wounded, but the *greater part without leave*.[26] I hope you will conclude to leave the State; am ashamed to own myself a Georgian.

I am sorry plantation affairs are not looking brighter. If we can make sufficient for a support tho' it will be well. Our syrup is now out & meat nearly so. We will wait for the former until some is made. It will be very expensive to buy the latter. What will you do about butter? I expect we have but few milch cows left. If the prospect is very bad could you not trade for a few good ones. We ought not to buy butter. I suppose we will make no sugar. when you come do not forget to bring the knitting thread & sewing thread.

Take the Boys' hats that Mr. Daniel had made; they were engaged at $16.00. You say nothing of the weaving! It will be a great disappointment not to get it done. Gus[27] has been down to see and consult Edward[28] about the disposition of the negroes on Mother's[29] lot. Edward thinks best for them to be sold as Gus says they will go to the Yankees, which will be a great loss to the family. There are some 4 or 6 very likely ones. Edward & Gus are awaiting your return & Mother is very anxious to see you. Should you be delayed any time you had best write. The Yankees can go to Athens when they like. Dr. Price has sent his bill, $350.00 & says he needs the

---

Times and True Union, 17 September 1864, 1, c. 5-6; and Stephen Davis, "The Conductor verses the Foreman: William Fuller, Anthony Murphy, and the Pursuit of the Andrews Raiders," *Atlanta History* 34 (1990): 47. Also see the memoir of Atlanta Unionist "Miss Abbey" [Cyrena Bailey Stone], MS 1000, Hargrett Rare Books and Manuscripts Library, University of Georgia Libraries and Thomas G. Dyer, "Atlanta's Other Civil War Novel: Fictional Unionists in a Confederate City," *Georgia Historical Quarterly* 79 (1995): 147-168.

[26]Confederate President Jefferson Davis and Georgia Senator Benjamin H. Hill visited Macon, Georgia on 23 September 1864 and addressed a public meeting at the First Baptist Church of Macon. Davis explained his purpose in removing General Joseph E. Johnston from command at Atlanta and the strategy of sending General Hood's army to Tennessee in hopes of cutting off General Sherman's federal army in Georgia. He made an appeal to the South's women to encourage the return to the Confederate army of men absent without leave. Davis claimed that two thirds of his soldiers were either at home sick or deserted. Ida Young, Julius Gholson, and Clara Nell Hargrove, *History of Macon, Georgia* (Macon: Macon Woman's Club, 1950), 262-263.

[27]Augusta Columbiana Clayton King. See note 11 above.

[28]Edward Patrick Clayton, b. Athens, Georgia 14 July 1820, d. Augusta, Georgia 1888, was the brother of William Wirt Clayton. Torrence, *Rootes of Rosewall*, 71.

[29]Julia Carnes Clayton, William Wirt Clayton's mother. See note 12 above.

money. Shall I settle it? write at once. If this should be as long reaching you as the rest of my letters I shall get an answer sooner in person. Tell Smith[30] to write a long letter. All join in love & kisses to you all.

Your devoted wife,
M.C. [Carolina Maria Clayton]

---

[30]See note 17 above.

SELECTED BIBLIOGRAPHY

Adams, Lewis Mulford, ed. *Webster's Unified Dictionary and Encyclopedia*. New York: H. S. Stuttman Co., 1961.

Allardice, Bruce S. *More Confederate Generals in Gray*. Baton Rouge: Louisiana State University Press, 1994.

Alphabetical Card File of the Confederate Pension Office. Georgia Department of Archives and History.

Amos, Harriet E. *Cotton City: Urban Development in Antebellum Mobile*. Tuscaloosa: University of Alabama Press, 1985.

Andrews, J. Cutler. *The South Reports the Civil War*. Pittsburgh: University of Pittsburgh Press, 1985.

Andrews, Sidney. *The South Since the War: As Shown by Fourteen Weeks of Travel and Observation in Georgia and the Carolinas*. Boston: Tucknor and Fields, 1866.

Approved Georgia Claims Before the Southern Claims Commission. National Archives. RG 217. Microcopy M1658.

Atlanta Historical Bulletin and *Atlanta Historical Journal* card catalog index. Atlanta Historical Society.

Atlanta Pioneer Women's Society. Papers collection. Atlanta Historical Society.

Austin, Jeannette Holland. *Georgia Obituaries (1905-1910)*. n.p., n.d.

Baldwin, Lucy Hull. Autobiography. Southern Historical Collection. University of North Carolina at Chapel Hill.

Ball, Douglas B. *Financial Failure and Confederate Defeat*. Urbana: University of Chicago Press, 1991.

Barker, Meta. "Some High Lights of the Old Atlanta Stage." *Atlanta Historical Bulletin* 1/3 (1928): 32-5.

Barnwell, V. T. *Barnwell's Atlanta City Directory and Stranger's Guide*. Atlanta: Intelligencer Book and Job Office, 1867.

Barrett, John G. *Sherman's March Through the Carolinas*. Chapel Hill: University of North Carolina, 1956.

Bartow County Deed Book P (1861-1867). Bartow County Courthouse, Cartersville, GA.

Battey, George Magruder. *A History of Rome and Floyd County*. Atlanta: Webb and Vary Company, 1922.

Beers, Henry Putney. *The Confederacy: A Guide to the Archives of the Government of the Confederate States of America.* Washington, DC: National Archives and Records Administration, 1986.

Benjamin E. Crane. File II Names. Georgia Department of Archives and History.

Bergeron, Arthur W. Jr. *Guide to Louisiana Confederate Military Units 1861-1865.* Baton Rouge: Louisiana State University Press, 1989.

Black, Nellie Peters. *Richard Peters His Ancestors and Descendants 1810-1889.* Atlanta: Foote & Davies Company, 1904.

Blanco, Richard L., ed. *The American Revolution 1775-1783: An Encyclopedia.* New York: Garland Publishing, 1993.

Board of Physicians Registry of Applicants 1826-1881. Georgia Department of Archives and History. RG 6-10-10.

Boatner, Mark M. III, ed. *The Civil War Dictionary.* New York: Vintage Books, 1987.

Boatwright, Eleanor Miot. *The Status of Women in Georgia, 1783-1860.* Brooklyn NY: Carlson Publishing, 1994.

Boney, William F. *Rebel Georgia.* Macon GA: Mercer University Press, 1996.

Bonner, James C. *Milledgeville: Georgia's Antebellum Capital.* Athens: University of Georgia Press, 1988.

Bowman, John S., ed. *The Civil War Almanac.* New York: Bison Books, 1983.

Bransford, John S. Letters. Incoming Correspondence of Governor Joseph E. Brown. Record Group 1-1-5, Georgia Department of Archives and History.

Briant, Huldah Annie. Papers. William R. Perkins Library, Duke University.

Brief Biographies of the Members of the Constitutional Convention July 11, 1877. Atlanta: The Constitution Publishing Company, 1877.

Broussard, James H. *The Southern Federalists 1800-1816.* Baton Rouge: Louisiana State University Press, 1978.

Bryan, Thomas Conn. *Confederate Georgia.* Athens: University of Georgia Press, 1953.

Byrne, Frank J. "Rebellion and Retail: A Tale of Two Merchants in Confederate Atlanta." *Georgia Historical Quarterly* 79 (1995): 30-56.

Carter, Dan T. *When the War Was Over: The Failure of Self Reconstruction in the South, 1865-1867.* Baton Rouge: Louisiana State University Press, 1985.

Carter, Samuel III. *The Siege of Atlanta, 1864*. New York: Bonanza Books, 1973.

Cashin, Edward J. *The Story of Augusta*. Augusta: Richmond County Board of Education, 1980.

Cashin, Joan E., ed. *Our Common Affairs: Texts from Antebellum Southern Women* Baltimore: John Hopkins University Press, 1996.

Castel, Albert. *The Campaign for Atlanta*. Washington: Eastern National Park and Monument Association, 1996.

——. *Decision in the West: The Atlanta Campaign of 1864*. Lawrence: University of Kansas Press, 1992.

Censer, Jane Turner. *North Carolina Planters and Their Children, 1800-1860*. Baton Rouge: Louisiana State University Press, 1984.

Chesnut, Mary. *The Private Mary Chesnut: The Unpublished Civil War Diaries*. Edited by C. Vann Woodward and Elisabeth Muhlenfeld. New York: Oxford University Press, 1984.

Clayton, Bruce. "Dixie's Daughter: The Life of Margaret Mitchell." *Georgia Historical Quarterly* 77 (199)

Clayton, Claud Franklin. *Family Notes and Recollections*. Knoxville: self published, 1959.

Clayton, P. A *Vindication of the Hon. Augustin S. Clayton*. Washington DC: G. S. Gideon, 1855.

Cleaves, Freeman. *Rock of Chickamauga: The Life of General George H. Thomas*. Westport CT: Greenwood Press, 1948.

Clinton, Catherine. *The Devil's Lane: Sex and Race in the Early South*. New York: Oxford University Press, 1997.

——. *The Other Civil War: American Women in the Nineteenth Century*. New York: Hill and Wang, 1984.

——. "In Search of Southern Women's History: The Current State of Academic Publishing." *Georgia Historical Quarterly* 76 (1992): 420-27.

——. *Tara Revisited: Women, War, & The Plantation Legend*. New York: Abbeville Press, 1995.

Coleman, Kenneth. *Confederate Athens*. Athens: University of Georgia Press, 1967.

Coleman, Kenneth and Stephen Gurr, editors. *Dictionary of Georgia Biography*. Athens: University of Georgia Press, 1983.

Compiled Service Records of Confederate General and Staff Officers, and Non-Regimental Enlisted Men. National Archives. RG 109. Microcopy M331.

Compiled Service Records of Confederate Soldiers Who Served in Organizations from the State of Georgia. National Archives. RG 109. Microcopy M266.

Compiled Service Records of Confederate Soldiers who Served in Organizations from the State of Mississippi. National Archives. RG 109. Microcopy M269.

Compiled Service Records of Confederate Units Not Raised by State. National Archives. Microcopy M258.

Confederate Pensions, Fulton County. Georgia Department of Archives and History.

Conley Family Folder. Family Files Collection. Alabama Department of Archives and History.

Cook, D. Louise, ed. *Guide to the Manuscript Collections of the Atlanta Historical Society*. Atlanta: Atlanta Historical Society, 1976.

Cooper, Walter G. *Official History of Fulton County*. Atlanta: self published, 1934.

Corley, Florence Fleming. *Confederate City: Augusta, Georgia 1860-1865*. Columbia: University of South Carolina Press, 1960.

Cozzens, Peter. *The Shipwreck of Their Hopes: The Battles for Chattanooga*. Chicago: University of Illinois Press, 1994.

Crannell, Carolyn Gaye. "In Pursuit of Culture: A History of Art Activity in Atlanta." Ph.D. dissertation, Emory University, 1981.

Cunningham, H. H. *Doctors in Gray: The Confederate Medical Service*. Baton Rouge: Louisiana State University Press, 1958.

Cunyus, Lucy Josephine. *The History of Bartow County Formerly Cass*. Cartersville GA: Tribune, 1933. Reprint, Easley SC: Southern Historical Press, 1976.

Current, Richard N., ed. *Encyclopedia of the Confederacy*. New York: Simon and Schuster, 1993.

Davis, Burke. *The Long Surrender*. New York: Random House, 1985. Reprint, New York: Vintage Books, 1989.

——. *Sherman's March*. New York: Random House, 1985. Reprint, New York: Vintage Books, 1988.

Davis, George B., Leslie J. Perry, and Joseph W. Kirkley. *Atlas to Accompany the Official Records of the Union and Confederate Armies*. Washington, DC: United States Government Printing Office, 1891.

Davis, Robert S. Jr., ed. "The General Sherman Census of Atlanta, September 1864." *Georgia Genealogical Magazine* 31 (1991): 132-41.

——, ed. "Georgia Cities on the Eve of the Civil War: The Insurance Reports of C. C. Hines," *Atlanta History* 31 (1987): 50-58.

Davis, Stephen. "'A Very Barbarous Mode of Carrying on War': Sherman's Artillery Bombardment of Atlanta, July 20- August 24, 1864," *Georgia Historical Quarterly* 79 (1995): 57-90.

——. "The Conductor versus the Foreman: William Fuller, Anthony Murphy, and the Pursuit of the Andrews Raiders." *Atlanta History* 34 (1990): 38-54.

Davis, William C. *Memorabilia of the Civil War*. New York: Mallard Press, 1991.

——. *The Confederate General*. Washington, DC: National Historical Society, 1991.

[Dawson, Francis, comp.] *"Our Women in the War." The Lives They Lived; The Deaths They Died. From The Weekly News and Courier, Charleston,* S.C. Charleston: The News and Courier Book Presses, 1885.

Death certificate of Sarah C. Crane. Vital Records Service. Georgia Department of Human Resources.

Degler, Carl N. *The Other South: Southern Dissenters in the Nineteenth Century*. New York: Harper & Row, 1974.

Dennett, John Richard. *The South As It Is: 1865-1866*. New York: The Viking Press, 1965.

Douglas, Henry Kyd. *I Rode With Stonewall*. Chapel Hill: University of North Carolina Press, 1959.

Doyle, Don H. *New Men, New Cities, New South: Atlanta, Nashville, Charleston, Mobile, 1860-1910*. Chapel Hill: University of North Carolina Press, 1990.

Duke, Basil W. *A History of Morgan's Cavalry*. Bloomington: Indiana University Press, 1960.

Dutcher, Salem and Charles C. Jones, Jr. *Memorial History of Augusta*. New York: D. Mason, 1890. Reprint, Spartanburg SC: The Reprint Company, 1980.

Dyer, Thomas G. "Atlanta's Other Civil War Novel: Fictional Unionists in a Confederate City." *Georgia Historical Quarterly* 79 (1995): 147-68.

Edwards, Anne. *Road to Tara: The Life of Margaret Mitchell*. New Haven: Ticknor & Fields, 1983.

Eighth Census of the United States (1860). National Archives. RG 29. Microcopy M653.

Evans, Clement, ed. *Confederate Military History*. 17 vols. Atlanta: Confederate Publications, 1899. Reprint, Wilmington NC: Broadfoot Publishing Company, 1988.

Evans, David. *Sherman's Horsemen: Union Cavalry Operations in the Atlanta Campaign*. Bloomington: Indiana University Press, 1966.

Evans, William David. *Rousseau's Raid, July 10-July 22, 1864*. Ann Arbor MI: University Microfilms International, 1994.

Farnham, Christie Anne. *The Education of the Southern Belle: Higher Education and Student Socialization in the Antebellum South*. New York: New York University Press, 1994.

Faust, Patricia L., ed. *Historical Times Illustrated Encyclopedia of the Civil War*. New York: Harper & Row, 1986.

Fleming, Berry. *Autobiography of a City in Arms: Augusta, Georgia 1861-1865*. Augusta: Richmond County Historical Society, 1976.

Foner, Eric. *Reconstruction: America's Unfinished Revolution, 1863-1877*. New York: Harper & Row, 1988.

Foreacre, Mrs. G. J. Memoir. Atlanta Pioneer Women's Society Papers Collection, Atlanta Historical Society.

Fox-Genovese, Elizabeth. *Within the Plantation Household: Black and White Women of the Old South*. Chapel Hill: University of North Carolina Press, 1988.

Franklin, John Hope. *The Emancipation Proclamation*. New York: Doubleday & Company, 1963.

Fulton County Deed Book K (1867-1868). Georgia Department of Archives and History. Microfilm reel 100/64.

Fulton County Deed Book L (1868-1869). Georgia Department of Archives and History. Microfilm reel 100/65.

Fulton County Index to Grantees (1854-1871). Georgia Department of Archives and History. Microfilm reel 151/62.

Fulton County Marriage Book B. Georgia Department of Archives and History. Microfilm reel 110/66.

Fulton County Marriage Book C (1866-1873). Georgia Department of Archives and History. Microfilm reel 110/67.

Fulton County Marriage Book D (1873-1880). Georgia Department of Archives and History. Microfilm reel 110/68.

Fulton County Marriage Book H (1892-1895). Georgia Department of Archives and History. Microfilm reel 110/72.

Fulton County Tax Digest, 1864. Georgia Department of Archives and History. Microfilm reel 70/29.

Funeral Services at the Burial of the Reverend Leonidas Polk. Columbia SC: n.p., 1864. Georgia Department of Archives and History. Microfilm reel 81/8.

Garrett Necrology. Atlanta Historical Society.

Garrett, Franklin. *Atlanta and Environs*. 3 vols. New York: Lewis Historical Publishing Company, 1954.

Gay, Mary A. H. *Life in Dixie During the War*. Atlanta: C. P. Byrd, 1897. Reprint, Decatur: DeKalb County Historical Society, 1979.

Gibbes, James G. *Who Burnt Columbia?* Newberry SC: Elbert H. Aull, 1902.

Gibbons, Robert. "Life at the Crossroads of the Confederacy: Atlanta, 1861-1865." *Atlanta Historical Journal* 23/2 (1979): 11-72.

Gibbons, Tony. *Warships and Naval Battles of the Civil War*. New York: Gallery Books, 1989.

Glatthaar, Joseph T. *The March to the Sea and Beyond: Sherman's Troops in the Savannah and Carolinas Campaigns*. New York: New York University Press, 1985.

Gournay, Isabelle. *AIA Guide to the Architecture of Atlanta*. Athens: University of Georgia Press, 1993.

Grant, Donald L. *The Way It Was in the South: The Black Experience in Georgia*. Seraucus: Birch Lane Press, 1993.

Hall, Virginius Cornick Jr. *Portraits in the Collection of the Virginia Historical Society: A Catalogue*. Charlottesville: University of Virginia, 1981.

Hallock, Judith Lee. *Braxton Bragg and Confederate Defeat*. 2 vols. Tuscaloosa: University of Alabama Press, 1991.

Hamilton, Markley & Joyner file. Confederate Papers Relating to Citizens or Business Firms. National Archives, Washington, DC. Microcopy M346.

Hanson, Elizabeth I. *Margaret Mitchell*. Chapel Hill: University of North Carolina Press, 1991.

Harley, William Donald. *Thomas Jane Sheppard of Liberty County*. St. Simons Island GA: self published, 1957.

Harrell, Carolyn L. *When the Bells Tolled for Lincoln: Southern Reaction to the Assassination*. Macon GA: Mercer University Press, 1997.

Harris, Julia Collier. "Miss Sterchi's School." *Atlanta Historical Bulletin* 5/21 (1940): 107-23.

Harwell, Richard Barksdale. *Gone With the Wind: As Book and Film.* Columbia: University of South Carolina Press, 1983.

——. "Our Confederate Dead." *Atlanta Historical Bulletin* 20 (1976): 97-111.

——. "Technical Advisor: The Making of Gone With the Wind The Hollywood Journals of Wilbur G. Kurtz." *Atlanta Historical Journal* 22 (1978): 8-11.

Hayden, John O. *Scott: The Critical Heritage.* New York: Barnes & Noble, 1970.

Haynes, John Edward. *Pseudonyms of Authors Including Anonyms and Initialisms.* Detroit: Gale Research, 1969.

Hays, Louise Frederick. "Adjutant General's Office Book of Commissions Military Records 1861-1865 Volume B–49." Unpublished typescript. Atlanta: Georgia Department of Archives and History, 1939.

Hemperley, Marion R. *Cities, Towns and Communities of Georgia.* Easley SC: Southern Historical Press, 1980.

Henderson, Lillian. *Roster of the Confederate Soldiers of Georgia 1861-1865.* 6 vols., Hapeville GA: Longino & Porter, 1958.

Hewett, Janet B., Noah Andre Trudeau, and Bryce A. Suderow. *Supplement to the Official Records of the Union and Confederate Armies.* 100 volumes to date. Wilmington NC: Broadfoot Publishing Co., 1996.

History of the Confederate Memorial Associations of the South. n. p.: Confederate Southern Memorial Association

Hitz, Alex M. "The Origin of and Distinction Between the Two Protestant Episcopal Churches Known as St. Luke's, Atlanta." *Georgia Historical Quarterly* 34 (1950): 1-7.

Hoehling, A. A. *Last Train From Atlanta.* New York: Bonanza Books, 1958.

Holloway, J. B. *Consolidated Index of Claims Reported by the Commissioner of Claims.* Washington, DC: United States Government Printing Office, 1892.

Howard, Charles Wallace. Autobiographical Questionaires. Georgia Department of Archives and History. Microfilm reel 154/6.

Howard, Frances Thomas. *In and Out of the Lines.* New York: Neale Publishing, 1905.

Huff, Sarah. *My 80 Years in Atlanta.* Atlanta: n.p., 1937.

Husband, M. F. A. *A Dictionary of the Characters in the Waverley Novels of Sir Walter Scott.* London: George Rutledge and Sons, 1910.

Hunt, Roger D. and Jack R. Brown. *Brevet Brigadier Generals in Blue.* Gaithersburg MD: Olde Soldier Books, 1990.

Jackson, Ronald Vern. *1870 Census Index of Georgia: Atlanta, Augusta, and Savannah*. North Salt Lake: Accelerated Indexing Systems, 1991.

Jarvis, Grace H. *1850 Census, Clarke County, Georgia (Seventh Census of the United States)*. Jacksonville: Jacksonville Genealogical Society, 1981.

Jones, Charles Edgeworth. *Georgia in the War 1861-1865: A Compendium of Georgia Participants*. Atlanta: Foote & Davies, 1909.

Jones, Joseph. "Roster of the Medical Officers of the Army of Tennessee." *Southern Historical Society Papers*. 22 (1894): 165-280.

Jones, Katherine M. *When Sherman Came: Southern Women and the "Great March."* New York: Bobbs-Merrill, 1964.

——. *Heroines of Dixie: Confederate Women Tell Their Story of the War*. New York: Bobbs-Merrill, 1955.

Johnson, Frank Roy. *The Nat Turner Slave Insurrection*. Murfreesboro: Johnson Publishing Company, 1966.

Karlovich, Audrey. "E. B. D. Julio Memorial." *Northwest Georgia Historical and Genealogical Society Quarterly* 28/1 (1996): 5-7.

Katcher, Philip. *The Civil War Source Book*. New York: Facts on File, 1993.

Kennett, Lee. *Marching Through Georgia: The Story of Soldiers and Civilians During Sherman's Campaign*. New York: HarperColins, 1995.

Kimberly, John. Papers. Southern Historical Collection. University of North Carolina at Chapel Hill.

Kingston files. Special Collections. Bartow County Public Library, Cartersville GA.

Kinney, Shirley; Tate, Madge; and Jenkins, Sandra. *Floyd County, Georgia Cemeteries*. Rome: Northwest Georgia Historical and Genealogical Society, 1985.

Knight, Edgar W., ed. *A Documentary History of Education in the South Before 1860*. 5 vols. Chapel Hill: University of North Carolina Press, 1990.

Knight, Lucian Lamar. *History of Fulton County Georgia*. Atlanta: A. H. Cawston, 1930.

——. Scrapbooks. 30 volumes. Georgia Department of Archives and History.

Kolchin, Peter. *America Slavery 1619-1877*. New York: Hill and Wang, 1993.

Kunkle, Camille. "'It Is What It Does to the Souls': Women's Views on the Civil War." *Atlanta History* 33 (1989): 57-70.

Kurtz, Elma S. "War Diary of Cornelius R. Hanleiter." *Atlanta Historical Bulletin* 14/3 (1969): 9-13.

Kurtz, Henry H., Jr. "Hijack of a Locomotive: The Andrews Raid Revisited." *Atlanta History* 34 (1990): 5-14.

Kurtz, Wilbur G. *Atlanta and the Old South*. Atlanta: Atlanta Lithograph Company, 1969.

——. "The Andrews Raid," *Atlanta Historical Journal* 13 (1968): 9-29.

Lane, Mills B. *Times That Prove People's Principles: Civil War in Georgia*. Savannah: Beehive Press, 1993.

Lawley, Francis. *Francis Lawley Covers the Confederacy*. Edited by William Stanley Hoole. Tuscaloosa: Confederate Publishing Company, 1964.

Lawrence, Harold. *Methodist Preachers in Georgia 1783-1900*. Duluth, Georgia: self published, 1984.

Leas, Susan Elisabeth. *Alive in Atlanta: A History of St. Luke's Church, 1864-1974*. Atlanta: self published, 1976.

Livingston, Gary. *Fields of Gray: The Battle of Griswoldville*. Cooperstown NY: Caisson Press, 1966.

Luraghi, Raimondo. *The Rise and Fall of the Plantation South*. New York: New Viewpoints, 1978.

Malone, Alberta. *History of the Atlanta Ladies Memorial Association 1866-1946 Markers and Monuments*. Atlanta: n.p., 1946.

Margaret Mitchell Marsh Collection. Hargret Rare Book and Manuscripts Library, University of Georgia Libraries.

Marshall, Charlotte Thomas. *Oconee Hill Cemetery*. Athens: Athens Historical Society, 1971.

Marszalek, John F. *Sherman: A Soldier's Passion for Order*. New York: The Free Press, 1993.

Marvel, William. *Andersonville: The Last Depot*. Chapel Hill: University of North Carolina Press, 1994.

Massey, Mary Elizabeth. *Refugee Life in the Confederacy*. Baton Rouge: Louisiana State University Press, 1964.

McCash, William B. *Thomas R. R. Cobb: The Making of a Southern Nationalist*. Macon GA: Mercer University Press, 1983.

McCoy, Christina M. "The Ante-Bellun Churches of Atlanta." Masters Thesis, Georgia State University, 1996.

McDonald, Roderick A. *The Economy and Material Culture of Slaves: Goods and Chattels on the Sugar Plantations of Jamaica and Louisiana*. Baton Rouge: Louisiana State University Press, 1993.

McDonough, James Lee. *Chattanooga–A Death Grip on the Confederacy*. Knoxville: University of Tennessee Press, 1984.

McElreath, Walter. "Sidney Root: Merchant Prince and Great Citizen." *Atlanta Historical Bulletin* 7/29 (1944): 171-183.

McMahon, Doreen. "Pleasure Spots of Old Atlanta." *Atlanta Historical Bulletin* 7/29 (1944): 231.

McPherson, James M. *Battle Cry of Freedom: The Civil War Era*. New York: Ballantine Books, 1989.

Menn, Joseph Carl. "The Large Slave Holders of the Deep South, 1860." Ph.D. dissertation, University of Texas, 1964.

Miers, Earl Schenck Miers. *The General Who Marched to Hell: William Tecumseh Sherman and His March to Fame and Infamy*. New York: Alfred A. Knopf, 1951.

Miller, Joseph C. *Slavery and Slaving in World History: a Bibliography, 1900-1991*. Millwood NY: Kraus, 1993.

Miller, Randall M. and John David Smith. eds. *Dictionary of Afro-American Slavery*. New York: Greenwood Press, 1987.

The Miscellaneous Documents of the House of Representatives for the Second Session of the Fifty-third Congress 1893-1894. Washington, DC: United States Government Printing Office, 1896.

Mitchell, Margaret. *Margaret Mitchell's "Gone With the Wind Letters."* ed. Richard Harwell. New York: Collier MacMillan Publishers, 1976.

Mitchell, Stephens. "Atlanta: The Industrial Heart of the Confederacy." *Atlanta Historical Bulletin* 1/3 (May 1930): 20-7.

Moebs, Thomas Truxton. *Confederate States Navy Research Guide*. Williamsburg VA: Moebs Publishing Company, 1991.

Mohr, Clarence L. *On the Threshold of Freedom: Masters and Slaves in Civil War Georgia*. Athens: University of Georgia Press, 1986.

Montgomery County Conveyances Volume T (1843-1844). Alabama Department of Archives and History.

Montgomery County Estate Case Files (1838-1946). Alabama Department of Archives and History.

Montgomery, Florence M. *Textiles in America 1650-1870*. New York: W. W. Norton & Company, 1983.

Mullinax, Martha H. *We Remember Kingston*. Marietta GA: Woman's History Club and Others, 1992.

——. Interview by the author. 25 January 1997.

Myers, Robert Manson. *The Children of Pride: A True Story of Georgia and the Civil War*. New Haven: Yale University Press, 1972.

The National Cyclopedia of American Biography 63 vols. New York: James T. White & Company, 1904.

Neely, Mark E. Jr., ed. *The Abraham Lincoln Encyclopedia.* New York: McGraw Hill, 1982.

Newman, Harry Wright. *The Maryland Semmes and Kindred Families.* Baltimore: Maryland Historical Society, 1956.

Newman, Harvey K. "The Role of Women in Atlanta's Churches, 1865-1906." *Atlanta History* 23 (1979-1980): 18.

Nicolson Family Papers Collection. Atlanta Historical Society.

Ninth Census of the United States (1870). National Archives. RG 29. Microcopy M593.

Noll, Arthur H. *Doctor Quintard, Chaplain* C.S.A. Suwanee: University of the South, 1905.

O'Briant, Don. *Looking for Tara: The Gone With the Wind Guide to Margaret Mitchell's Atlanta.* Atlanta: Longstreet Press, 1994.

O'Connor, Richard. *Thomas: Rock of Chickamauga.* New York: Prentice-Hall, 1948.

Official Army Register of the Volunteer Force of the United States Army For the Years 1861, '62, '63, '64, '65. Washington, DC: United States Government Printing Office, 1865.

O'Neill, Charles. *Wild Train: The Story of the Andrews Raiders.* New York: Random House, 1958.

O'Shea, Richard and David Greenspan. *American Heritage Battle Maps of the Civil War.* New York: Smithmark, 1994.

Osthaus, Carl R. *Partisans of the Southern Press: Editorial Spokesmen of the Nineteenth Century.* Lexington: University of Kentucky Press, 1994.

Otto, Rhea Cumming. *1850 Census of Georgia (Fayette County).* Savannah: self published, 1983.

Pardon Petitions and Related Papers Submitted in Response to President Johnson's Amnesty Proclamation of May 29, 1865. National Archives. RG 94. Microcopy M1003.

Parks, Joseph H. *General Leonidas Polk, C.S.A.: The Fighting Bishop.* Baton Rouge: Louisiana State University Press, 1962.

Patton, James W. and Clyde Edward Pitts. *The Benjamin Cudsworth Yancey Papers in the Southern Historical Collection of the University of North Carolina Library.* Chapel Hill NC: Southern Historical Collection, 1967.

Perry, Leslie J. and Joseph W. Kirkley. *Atlas to Accompany the Official Records of the Union and Confederate Armies*. Washington, DC: United States Government Printing Office, 1891.

Pioneer Citizens' Society of Atlanta. *Pioneer Citizens' History of Atlanta 1833-1902*. Atlanta: Byrd Publishing, 1902.

Piston, William Garrett. *Lee's Tarnished Lieutenant: James Longstreet and His Place in Southern History*. Athens: University of Georgia Press, 1987.

Pyron, Darden Asbury. *Southern Daughter: The Life of Margaret Mitchell*. Oxford: Oxford University Press, 1991.

Quarles, Benjamin. *Lincoln and the Negro*. New York: Oxford University Press, 1963.

R. G. Dun Collection of Credit Reports. Baker Library, Harvard University.

Rable, George C. *Civil Wars: Women and the Crisis of Southern Nationalism*. Urbana: University of Illinois Press, 1989.

Ramage, James A. *Rebel Raider: The Life of General John Hunt Morgan*. Lexington: University of Kentucky Press, 1986.

Reed, Wallace P. *History of Atlanta, Georgia*. Syracuse NY: D. Mason & Co., 1889.

Report on the Treatment of Prisoners of War by the Rebel Authorities. Washington, DC: United States Government Printing Office, 1869. 40th Congress, 3d Session, Report 45.

Richards, William A. "'We Live Under a Constitution': Confederate Martial Law in Atlanta." *Atlanta History* 33 (1989): 25-33.

Richmond County Deed Book QQ (1860-1863). Georgia Department of Archives and History. Microfilm reel 138/28.

Richmond County Tax Digests, 1861-1865. Georgia Department of Archives and History. Microfilm reel 186/6.

Roberts, W. Adolphe. *Semmes of the Alabama*. Indianapolis: Bobbs-Merrill, 1938.

Robson, Kate Hester. Memoirs. Atlanta Historical Society.

Rodgers, Robert L. *History Confederate Veterans' Association of Fulton County, Georgia*. Atlanta: V. P. Sisson, 1890.

Rose, Anne C. Rose. *Victorian America and the Civil War*. Cambridge: Cambridge University Press, 1992.

Rowe, Carolyn McGough. *Index to Individual Pardon Applications From the South 1865-1898*. Pensacola: self published, 1996.

Rowland, Dunbar, ed. *Jefferson Davis Constitutionalist: His Letters, Papers and Speeches*. 10 vols. Jackson: Mississippi Department of Archives and History, 1923.

Russell, James Michael. *Atlanta 1847-1890: City Building in the Old South and the New*. Baton Rouge: Louisiana State University Press, 1989.

Schott, Thomas E. Schott. *Alexander H. Stephens of Georgia*. Baton Rouge: Louisiana State University Press, 1988.

Schroeder-Lein, Glenna R. *Confederate Hospitals on the Move: Samuel H. Stout and the Army of Tennessee*. Columbia: University of South Carolina Press, 1994.

—. " 'To Be Better Supplied Than Any Hotel in the Confederacy': The Establishment and Maintenance of the Army of Tennessee Hospitals in Georgia, 1863-1865." *Georgia Historical Quarterly* 76 (1992): 809-36.

Scott, H. L. *Military Dictionary*. New York: D. Van Nostrand, 1864.

Scott, Robert N., comp. *The War of the Rebellion: A Compilation of the Official Records of the Union and Confederate Armies*. 128 vols., Washington, DC: United States Government Printing Office, 1888-1900.

Scruggs, Carroll Proctor. *Georgia Historical Markers*. Helen: Bay Tree Grove, 1973.

Semmes, Benedict J. Papers. Southern Historical Press. University of North Carolina at Chapel Hill.

Seventh United States Census (1850). National Archives. RG 29. Microcopy M653.

Shavin, Norman. *Days in the Life of Atlanta*. Atlanta: Capricorn Corporation, 1987.

—. *Whatever Became of Atlanta?*. n.p., n.d.

Shavin, Norman and Galphin, Bruce. *Atlanta: Triumph of a People*. 2nd ed., Atlanta: Capricorn Corporation, 1985.

Sherman, William T. *Memoirs of General T. Sherman*. New York: D. Appleton, 1875. Reprint, New York: De Capo Press, 1984.

Sifakis, Stewart, ed. *Who Was Who in the Confederacy*. New York: Facts on File, 1988.

Singer, Ralph Benjamin "Confederate Atlanta." Ph.D. dissertation, University of Georgia, 1973.

Smedlund, William S. *Camp Fires of Georgia's Troops, 1861-1865*. Lithonia: self published, 1994.

Smith, Charles Henry. *Bill Arp, So Called. A Side Show of the Southern Side of the War*. New York: Metropolitan Record Office, 1866.

Smith, George. *Dictionary of National Biography*. 22 vols. Oxford: Oxford University Press, 1882-1952.

Sneed, Delia Foreacre. "Sketch of G. J. Foreacre." MS 89, Foreacre Willett Papers. Atlanta Pioneer Women's Society Papers Collection. Atlanta Historical Society

Southern Historical Association. *Memoirs of Georgia Containing Historical Accounts of the State's Civil, Military, Industrial and Professional Interests*. 2 vols. Atlanta: Southern Historical Association, 1895.

Spencer, Warren F. *Raphael Semmes: The Philosophical Mariner*. Tuscaloosa: University of Alabama Press, 1977.

Steuart, Bradley W. *Georgia 1870 Census Index*. Bountiful, Utah: Precision Indexing, 1990.

Stone, Cyrena Bailey. Miss Abbey's Diary. Hargrett Rare Books and Manuscripts Library, MS 1000. University of Georgia Libraries.

Stroud, David. *Flames and Vengeance: The East Texas Fires and the Presidential Election of 1860*. Carrollton TX: Alliance Press, 1997.

Taylor, Joe. "Atlanta Mortality Trends: 1853-1873." *Atlanta Historical Bulletin* 20 (1976): 17-20.

Temple, Sarah Blackwell Gober. *The First Hundred Years: A Short History of Cobb County, In Georgia*. Atlanta: Walter Brown, 1935.

Thomas, Emory M. *The Confederacy as a Revolutionary Experience*. Englewood Cliffs NJ: Prentice-Hall, 1971.

Thornton, Ella May. "Captain John Keely: An Informal Reminiscence." *Atlanta Historical Bulletin* 4 (1939): 73-6.

Torrence, William Clayton. *Rootes of Rosewall*. n.p., 1906.

Tragle, Henry Irving Tragle. *The Southampton Slave Revolt of 1831*. Amherst: University of Massachusetts Press, 1971.

Trudeau, Noah Andre. *Out of the Storm: The End of the Civil War, April-June 1865*. Boston: Little, Brown & Co., 1994.

US Congress. House. William W. Clayton Pardon File, HR 40A-H21.8, RG 323, Records of the US House of Representatives, National Archives, Washington, DC.

US Congress Joint Select Committee to Inquire into the Condition of Affairs in the Late Insurrectionary States. *Testimony Taken by the Joint Select Committee to Inquire into the Condition of Affairs in the Late Insurrectionary States*. 42nd Congress. 2nd Session. Georgia Volume 2. Rept. 41.

Van Duzer, John C. Collection. Special Collections. Perkins Library, Duke University.

Wakelyn, Jon L., ed. *Biographical Dictionary of the Confederacy*. Westport CT: Greenwood Press, 1977.

Warner, Ezra J. *Generals in Blue: Lives of Union Commanders*. Baton Rouge: Louisiana State University Press, 1964.

——. *Generals in Gray: Lives of Confederate Commanders*. Baton Rouge: Louisiana State University Press, 1964.

Waugh, John C. *The Class of 1846: Stonewall Jackson, George McClellan, and Their Brothers*. New York: Warner Books, 1994.

Weinreb, Ben and Christopher Hibbert. *The London Encyclopedia*. London: Book Club Associates, 1983.

Welsh, Jack D. *Medical Histories of the Confederate Generals*. Kent OH: Kent State University Press, 1995.

White, George. *Historical Collections of Georgia*. New York: Pudney & Russell, 1854.

White, Lee Ann. *The Civil War as a Gender Crisis: Augusta, Georgia, 1860-1890*. Athens: University of Georgia Press, 1995.

Whitehead, A. C. *Makers of Georgia's Name and Fame*. Boston: Educational Publishing Company, 1913.

Wilbur Kurtz Collection. MS 130. Atlanta Historical Society.

Wiley, Bell I. *Civil War Times Illustrated Photographic History of the Civil War Vicksburg to Appomattox*. New York: Black Dog & Leventhal, 1994.

William W. Clayton. File II Names. RG 4-2-46. Georgia Department of Archives and History.

William Wirt Clayton Bible. Private collection of Gordon Ford of Forest Park, GA.

Williams, C. S.*Williams' Atlanta Directory For 1859-60*. Atlanta: M. Lynch, 1859.

Winship Flournoy Family Papers, Atlanta Historical Society.

Winters, John D. *The Civil War in Louisiana*. Baton Rouge: Louisiana State University Press, 1963.

Women's Society Papers Collection. Atlanta Historical Society.

Wooten, Grigsby H. Jr. "New City of the South: Atlanta, 1843-1873." Ph.D. dissertation, John Hopkins University, 1973.

Wright, John H. *Compendium of the Confederacy: An Annotated Bibliography*. 2 vols. Wilmington NC: Broadfoot Publishing, 1989.

Young, Ida Young, Julius Gholson, and Clara Nell Hargrove. *History of Macon, Georgia*. Macon GA: Macon Woman's Club, 1950.

Newspapers

Bibliographic Note: No repository has microfilm copies of all of the surviving Civil War Atlanta newspapers. Most of the Georgia newspapers cited here are included among the microfilm of the Georgia Newspaper Project (GNP) of the University of Georgia. The author donated to the GNP microfilm of newspapers of the Western Reserve Historical Society and the Southern Baptist Historical Commission. Other Atlanta newspapers cited came from the Boston Athenaeum, which has, at the author's request, offered to loan their Georgia newspapers to the GNP for microfilming. Tennessee newspapers cited here are on microfilm at the Tennessee State Library and Archives.

Atlanta Daily Intelligencer.
Atlanta Daily Reveille.
Augusta (GA) *Daily Constitutionalist*.
Chattanooga (TN) *Daily Rebel*.
The Commonwealth (Atlanta).
Daily Chronicle & Sentinel (Augusta).
Daily Intelligencer (Atlanta).
Daily Southern Confederacy (Atlanta).
Louisville (KY) *Daily Press & Times*.
Macon (GA) *Daily Telegraph and Confederate*.
Nashville (TN) *Daily Times & Press*.
Nashville (TN) *Daily Times & True Union*.
Nashville (TN) *Dispatch*.
Southern Banner (Athens)
Southern Confederacy (Atlanta).
Southern Watchman (Athens).
Sunny South (Atlanta).
Weekly Atlanta Intelligencer.

INDEX